ALTERNATIVES
IN EDUCATION

Edited by Mark and Helen Hegener

Home Education Press

Alternatives In Education

Edited by Mark and Helen Hegener

published by
  Home Education Press
  Post Office Box 1083
  Tonasket, WA 98855
  509-486-1351

First printing 1987.
Second printing 1988.
Third printing 1988.
Revised fourth printing 1992.
Printed in the United States of America.

ISBN   0-945097-15-8

Library of Congress Cataloging-in-Publication Data

Hegener, Mark
  Alternatives In Education

  Bibliography: p.
  Includes index.
  1. Non-formal education 2. Education--experimental methods. I. Hegener, Helen. II Title.
LC45.3.H44   1992   371'.04   87-36257

For Michael, Christopher, Jody Ellen, Jim and John.

We would like to thank these people who have helped us make this book possible: Britt Barker Bennett, Patricia Smith-Carsten, Craig Conley, Patrick Farenga, John Taylor Gatto, Daniel Greenberg, Bobbie Groth, Katharine Houk, Sandra Hurst, Catherine Johns, Thomas Kane, Larry and Susan Kaseman, Ron Miller, Jerry Mintz, Pat Montgomery, Susan Nelson, Becky Olson, Donn Reed, Seth Rockmuller, Susan Mayelin Stephenson, and Jane Williams.

Special thanks to Agnes Liestico for her proofreading and copy-editing, and to Earl Stevens for his introduction.

TABLE OF CONTENTS

PREFACE

The first edition of *Alternatives In Education* was published in the fall of 1987. It was an attempt to fill what we saw as an information gap in education. There were literally dozens of ways children could learn and grow, and yet many people were simply unaware that these options existed, because it was difficult to find out about alternative schools, or homeschooling, or how children might get into college without a high school diploma.

As the parents of five children, and as publishers of a national magazine for homeschooling families, we were becoming increasingly aware of the need for information about what was really available to families in education. Too many people had believed for too long that public schooling, expensive private schooling, or church schooling were the only choices available for the education of their children.

The first edition of *Alternatives In Education* received glowing reviews, was picked up by two book clubs, made a library top forty listing, and went through three printings in eighteen months. Then, because we were becoming increasingly occupied with concerns specific to the burgeoning homeschooling movement and our publishing of homeschooling books and a magazine, we let *Alternatives In Education* go out of print. We honestly never expected to either revise or reprint it.

But we kept receiving orders for the book long after we'd made it clear that it was no longer available. People had a need for the kind of information it presented, information which was only available from widely scattered, sometimes difficult to locate sources. *Alternatives In Education* was the only complete guide to the options available to families outside the public and traditional private school systems. The more we asked around, the more we found people who believed that yes, we should reprint the book, that we needed to keep the information available, and, if possible, we should expand the content in a new edition. So we began the long process of revision.

Once the decision was made to go ahead, we mailed letters to our colleagues in the various fields of alternative education, asking for input and information, and they responded enthusiastical-ly. We read and reread through our own files for articles and es-says, interviews and excerpts to include in this new volume. The book grew, and the edition you hold in your hands is quite differ-ent from the first effort we published in 1987. And yet this book merely provides a starting point for your own explorations in edu-cation.

Education is an interactive process, and we are all teachers as well as students. In the compiling of this book we were reminded over and over again that learning is a lifelong process, that the best and most valuable lessons are the ones we choose for our-selves, not the ones decreed necessary to pass a test or to earn a certificate. And we were reminded that the best teachers are usu-ally found in the relationships that make a book such as this one possible, relationships born of a shared interest, a philosophical agreement, and sometimes even a disagreement. We learned an inestimable amount while working on this book, and for that, dear reader, we thank you.

Mark and Helen Hegener
Wauconda, Washington
July, 1992

INTRODUCTION

by Earl Stevens

Most of us can remember a time when we thought in very conventional ways about the education of children. Education meant the public school classroom or at least some imitation of it. There is a mythological golden age of public education in our consciousness, captured in Norman Rockwell paintings, cinema, television, and modern literature, in which the public school is a positive place where the children of our nation come together to learn academics and social skills.

However, we do not all agree on the value of public school education. Some adults claim to have benefited from their school days; others feel that their time was largely wasted or that they suffered damage through relentlessly dictatorial classroom training and through too many negative social experiences. Because they were children with different backgrounds, different needs, different talents, and different hopes, there was no single model of learning that could have been suitable for all of them, and, for the most part, there was only one model available.

My interest in alternative education has its roots in my own childhood public school experiences. They were almost uniformly negative, and I don't think I'm being dramatic in saying that it took me years to recover from some of them. I needed an alternative setting, but none existed for me. I wasn't having problems with my daily life in the community, but I was one of the kids who turned out to be a problem at school.

I don't know what language would be used these days to describe my condition as a student. It might now be called "attention deficit disorder," although I always thought of it as "boredom." I couldn't tear myself away from daily life long enough to memorize the stuff for which my teachers held me responsible. I simply didn't care, and I couldn't be made to care. When I was inside the classroom I dreamed about being outside. I rarely finished my school work except at the last minute to save myself from certain disaster, and often I was too late. Everybody was very disappointed.

Most of my friends received high grades consistently, but some of them were as discontented with schooling as I. In spite of their success they disliked school because it gobbled up so much of their lives and left them little time to engage in activities that held meaning for them. Some of them had wised up enough by high school to sense that their time was being wasted on a grand scale. But, they reasoned, this was something you had to do, right?

My teachers, my guidance counselor, and my parents told me again and again that I was more than capable of doing the work. Since it had been decided that I could do the work the problem seemed to be that for some perverse reason I wouldn't. Why I didn't just go ahead and do the work was a mystery that was possibly rooted in some defect of my character. My consistent academic downward spiral was "what happens to kids when they don't apply themselves." But I couldn't seem to make myself apply myself. Philosophic implications aside, it seemed to be an impossible task.

I tried not to make anybody too uncomfortable. I wasn't a rebel. I wasn't even a resister. I was a perpetual escapee. There were other escapees and rebels and resisters who got into trouble for carelessness, or breaking the rules, or falling asleep in class, or forgetting to do their homework. The children who didn't fit were very difficult to classify, perhaps because there were so many of them.

At the end of my sophomore year I quit high school simply because I couldn't subject myself to two more years of it. A few years later I went to college. Although I had missed more than 20 one-semester courses in high school, I was accepted by a local university, where I discovered that having missed high school seemed to make no difference at all. So much fuss is made in high school about the importance of a successful high school career as a prerequisite for college. How is it, I wondered, that a high school dropout failure like me could just simply bypass it all and, without inconvenience, go on to earn high grades in college?

After graduation I became a high school English teacher. Perhaps it was my subconscious mind luring me back to fix things. I would return as a school reformer. No losers, only winners. But it didn't work out so well. For some reason the kids weren't all that interested in being saved, by me or by anybody else. They seemed to be preoccupied with their own lives, and were only politely interested in my plans for them. Most of those who cared about anything at all connected with the school were obsessed with grades. As well they might be! Everything depended upon grades and class standing. I found that no matter how much I cared about the kids, no matter how interesting or even provocative I made my classes, no matter how well-meant my intentions, I would never get thirty different personalities to engage with me simultaneously, except through coercion. Since the system is based upon grades, I was always making them an offer that they couldn't refuse. Under these circumstances the kids cared only about getting it over with and recording the grade. Who could blame them?

I had a lot of difficulty assigning grades. I'm not sure now how I made those decisions. It didn't seem to matter. Everybody, even the ones who received low grades, accepted the grades as though they meant something. The students must have figured that they got what they deserved. Their report cards would say things like "Needs to apply himself more" or "Needs to participate in class." These comments would magically appear on computerized report cards at the end of each marking period as a result of teachers filling in little circles with a #2 lead pencil. Many of the teachers used the phrase "Nothing seems to be happening."

Some of the kids who typically earned high grades were not enthusiastic about being high school students, similar to my own classmates years before. Despite favorable report cards they were no more satisfied with their lot in the classroom than were the kids at the bottom of the bell curve. The difference was that nobody yelled at them if they stayed on top. Although they did the work, it held little meaning for them except as a way of keeping parents and teachers at bay. Winning loses some of its appeal when the game itself offers little satisfaction and one must depend mostly upon applause.

I left after four years. I found that I could no longer make a case to my students for staying in our school, one of the best high schools in a very affluent town. I couldn't even make a case for what I was teaching. I had no idea what children should be taught or even if we should be teaching them, and I felt that, with only a few exceptions, my peers in the teachers' lounge no longer even thought much about the why of what they were doing.

Some years later, living in a smaller town and having a child of my own now, I joined with a group in my community to badger the school board into launching an alternative public elementary school. It was to be a modest beginning, a step away from the rigid, age-segregated, test-driven 19th-century classrooms that were ubiquitous in the local school system. After two years of struggle with the school board, this alternative school was begun with one class each of first, second, and third graders. Today it reaches all the way to the start of middle school and is so popular that many parents who want it for their children find there is no place for them there, and they are bitter. A neighboring town with the same problem instituted a lottery by which the winners could send their children to the alternative school and the losers would be left with the "old-fashioned" school. For many parents, any alternative school is a step in the right direction.

There isn't enough money and there will never be enough imagination for the public schools to find what is needed for each child. But what the schools could do is provide children with enough freedom of speech and movement so that they can learn how to look for it for themselves. When that is seen as impossible, as it usually is, then parents must do their own thinking and must be willing to act upon their surmises. The idea behind "alternative" is to find what works, and not to rely entirely on what is expected to work. Finding what works sometimes involves trial and error. To some parents this may feel a little scary, but it is only a simple process of growth which has been long neglected by the schools.

For my own child, I chose home education. As Seth Rockmuller says in this book, home education "frees you to create all sorts of other educational alternatives. You can use home education as a base and build anything from it." I sometimes use the term "home-based education" because the child is growing up in a community as well as in a home, and the family can take advantage of whatever the community has to offer. To me it means that the family has taken over the selection and the management of educational objectives instead of leaving these matters to somebody else. Even relatively small communities have much to offer a family who is looking for academic and social experiences out in the world.

The point is not whether or not families should choose home education or an alternative school or any other way of helping their children become educated. When we take responsibility for the management of education we can choose from all these alternatives, and we can change our minds. It is not just a myth that we need to find what's right and stick to it; finding what is right, once and for all, is an impossibility. As we change, as our children change, so does our vision. What matters is that families break their dependency on institutions so that they can act upon their own perceptions.

Parents and children look for alternatives from many different situations and perspectives. They may question the common assumption that the purpose of education is to train children for global economic warfare. They may feel that schools breed peer-dependency and consumerism. They may be dealing with a handicap or a special talent or both in the same child. They may have a child who looks or acts "different" and they know that public school is the place where children who are different are tormented in ways that have no counterpart in adult life. Or they may feel that the community, not the public school classroom, is the "real" world. They may decide for any number of reasons that they can find a better way. Some parents choose alternatives after long and careful planning, while others arrive at these choices as refugees from painful conflicts with public school authorities. If there is no support from friends and relatives, it can be lonely and difficult, but the rewards are great and long-lasting.

The most important lesson that I have learned about the education of children is that it must be a family affair before it can be anything else. Only when the meaning and the content of daily life springs from the collective needs and aspirations and vision of the family can there be success. Perhaps more than at any other time since the beginning of public education in this country, parents and children are aware that they have the power and the responsibility to take charge of their education and their daily lives. Here, in this book, is both information and inspiration for those who are ready to act on that awareness.

Not so long ago, many of us didn't know we had any choices. Now we can see that our choices are unlimited. There have always been alternatives, but perhaps we have never felt the need for them so intensely as we do now. This book is about why it is important to search for alternatives and where to begin looking. There are many voices here and much to think about. This is not simply a list of alternative educational situations, it is about alternative ways of looking at life. This book is about family empowerment and the future of our children.

Portland, Maine
July, 1992

CHAPTER ONE

Alternative Education

Alternative Education:
The Road Less Travelled

By its very definition, alternative education indicates a departure from the norm, a side road travelled by only a few "differently thinking" parents who are searching for something that cannot be found in today's most popular education system: the public and traditional private schools. Stating that you're interested in alternative education for your children usually makes people wonder why you would want to strike off on such a tangent. Among friends and relatives it often sets off a barrage of well-intentioned admonitions such as, "Why can't you just send your kids to public school like everyone else?"

Two roads diverged
in a wood, and I-
I took the road less
travelled by,
And that has made all
the difference.
Robert Frost
The Road Less Travelled

Whether your interest is in homeschooling, an alternative school, locating a Waldorf school for your child, or any of the dozens of other options, you're going to be swimming against the tide of common educational practice in this country. You're making a social statement by going to the often considerable trouble of seeking out and providing a different kind of education for your children.

The word "alternative" simply means a choice between two or more things. Which do you prefer, apples or oranges or bananas? So how did the term "alternative education" get it's unmistakably second-class rating? It's a direct function--and a classic example--of good old peer pressure at work.

In the traditional public schools

most of us attended, and to which we're expected to send our own children, we were taught, both directly and indirectly, to conform. Classrooms could only be managed efficiently when all the children in them behaved in a predictable manner, and if they lost some of their individuality along the way that was probably just as well. The primary function of the schools was to produce a cooperative work force for an industrialized country (surprised? You probably thought they were supposed to teach children to read and write...). Adults who conformed and "went along" would fit much more readily into the factories and assembly lines and sales positions for which they were being groomed. The teenagers' natural sense of wanting to belong, of wanting to be part of the group, and winning peer and adult approval through being like everyone else was encouraged. (Remember how important it was to be dressed like your classmates, to have the same hairstyle, the same notebook covers, the same shoes?) You were encouraged to be painfully aware of what others would think about everything you did, and those individuals who refused to play the game were branded as rebels and non-conformists. They were always a little different, and according to the rules of the game, being different made them suspect. In our present society, alternative forms of education are a little different, and, to many, they're a little suspect.

So why, in view of all the negative publicity, would anyone choose to homeschool their children, or send

"The crazy combative patriotism that plainly threatens to destroy civilization is very largely begotten by the schoolmaster and the schoolmistress in their history lessons. They take the growing mind at a naturally barbaric phase and they inflame it and fix its barbarism."
–George Herbert Wells
The Informative Content of Education

them to an alternative school? Wouldn't it be easier to just "play the game," and to teach our childen to play along as well? Not necessarily.

Our public and most traditional private schools are bogged down in a bureaucratic quagmire that will not allow them to address the real needs of children. Overly concerned with their own survival, they have trouble enough simply categorizing and controlling children, and making it appear that they're doing a good job of that. It would just be too much trouble to provide those children with a challenging, stimulating, and exciting education as well. The alternative educational programs, on the other hand, generally consider the inspiration of learning their whole reason for being. Many of the educators in alternative and community schools work for love, and very little, if any, money (don't confuse them with the often expensive traditional private schools).

Parents who choose to educate their children at home take on the challenge knowing that it will cost time, money, and more than a little parental freedom. The volunteers who donate time and energy to run support groups, learning and resource centers, national organizations, and the other necessities that keep these educational options available are giving of themselves because they know that alternative education is worth supporting.

In the summer of 1986, Jerry Mintz, then Executive Director of the National Coalition of Alternative Community Schools, wrote, "People who have their finger on the pulse of change

"Thou hast most traitorously corrupted the youth of the realm in erecting a grammar-school; and whereas, before, our forefathers had no other books than the score and the tally, thou hast caused printing to be used; and, contrary to the king, his crown, and dignity, thou hast built a paper-mill."

–William Shakespeare
King Henry VI

in this country know that something significant is beginning to happen." Jerry was right. Education in America *is* changing. But real change, lasting change, never happens overnight.

Slowly, but ever so surely, we are finding better ways to educate our children. But the real battles will not be fought over educational methods. Teachers, even in public schools, usually know how children learn best, and they usually have the children's best interests at heart, that's why they chose to become teachers. The real battles will be over who's going to control our children's lives, and how -- and more importantly, what -- they will learn. Whether we like it or not, whether we're aware of it or not, our children are merely pawns in a high stakes game being played by bureaucrats and politicians and business interests. Find out what's *really* happening in education today, and be prepared for a severe shock.

In time, the word "alternative" will undoubtedly be dropped from those educational methods this book addresses. They will be, as they rightfully should be, simply different routes to learning, a series of choices for parents and their children to make. But until then, those of us who choose these routes will be the ones taking the road less travelled by.

"There is no absurdity so palpable but that it may be firmly planted in the human head if you only begin to inculcate it before the age of five, by constantly repeating it with an air of great solemnity."

—Arthur Schopenhauer

Educating for Wholeness--A Challenge To Modern Schooling

—— Ron Miller, Ph.D. ————————————————————————

"Alternative education" is a phrase that refers to a number of very different philosophies of teaching and learning. There are "alternative schools" in the public education system that generally serve students who have been discouraged or alienated by conventional methods. A network of independent alternative schools, sometimes called "democratic" or "free" schools, are comprised of small, informal communities of families, teachers and students. There are nearly 100 Waldorf schools in the U.S., based on the very carefully designed plan of the spiritual philosopher Rudolf Steiner, and many hundreds of Montessori schools--also carefully designed, but in a very different way, according to principles established by the physician/educator Maria Montessori. And there are still other "alternative" approaches, including homeschooling.

In order to appreciate what makes these educational approaches "alternative," it is necessary to understand the essential qualities of conventional, traditional schooling that they are alternative *to*. Our culture (the modern, industrialized Western world) has defined *education* as the transmission - from the adult generation to the young - of several basic intellectual skills and a "curriculum" of selected facts. And the decisions about which skills and which facts are selected depends a great deal on the economic, technological, social and political goals of those in positions of authority in our society.

Modern public school systems (in the U.S. as well as in Europe) were set up during the early decades of the nineteenth century in order to serve the rapid expansion of industrializing nations. Then, as now, political and educational leaders saw a direct connection between the intellectual and social disciplining of children through schooling, and a nation's success in economic development. Then, as now, children were viewed primarily as a natural resource to be exploited for the sake of the materialistic and nationalistic goals of adults - or more specifically, of the few white, male adults who have made the economic and political decisions for most nations.

Some educators have opposed this definition of education. They point out that the Latin roots of the word - "educare" or "ex ducere" - have nothing to do with transmitting a curriculum or disciplining young workers and citizens; they literally mean *drawing forth* the human possibilities contained within the soul of every child. These educators have argued that every child is a precious, spiritual being, who has potentials and aspirations that deserve to be nurtured for the sake of the child's own unique development. The most influential educators and philosophers who have held this view in the past two centuries include Rousseau, Pestalozzi, Froebel, Channing, Emerson, Alcott, Parker, Montessori, Steiner, Neill, Goodman, and Holt. Although there are many differences in their views, I consider them all to be *holistic* educators, because they have all defined education in terms of wholeness—the whole, integrated person; a whole, democratic community life; and a respect for the whole cultural, global, ecological and even cosmic context of human life. In their diverse ways, these alternative educators have argued that conventional education is inadequate in four respects:

1. Education should nurture the development of the whole person. It is not enough to train people for academic achievement and vocational skills alone. The human personality is an integrated system of intellectual, physical, social, moral, emotional, creative, and spiritual possibilities. To arbitrarily focus on one or two limited aspects does violence to human development.

2. Education should hold a reverence for life - for the mysterious unfolding of life in the soul of every child. The human being should be appreciated as a spiritual being, and not treated with reductionistic labels (such as "IQ" or "learning disabled"). "Spirituality" may or may not mean conventional religious beliefs; it is essentially a respect for the vast contexts that provide meaning to human life.

3. Education should be a mutually respectful relationship - indeed a friendship - between the teacher and the student. The teacher must not be a taskmaster, wielding weapons such as grades, corporal punishment, anti-"hyperactivity" drugs and a bagful of institutional tricks to control children's minds and bodies. Children should be valued as individuals; true education is grounded in love and occurs most naturally in a democratic community.

4. Education must confront the dehumanizing tendencies of modern culture. Once we seek to nurture the finer potentials in the human spirit, it becomes evident that the competitive, hierarchical, materialistic, violent and hedonistic qualities of our dominant worldview are highly destructive of these potentials. Schools

must not serve as training centers for "success" in such a society; they must stand for more humane values.

Any educational approach which honors these four premises is, despite variations in particular methods and practices, holistic. Other terms, closely associated with holistic approaches, are sometimes used synonymously (although they are not as all-encompassing): ecological, integrative, contextual, and global. These terms remind us that a concern for human development must extend beyond the individual, family, clan, nation, or even all of humanity; they remind us that a true reverence for life involves a deep respect for the interconnectedness of all life on Earth. In this sense, "global education" does *not* mean teaching our children Japanese so they can cut sharper business deals in Japan; it means cultivating a respect for all of humanity, all of life, and working to overcome the prejudices and hostilities that divide cultures and nations. At this point in history, we must learn to work in harmony with other peoples and with the Earth, or else we are all doomed together.

Holistic education is related to two previous reform efforts in American education in this century--humanistic and progressive education. "Humanistic education" is a movement of the past twenty years based on the work of humanistic psychologists such as Carl Rogers, Abraham Maslow and Fritz Perls. Humanistic educators are concerned with the student's healthy emotional life and ability to choose life-affirming values - as well as their intellectual development. They have developed classroom techniques aimed at increasing self-esteem and helping young people "clarify" their values; they may be interested in various meditative or imagery practices which help students discover deeper levels of self-understanding. This humanistic approach is *not* the same as the "secular humanist" movement which is stridently atheistic and narrowly scientific in orientation. It is unfortunate that the same name is claimed by both groups.

"Progressive education" was quite popular earlier in this century, based on the ideas of Francis W. Parker, John Dewey, and others. It sought to develop children's creativity and self-expression through the use of arts and group projects. It attempted to make schools into democratic communities, and to link educational experiences with real life problems. The movement was severely criticized during the 1950's (when American culture was engaged in a fierce crusade against intellectual and political dissent) and until recent years was limited to a few, rather elite, private boarding schools. But lately, the progressive education movement has shown signs of reviving and forming a new network of educational reformers.

In addition, the term "progressive" has been picked up by many political activists (for example, Jesse Jackson's followers are called the "progressive" wing of the Democratic party), and a few of these activists who work in education are attempting to re-establish "progressive education" as a political, as well as pedagogical, reform movement. They are concerned with the problems of racism, sexism, poverty and the unequal distribution of wealth and power in this society, and the effects these have on children's lives and development.

In general terms, I would argue that holistic education, in all of its expressions, is most definitely *alternative* to the aims and practices of mainstream education. It is not surprising that conventional educators, and many parents, do not fully recognize how different these approaches really are. The "reforms" and "restructuring" that politicians and commissions are always talking about are *not* holistic approaches; they consistently fail to question the limited, nationalistic goals of public education. It is my belief that holistic education, which for two hundred years has been a small, ineffective movement on the fringes of American education, is exactly the approach to teaching and learning which we will need in the twenty-first century. The global and ecological challenges now facing humankind are unprecedented. We desperately need an education that will encourage the fullest development of human abilities - our inherent intellectual, physical, moral, social, creative and spiritual potentials.

The Educational Marketplace

—— Jane Williams ————————————————————————

Educational environments are usually categorized into one of the following four groups: private schools, state schools, church-affiliated schools, and alternative learning environments. Clear-cut distinctions, however, do not always exist between these groups. Some private schools consider themselves Christian schools, but they may not be affiliated with any specific church. A private school that touts a particular educational philosophy, for example the Montessori method, may be either Christian or non-sectarian. Church-affiliated schools can practice a very traditional approach to education, or they may resemble more closely a throw-back to the one-room schoolhouse where peers help each other. Religious instruction in the church-affiliated school may comprise one class period, or might permeate every subject of the educational program. Consequently, the best way to learn about a school's educational philosophy and attitude towards children is to interview the administrator and/or its teachers. Because you think you understand, for example, the Montessori method, is no guarantee that each Montessori school has interpreted and applied Montessori in the same way.

Among private schools, Carden, Montessori and Waldorf are the predominate franchise, or chain-like, schools available in the United States. Other private schools are usually one-of-a-kind enterprises and can be either religious or nondenominational. Carden, Montessori and Waldorf each claim to nurture a child's self-esteem and address the needs of the individual. Each believe their approach to education is unique and each has its own curriculum program and instructional materials. In fact, Carden is considered a "method" that can be adapted by any school.

One of the objectives of Montessori is to assure that the child does not fail when attempting new tasks. Montessori believes that failure can have negative effects on the child, so Montessori instructors do everything they can to assure that this doesn't happen. A prominent feature of Montessori education is the prepared learning environment. For example, if a three year old child wants to try a task that has been judged appropriate to the mechanical abilities and intellectual level of a five year old, then the three year old will not be permitted to attempt the task because he might fail. Montessori uses a very physical approach to learning and uses a lot of manipulatives, like blocks and Cuisenaire rods.

Waldorf School proponents believe that learning should be in harmony with nature and the arts; so art, music, and nature predominate the Waldorf curriculum. In the early years a child is not given letter grades, but rather a written report is made of the child's intellectual, emotional, and educational progress. In an effort to provide the young child with a secure learning environment the same teacher moves with her class through the elementary grade levels.

Carden School is disciplined. Carden offers a traditional curriculum, emphasizing the classics in literature, phonics, comprehension, and ethical values, among other things. Competition is not a part of the learning experience. A prerequisite for teaching at Carden is to sincerely like children, and Carden teachers are required to attend regularly scheduled Carden educational programs.

A large percentage of church-affiliated schools are teaching arms of the large churches like the Catholic Church. Many smaller churches, however, are providing educational facilities to be used by members of their congregations. Usually the parents of those children attending these small church schools share the responsibility for instruction. By meeting in church facilities and teaching religion, the legal question of separation of church and state complicates the possibility for state intervention. These schools are usually very small, comprising just a few families—perhaps five to twelve. The educational philosophy is as varied as the schools and usually develops from the beliefs of the families involved.

Some private schools provide home study curriculums as an alternative to on-site instruction. The school provides the curriculum materials and the student follows the course guidelines. Some of these curriculums require the parent to act as teacher, while some are designed for the student to work through the program independently. Whereas some private schools provide a correspondence teacher to grade work and provide comments, others provide an on-site visiting teacher who comes to the home on a pre-arranged schedule. These correspondence curriculums are generally utilized by students learning at home exclusively, by conventionally schooled students to supplement their regular curriculum, or by missionaries or military families on overseas duty. Again, these schools and their curriculums can be very traditional and rigid, or very open and unstructured.

Homeschooling has many variations. In a homeschool, the degree of freedom the child has in relation to his learning is largely dependent on his parents. Homeschools can be as rigidly formal as the most structured state school or so free as to allow the child to pursue his education based on the child's own motivation, curiosity, and interests about the world. This latter approach has been called natural learning, organic learning, interest-initiated learning, independent learning, or invited teaching.

In a natural learning environment a child is permitted to pursue whatever direction his curiosity takes. If the child wants to attempt a task that an older sibling is doing, then he can. Through failure comes knowledge. Seldom does a child get so frustrated that the situation becomes negative. Usually he knows his limits and will stop himself when he has reached that limit. In the natural learning environment frustration does not come from failure, but rather from the inability to be able to try. Since many adults have preconceived notions of what children are capable of doing, adults oftentimes underestimate children's abilities. In natural learning the parent learns to reevaluate his ideas about children and look to the child for information about what he is capable of accomplishing.

Another form of homeschooling is one in which the parent supplements what is lacking or misrepresented in the curriculum of the institutionalized school, either private or state. This might mean the study of free market economics, critical thinking, reasoning skills, and a more complete presentation of our American heritage.

Working within some state systems a student may choose independent study, another variation of homeschooling, if the district offers such a program. Independent study allows the parents to work with a state school liaison teacher to develop a home study program acceptable to all parties concerned. The degree of freedom the parent has to design the curriculum is determined in large part by the attitude of the liaison teacher. If an independent study program is not available, a family may ask that the district start a program, or they can try to transfer to a district that does offer independent study.

Tutoring is a statute option available in many states. A teacher instructs the child on a one-to-one basis in the home.

Within the confines of state education, a student can attend the state school which is assigned to him based on the geographical location of his home. However, some schools are offering alternative educational environments within their districts, allowing the parent the choice of sending his child to a back-to-basics school, open school, or a traditional classroom.

Intradistrict or interdistrict transfers can be requested. The parent requests that his child be transferred to another school within the same district (intradistrict), or to a school in a completely separate district (interdistrict).

If the state school does not offer a choice of educational environments within its district, a parent can try to enroll his child in a particular teacher's class at the state school the child is attending. By interviewing teachers, a parent and/or a student may find one that most meets the student's educational goals and is consistent with the parent's and/or student's philosophy of learning.

The State of California offers a program called the Regional Occupational Program (ROP). Through ROP a student who wants to explore a vocational career signs up for a block of time in ROP and works, for example, as an apprentice in a cafeteria, in an office as a secretary, or as a helper in an auto shop.

If the student feels he has learned everything his school (either public or private) has to offer him, he may try to exit the system early. The student may then begin college or vocational training, or try to find employment.

Some of these educational options depend on the laws in force in each state, and each parent should discern the locally enforced legal answers for himself.

Since most children spend seventeen or eighteen years in a school environment, it is essential for parents to be aware of the educational choices available. Without this knowledge, it is virtually impossible to select a learning environment which can realistically accommodate a family's budget, life style, and philosophies of learning and of life.

GATE and the Education Revolution of the 1990's

—— Ron Miller, Ph.D. ——————————————————————

In June, 1990, eighty people, sharing a common goal of drastically changing the ways young people are educated in the modern world, gathered at a retreat near Chicago. Homeschoolers were there, along with Waldorf and Montessori educators, public and private alternative school people, global and environmental educators, and advocates of other innovative, person-centered approaches. Several college professors, editors, and even a researcher from the U. S. Department of Education also attended. The group issued The Chicago Statement on Education, which proclaimed that old ways of thinking about teaching and learning are obsolete, given the social and environmental problems in the world today.

Although the group represented a great variety of educational methods, there was general agreement that the established, factory-model approach to education needs to be replaced by a more democratic, person-centered, and flexible model, a model based on ecological awareness, global and multi-cultural sensitivity, and a respect for the spiritual dimension of human life; the general term for this model is "holistic education." The Chicago Statement makes it clear that "holistic education is not one particular curriculum or methodology," but a set of broad philosophical principles that parents and educators from diverse backgrounds and organizations can agree upon. These principles pose a humane, decentralized alternative to the authoritarian, bureaucratic system of schooling we have today.

In August, 1990, a steering committee (comprised of people who had planned the conference plus several new members) launched the Global Alliance for Transforming Education (GATE), a non-profit organization dedicated to promoting these principles. GATE's role is to be a networking link, a catalyst, a clearinghouse serving *all* holistically oriented educational movements. For many years, alternative educators have worked in isolation from each other: homeschoolers, Montessorians, Waldorf educators, progressive educators, alternative school people, and other groups all have their own publications, their own conferences, their own internal politics, and they all make their own separate attempts to change the educational system. While the system is entrenched and monolithic, these radical reform efforts are marginal and fragmented—no one by itself has been able to bring about the significant changes that are needed.

The idea behind GATE is that by joining forces, these groups could exert a far greater influence than by continuing to work separately. A key idea in holistic thinking is that the whole is greater than the sum of its parts. By joining together to support common principles that are more comprehensive than any one group's particular perspective, a new force for educational change is created. Yet the advantage to building a *coalition* is that each constituent part offers its distinctive perspective, and particular strengths and insights that no other part offers in quite the same way. GATE has no intention to replace or compromise the work that any constituent member has been doing—its aim is to find unity by means of this diversity. GATE's role is like an orchestra conductor—it does not seek to become a new, loud instrument that will drown out any others. The goal is to open up the educational system to new possibilities, enabling young people, families and communities to choose how, what and where they wish to learn.

In 1991 GATE held an exciting conference in Colorado, issued a 16 page mission statement entitled *Education 2000: A Holistic Per-*

spective, and after receiving a foundation grant, hired Phil Gang as full-time director. During the next several months, Phil travelled around the U. S., to Europe, South America and Japan, and worked with the steering committee and regional GATE coordinators to start building "partnerships" with parents, local communities, universities, business leaders, United Nations agencies, and other constituencies. GATE holds annual conferences, as well as educational institutes, leadership training weekends, and meetings of representatives from key educational movements. Many of us who have been involved in the growth of this coalition are extremely encouraged by the response it has received, and we are hopeful that it may ultimately succeed in bringing about a genuine revolution in the way people think about education.

GATE is different from all previous educational reform efforts, not only because it is bringing together many alternative voices, but because it intends to shift the focus of education away from job and citizenship training and national economic goals, to a deep concern for the full, healthy growth of human beings. Education 2000 calls for an explicit recognition of the spiritual dimension of human existence, but there is no intention to represent any particular religious philosophy. GATE's steering committee, for example, includes people who are Unitarian, Catholic, Quaker and Jewish, as well as a Mormon, who was a principal of public schools in Utah for over 30 years. GATE could not embrace this diversity if it were pushing one particular religious viewpoint.

Homeschoolers may wonder: "Isn't GATE largely a group of professional educators who are mainly concerned about schools? Won't GATE compromise its principles as it works with mainstream institutions?" These are valid questions. So far, GATE *is* primarily comprised of educators. But we are profoundly dissatisfied educators who have given a great deal of thought to what is wrong with the educational system and what needs to be changed. We are not only concerned about schooling, we are much more generally concerned with building a society that will nurture the healthy growth of human beings. Our mission statement asserts that "education means caring enough to draw forth the greatness that is within each unique person." The emphasis is not on schooling, or instruction, or curriculum, but on *caring* and personal individuality.

The educators who have joined the GATE coalition welcome parents, families, and young people themselves as equal partners in this quest for a nurturing society. GATE recognizes the homeschooling option: a section of *Education 2000* called "Freedom of Choice," in addition to calling for more genuine options in public and private schooling, explicitly states: "Families should have freedom to educate their children at home, without undue interference from public authorities. Homeschooling has proven to be educationally, socially and morally nourishing for many children and families." GATE recognizes that homeschoolers have distinctive interests and goals that are of special concern to them; still, we believe that when homeschoolers describe *why* they care so passionately about nurturing their children, they are expressing a point of view--a reverence for life, really--that is much larger than homeschooling *per se* and is sincerely shared by all other members of GATE; indeed, it is the very basis for GATE's existence. We believe that it is time for all of us to work for this nurturing, caring point of view *together*, because the larger society, and its educational system, have proven to be hostile to it.

GATE exists "to proclaim and promote a vision of education that fosters personal greatness, social justice, peace, and a sustainable environment." As a coalition, GATE enables diverse people and diverse communities to strive for this vision in their various ways. We may disagree, sometimes passionately, about particular approaches. But our hope is that the principles upon which this vision is based are inspiring, unifying, and beyond compromise.

For more information about GATE, including a copy of *Education 2000: A Holistic Perspective*, contact Dr. Phil Gang, GATE, 4202 Ashwoody Trail, Atlanta, GA 30319. 404-458-5678.

The Alternative Education Resource Organization

—— Jerry Mintz ——————————————————————————

The Alternative Education Resource Organization (AERO) helps people who want to change education to a more empowering and holistic form. We help individuals and groups of people who want to start new community schools, public and private, or change existing schools. We also provide information to people interested in homeschooling their children.

We publish a newsletter, *AERO-Gramme*, which offers networking news from many different realms of alternative and holistic education. We have a directory of alternative schools and homeschool resources, consulting services, and have organized television and radio presentations about educational alternatives. We have made videos on topics such as the 70th anniversary celebration of Summerhill School in England, the first New Schools Festival in the USSR, footage from 12 alternative schools around the country, and a description of educational alternatives and communities starting at the turn of the century by 98 year old Nellie Dick, an educational pioneer. Also included are videos of over 70 alternative schools and programs. We are supported by individual contributions and foundation grants, and are a part of the School of Living, a non-profit corporation.

Some of the goals of The Alternative Education Resource Organization are to work to change our educational system, learn how to use the media toward this end, help people become aware of their educational options and to find the resources they need, and to learn how to better get communication going across the "parallel universes" of alternative educational systems. This includes all of the networking, both through the office and through the publication of the *AERO-Gramme* newsletter.

We have travelled thousands of miles to help promote educational alternatives, and to help people who want to create new alternatives in their communities. This has included organizing several new independent alternative schools in Missoula, Montana; helping people set up new homeschool resource centers in Virginia, Rhode Island, and New York; helping public alternative schools set up self governing democratic meetings.

In the summer of 1991 we travelled to the Crimea, USSR, to the first New Schools Festival in the USSR. We have never been in a situation in which people were so hungry for information about ways to change the education system. People took seriously the idea that proper preparation for a democratic society is participatory and democratic education. We will be returning to lead a teacher education seminar in alternative educational systems, taking five homeschooled and alternatively schooled students with us, to meet five of their counterparts in Russia.

The *AERO-Gramme* was originally sent out to just fifty individuals and alternative schools in 1989 to help provide materials for the Kee Way Win Indians, to match a grant that was given to us to support a trip to northern Ontario to help them start a new school. Subsequently, *AERO-Gramme* has grown to a circulation of over 1,000 individuals, homeschools, programs, and alternative schools.

To illustrate the kind of work we do, a detailed description of one of our first trips might be helpful: I heard about the Kee Way Wins on a trip to Canada, when their chief, Geordi Kakepetum came down to Toronto to tell the plight of his people, who had not received any of the housing and educational assistance that the Canadian government had promised. Since moving to Kee Way Win five years earlier, there had been no school at all, and some of their children were illiterate. It hadn't occurred to the people that they could teach their own children.

Back in 1985, when the tribe had returned to their ancestral land on the eastern shore of Sandy Lake, they were told by David Crombie, then Indian Affairs Minister, that reserve status would be forthcoming. Unfortunately Crombie was later transferred, and the status was never granted, leaving the tribe in limbo.

Having been the founder and director of an alternative school, and the Executive Director of an international alternative school organization,I felt that these innovative approaches could be used as models, and the schools themselves could be resources for the Kee Way Wins. Perhaps more to the point, in 1971 I helped the Mohawks at Akwesasne, in upstate New York, start the first Indian run survival school in North America. This school has helped the Mohawks (and other Native tribes who have used it as a model) retain their language and culture, while still preparing them for the modern world.

Chief Kakepetum, communicating to me by a battery powered microwave telephone, confirmed the details and we agreed that I would come to Kee Way Win and help the tribal council start a school, utilizing whatever available resources we could find.

Traveling first by train to Sioux Lookout, 250 miles east of Winnipeg, Manitoba, the next leg of the journey was by Bearskin Air, covering over 200 miles of frozen lakes and countless pine forests to Sandy Lake, in northwestern Ontario. From there I travelled 28 miles across the frozen lake in 30 below zero temperatures.

Meeting with the education council I stressed the idea of using the abilities of the community members, and organizing a curriculum that combined the new with the old, including a tribal council decision making process for the school itself. David Thompson, a Kee Way Win council member, asked what he could do personally, and I suggested that he could tutor the kids individually in reading. It was as if the idea had never occurred to him before, but now he was excited about it. He began furiously taking notes as he realized the possibilities of the approach. The elders knew such things as syllabics, the Cree written language, traditional trapping techniques, tribal history, crafts, etc.

The Kee Way Win children were also involved in the process. They had heard that I was a good ping pong player and asked me to teach them how to play. A dozen children participated in an impromptu model of a workable approach to education. By the time we had finished, five hours later and past midnight, I had brought them from the point of not even knowing the rules or how to hit a ball over the net to playing singles, doubles, and having a mini-tournament. They wanted to do the same thing the next night, my last evening at Sandy Lake, but I had meetings scheduled with some council members. I told them they would have to organize the whole thing themselves, and I would come over later. Cain Linklater, a 12 year old from the Kee Way Win band, organized the event. I had my meeting with the council and then went to join the ping pong games, which were going strong. The group had learned to organize this activity by themselves.

The tribal council subsequently got a community school going, and once this was achieved the Province of Ontario was legally required to support it, which they have done. Now, two years later, the school is flourishing.

The Alternative Education Resource Organization is now sponsored by the School of Living, a non-profit organization, which through the years has been consistently working for holistic living and empowerment of people. While not well known, the School of Living has been the parent group to many significant movements. It is de-centralist in philosophy, and has been low-profile during its 55 year history. Nevertheless, spinoffs from this group have been prime movers in health food, organic farming, land trust, alternative education, intentional communities, and environmental protection communities.

Ralph Borsodi, the originator of the land trust idea, was also the founder of the School of Living. The name comes from the home-school which he started for his own children in 1920. He is credited by some as the father of consumer protection, publishing his classic book, *The Advertising Age*, in 1925. The School of Living is credited with being one of the first proponents of the back to the earth movement and environmentalism, which has led to the newer concepts of bioregionalism and permaculture. People who have followed the work of the School of Living have said, "If you want to know what the important new movements will be thirty years from now, find out what the School of Living is doing today."

Networking and linkages are the key to the holistic approach, and one of our roles has become that of expediting these connections between the different alternative and holistic education systems. Some of these seemed not to be in communication with each other, so our task has been to get communication going across these parallel universes, helping these holistic systems become more of a whole. If these movements can become united, not identical, but working together in a global community, it is possible that the entire educational system could change, a true "paradigm shift," as some have called it.

We are now in the process of editing the *Alternative Education Almanac*, to be published by Solomon Press. It will present an overview of the different forms of educational alternatives, the history of alternative education, and specific how-tos for creating alternative schools, restructuring schools, and starting to home-school. It will also list, state by state, every known educational alternative in the United States, as well as many abroad, a total of more than 5,000 schools and programs. It will thus become a primary resource, uniting for the first time all forms of educational alternatives under one cover.

For information write to AERO, 417 Roslyn Road, Roslyn Heights, NY 11577; 516-621-2195.

Alliance for Parental Involvement in Education, Inc.
Empowering Families

The Alliance for Parental Involvement in Education emphasizes the importance of the family in education. ALLPIE encourages parents to become involved in the education of their children wherever that education takes place - in public school, in private school, or at home. By providing information about educational options, family rights in education, current educational trends, and useful resources, ALLPIE works to empower parents - the only true experts with respect to the unique learning styles of their own children (other than the children themselves). ALLPIE believes that parents have both the right and the responsibility to seek out and to work with educational programs that address the needs of the whole child.

The Alliance for Parental Involvement in Education is a grassroots, nonprofit, tax-exempt organization whose board of directors is comprised of parents with experience in different types of education. Information is provided through pamphlets on subjects such as parent/student rights, public education, alternative education, and home education; *Options in Learning*, the ALLPIE newsletter; and a book and resources catalog containing books about different educational options and learning resources. In addition, ALLPIE encourages direct contact among concerned parents by conducting workshops (Family Rights and Options in Education, Learning Materials, and Home Education), and by maintaining a referral service to connect people with others who have faced similar situations and with professionals and organizations which provide useful services.

For a free brochure, catalog, and sample newsletter, write to ALLPIE, P. O. Box 59, East Chatham, NY 12060-0059, or call 518/392-6900.

For Further Information

ORGANIZATIONS:

The Alliance for Parental Involvement in
Education (ALLPIE)
Post Office Box 59
East Chatham, New York 12060-0059
518-392-6900

National Coalition of Alternative
Community Schools (NCACS)
58 Schoolhouse Road
Summertown, Tennessee 38483
615-964-3670

The Global Alliance for Transforming
Education (GATE)
4202 Ashwoody Trail
Atlanta, Georgia 30319
404-458-5678

The Alternative Education Resource
Organization (AERO)
417 Roslyn Road
Roslyn Heights, New York 11577
516-621-2195

PUBLICATIONS:

The AERO-Gramme
The Alternative Education Resource
Organization
417 Roslyn Road
Roslyn Heights, New York 11577
516-621-2195

Options in Learning
The Alliance for Parental Involvement in
Education
Post Office Box 59
East Chatham, New York 12060-0059
518-392-6900

National Coalition News
National Coalition of Alternative
Community Schools
58 Schoolhouse Road
Summertown, Tennessee 38483
615-964-3670

SKOLE
72 Philip Street
Albany, New York 12202
518-432-1578

The GATE Newsletter
The Global Alliance for Transforming
Education
4202 Ashwoody Trail
Atlanta, Georgia 30319
404-458-5678

Changing Schools
c/o Colorado Options in Education
98 North Wadsworth Blvd. #127, Box 191
Lakewood, CO 80226
303-331-9352

Holistic Education Review
39 Pearl Street
Brandon, Vermont 05733-1007
802-247-8312

Rethinking Schools
1001 E. Keefe Avenue
Milwaukee, WI 53212
414-964-9646

BOOKS

Arons, Stephen *Compelling Belief: The Culture
of American Schooling* (McGraw-Hill, 1983)
Ashton-Warner, Sylvia *Teacher* (Simon &
Shuster, 1963)
Bruner, Jerome *The Process of Education*
(Harvard, 1960)
Copperman, Paul *The Literacy Hoax*
(Morrow Quill, 1978)
Deal, Terrance E. and Robert R. Nolan
*Alternative Schools: Ideologies, Realities,
Guidelines* (Nelson-Hall, 1978)
Dennison, George *The Lives of Children: The
Story of the First Street School* (Random
House, 1969)
Dewey, John *Education Today* (Putnam,
1940)
Dreikurs, Rudolf *Children: The Challenge*
(Hawthorn Books, 1964)
Elkind, David *Miseducation* (Knopf, 1987)
Gatto, John Taylor *Dumbing Us Down: The
Hidden Curriculum of Compulsory Schooling*
(New Society Publishers, 1991)
Goodman, Paul *Growing Up Absurd*
(Random House, 1960)
Goodman, Paul *Compulsory Mis-Education*
(Horizon, 1964)
Graubard, Allen *Free The Children: Radical
Reform and the Free School Movement*
(Pantheon Books, 1972)

Hemmings, Ray *Children's Freedom: A.S. Neill and the Evolution of the Summerhill Idea* (Schoken Books, 1973)

Hentoff, Nat *Our Children Are Dying* (Viking, 1967)

Herndon, James *The Way it Spozed To Be* (Simon & Shuster, 1968)

Hillesheim, James W. and George D. Merrill *Theory and Practice in the History of American Education* (Goodyear Publishing Company, 1971)

Holt, John, *How Children Fail* (Pitman Publishing, 1964)

Holt, John *How Children Learn* (Pitman Publishing, 1967)

Holt, John *Freedom and Beyond* (E. P. Dutton, 1972)

Holt, John *Escape From Childhood* (E. P. Dutton, 1974)

Holt, John *Instead of Education* (E.P. Dutton, 1976)

Holt, John *Teach Your Own* (Delacorte Press, 1981)

Holt, John *Learning All The Time* (Delacorte, 1989)

Illich, Ivan *Deschooling Society* (Harper & Row, 1970)

Kohl, Herbert *36 Children* (The New American Library, 1967)

Kohl, Herbert *The Open Classroom* (New York Review of Books, 1969)

Kohl, Herbert *The Question is College* (Times Books/Random House, 1989)

Kozol, Jonathan *Death at an Early Age* (Houghton Mifflin, 1967)

Kozol, Jonathan *Free Schools* (Houghton Mifflin, 1972)

Kozol, Jonathan *The Night is Dark and I Am Far From Home* (Simon and Schuster, 1975, 1990)

Leonard, George *Education and Ecstasy* (Delacorte Press, 1968)

Leue, Mary *Challenging the Giant: The Best of SKOLE, The Journal of Alternative Education* (Down-to-Earth Books, 1992)

Maeroff, Gene I. *Don't Blame the Kids* (McGraw-Hill, 1982)

Miller, Ron *What Are Schools For: Holistic Education in American Culture* (Holistic Education Press, 1990)

Neill, A. S. *Summerhill* (Hart Publishing, 1960)

Piaget, Jean *To Understand Is To Invent* (Grossman Publishers, 1973)

Popenoe, Joshua *Inside Summerhill* (Hart Publishing Company, 1970)

Postman, Neil, and C. Weingartner *Teaching As A Subversive Activity* (Delecorte Press, 1969)

Postman, Neil, and C. Weingartner *The School Book* (Delecorte Press, 1973)

Ravitch, Diane *The Troubled Crusade: American Education 1945-1980* (Basic Books, 1983)

Reimer, Eric *School is Dead: Alternatives in Education* (Doubleday and Company, 1971)

Rousseau, Jean-Jacques (Trans. by Allen Bloom) *Emile* or *On Education* (Basic Books, 1979)

Spring, Joel *The Sorting Machine: National Education Policy Since 1945* (McKay, 1976)

Spring, Joel *The American School: 1642-1985* (Longman, Inc., 1986)

CHAPTER TWO

The Politics of Education

American Education:
Our Ticket to Social Control

"It is the duty of a citizen in a free country not to fit into society, but to make society."

- John Holt

"Never doubt that a small group of thoughtful citizens can change the world. Indeed, it's the only thing that ever has."

- Margaret Mead

How our children live and learn is fundamental to the future. This nation's children live and learn in an illusory world called school, a world shaped and driven not by parents and teachers, nor by the apparent educational policy-makers, but by powerful political and economic forces within our society. In order to understand these forces, and the pivotal role they play in molding the future, we must first understand how we have been paralyzed as a society, duped into believing that we as individuals are powerless, and that only the "experts," with their institutions and degrees and policies and procedures, can conjure up real change.

The magnitude of the social problems we face today can leave us feeling personally paralyzed and powerless. While we would like to do something about these problems, we have been led to believe that someone, somewhere, knows what to do, is better qualified to come up with workable solutions and will somehow make things better. The attitude that we must leave the really big problems to the experts underscores our predicament, because the experts are the ones with the greatest stake in maintaining the status quo. Their solutions blatantly ignore the key to real change, that is, who wields the power in this country.

In a democracy the power is in the hands of an educated, knowledgeable populace, and to control education is to control the people. To this end, our compulsory attendance laws and their accompanying regulations assure a compliant and conforming populace, educated in accordance with the needs of those who have assumed control. This has been consistently understated and the real purposes of education have remained hidden behind a facade of teaching children to read and write and compute.

Educational reform has indirectly acknowledged that schooling does not meet the needs of children. But because the reformers are aware of the hidden agenda of schooling, and because they generally agree with its purposes, reform efforts have only served to tighten the grip of business and political interests. Big business says "Give us a compliant workforce," and the schools reply "Sure, we can do that. Just give us your unequivocal support." Politicians say "Give us a literate populace," and the schools reply, "Sure, we can do that. Just give us more money."

A populace that does not hold onto its understanding of empowerment can never effect change, but will only serve the purposes of the political and economic machinery. This is the job which has been given to the school system. Keep the people feeling helpless, and they'll turn to you for help. In a nation that considers itself leader of all the 'free nations' in the world, social control can never be blatantly repressive, but of necessity, will be subtle and pervasive. The challenges which we as alternative educators are facing today will not eradicate alternative education, nor force our children to attend government schools, but will ultimately bring national standards and uniform educational policies into our homes and alternative schools. Because they dare not take control by force, they will take control through rules and regulations, policies and procedures.

Our tightly controlled educational system mocks the promise of democracy. With a closed educational system we simply cannot have an open political system. The current situation allows the government and big business to manufacture and to maintain our culture for us, and in turn, control remains in the hands of the experts and institutions. The ability to change this situation is in the hands of the families and individuals who understand why change is necessary.

Becoming Involved In The Politics Of Alternative Education

—— Larry and Susan Kaseman ————————————————

Alternative education differs in important ways from conventional education. Nevertheless, alternative education exists within the context of education in general and American society as a whole. Today alternative education is facing increasing challenges from both short term threats aimed directly at it and from more subtle long range trends that will alter the fundamental nature of education in American society. Alternative education will only continue to exist in any meaningful sense—that is, as a true alternative and not just as a carbon copy of conventional education—if alternative educators become involved in the politics of alternative education. Alternative educators need to recognize and counter short term challenges that would allow the educational establishment, the state, and big businesses greater control over alternative education. Alternative educators must also be aware of larger, more subtle trends in education in general which would erode the choices that are available and weaken alternative education. Alternative educators are in a strong position to respond to these challenges. In fact, by being alert and aware, alternative educators can make important contributions not just to the future of alternative education, but to American education in general.

Today alternative educators, whether true conservatives or leftist radicals, are the potential vanguard for retaining freedom of thought and expression. In the 1920's and 30's the threat to freedom of thought came from attempts by public schools to create a monopoly in education. Today the threat is not that the public schools will have a monopoly. It is rather that the people of this country will allow legislation to be passed that will specify what children need to know and how they will be trained for work and citizenship and right behavior. This threat is far more insidious and serious since it will appear under the guise of choice in education and/or a voucher system and will affect all children. Therefore, alternative educators should be a vanguard that articulates what is happening and takes a stand against America 2000 and other "educational reform" packages that would actually change the fundamental role of education in our society.

Families involved in alternative education face questions such as:

- Can we afford to give our children an alternative education if it means that they then will be handicapped in getting a job or getting into college? If, as has been proposed, certification of employment skills were included with public school diplomas, would people with alternative educations be handicapped?
- How would our family deal with the loss of meaningful educational alternatives that would follow the implementation of proposals for "educational reform" such as America 2000?
- Should we support vouchers or oppose them?
- How can we counter attempts to increase government regulation of alternative education?

Such questions lead alternative educators to become involved in the politics of alternative education. "Politics" as it is used here is not limited to questions of Democrats versus Republicans or who is running for school board or how tax dollars will be divided among educational programs. Instead the word is used in its broader meaning, as the process of working together with a wide variety of people to establish and maintain laws that cover some part of our lives, in this case, education. "Law" in this sense includes both statutory law (which is passed by legislatures and written in the formal legal code) and common law (which is based on custom, common practice, and court decisions but is not formally written into law). And "alternative educators" means both those who are formally recognized as such and paid for their work (often called "teachers" or "administrators") and parents who are exercising the responsibility that all parents have for their children's education either by deciding to send their children to an alternative school or by educating their children themselves at home. To emphasize this point, the term "alternative educator/parent" will be used sometimes, although for the sake of readability it will sometimes be shortened to "alternative educator."

This chapter discusses contributions alternative educator/parents can make to educational policy and ways of recognizing and responding to direct and indirect challenges to alternative education.

Why Become Involved In The Politics Of Alternative Education

Some alternative educators/parents resist becoming involved in the politics of education. They may claim that they do not have time, or that politics detracts from their true mission of educating children, or that the system is simply too large and complex for an individual to have any influence, or that they do not want to criticize public education. However, compelling reasons draw many alternative educators into the arena of politics:

- By definition, alternative educators are unwilling simply to accept schools as they are, to take the easy way out, to go along with the system. Their questioning and searching lead them to realize that working with others to influence laws and policies is an inevitable part of what they are about. Many alternative educators are alert, socially aware, and accustomed to taking responsibility for various parts of their lives, perhaps including diet, medical self-care, voluntary simplicity, involvement in local government, and environmental activism.

- Alternative educators are on the cutting edge of educational developments. They have direct experience with innovative approaches to learning that work. They focus on the needs of children and families rather than on serving the state and the economy.

- Alternative educators see education as fundamental to each person's development, especially in a society that claims to value education so highly.

- Numerous forces threaten the existence and freedom of alternative education. People who have had direct personal experience with alternative education can best appreciate how important it is, and how serious would be its restriction or loss, to individuals and to our society as a whole. Alternative educators need to work together to counter threats to alternative education.

Some alternative educators become involved in the politics of education reluctantly, only because they feel they must. However, they discover it is more interesting and rewarding than they anticipated, they meet fascinating people and make new friends, their increased understanding of how our society operates informs many of the decisions they must make, and the empowerment they feel as a result of their actions spills over into other areas of their lives and strengthens their families.

Framing The Issue

A first step in solving a problem is to frame the issue clearly and carefully. This involves articulating the most important concerns, selecting the primary focus of the effort, choosing a direction to follow, and determining strategy. Often several options exist, and the results will be strongly influenced by the way the issue is framed. For example, the key issue facing alternative education can be seen as:

- Setting goals concerning the role education should play in a child's life, discussing alternative approaches to education, analyzing children's responses to these approaches, OR
- Promoting alternative education in general (or one particular approach such as wholistic, religious based, Montessori, Waldorf, or homeschooling) and encouraging people to choose an alternative approach rather than a conventional school, OR
- Finding additional sources of funds so the financial future of alternative education is more secure and more children can participate, OR
- Uniting to protect the freedoms, rights, and responsibilities of alternative educators and to introduce positive ideas and counter harmful trends in the current "educational reform movement" based on America 2000 to prevent it from overpowering alternative education.

We, the authors, feel that the last option is the one which should take precedence. Certainly debates about approaches to education are important and often very stimulating and enjoyable, and questions centered on gaining popular support and funding for alternative education are practical and important. But these will be meaningless if we do not exert some influence on the direction in which American education is going and counter current proposals that threaten the very existence of alternative education.

Sometimes the realities of a situation require that we work with other alternative educators whose approach to education and other aspects of life differ significantly from ours. This is inevitable in an area as varied as alternative education. We cannot work to protect the rights and responsibilities of only those alternative educators who agree with our particular approach. One basic tenet of alternative education is the need and right of each family to make its own decisions concerning its approach to education. As soon as alternative educators begin arguing that a certain approach should not be allowed, because it is too narrow-minded, or too one-sided, or too unstructured, or too limited, or too isolated, the rights and responsibilities of all alternative educators have been seriously diminished. It is only by setting aside our differences and uniting to work together to protect the rights and responsibilities of all alternative educators that any of us will be able to protect our own rights and responsibilities.

Positive Contributions That Alternative Educators Make

Alternative educators/parents have important contributions to make to the continuing debate over education. Among them are the following:

- Obviously alternative educators have a great deal of insight and experience with a wide range of approaches to learning that work well.
- As alternative educators, we often have a more realistic perspective on the conventional educational system simply because we have valuable experience outside that system. Because we know that it is not the only option, or even the best option, we are able to view the system in a more detached way.
  In addition, having had experience with approaches to learning that work better than those of the conventional educational system, we also have insights into what the real problems are and how they might be better approached.
- Alternative education has put the lie to some of the basic principles of conventional education. It has shown that special teacher education or training is unnecessary and in fact may be an obstacle to good teaching. It has demonstrated that there is no one right way to learn, that there are no techniques and texts that can be counted on to work better than others, and that tests do not validate the whole process.
- Another valuable asset is the international network that alternative educators have developed among people informed and concerned about children and learning.

Threats That Alternative Educators Must Counter

Opposition to alternative education exists for a number of reasons. Those with a strong vested economic interest in public schools want larger numbers of students in them and want to capture the market that private education represents. Those who are working to make the public schools serve the state and the economy resent the alternative that some private education presents. Some people feel that public schools are an essential aspect of our society, part of the glue which holds it together, part of the "melting pot." Therefore, they feel it is wrong not to support public schools in every way, including sending as many children as possible to them. Others feel that a public school education is an important experience for every child. They object to what they see as the "isolationism" and "elitism" of alternative educators. Some people distrust alternative educators because they are not strongly regulated by the state, because they are different, because they are considered a threat.

Alternative education can be restricted and compromised in two different ways. Short term threats appear in the form of direct attacks, precedents, new legislation, increased regulation, and policy changes that directly affect alternative education in negative ways. (Examples of these and ways of countering them are discussed under "Recognizing Direct, Short-Term Threats" and "Minimizing and Responding to Short-Term Threats.")

But even more dangerous are indirect threats to alternative education that arise from recent developments in education in America, and current proposals for "educational reform" such as those in America 2000, corresponding state and local 2000 plans, and similar programs. These proposals would change the fundamental role of education from that of providing a service to those who choose to attend a public school, to that of determining the way in which children are raised and the kind of adults they should become. These developments have the potential to radically reshape education in America, and the "reforms" would have serious and devastating effects on our whole society. As citizens we are very concerned about all of them. However, since this chapter is addressed primarily to alternative educators, the discussion here will focus on the effects these developments and reforms are having and will have on alternative education. (See below, "Recognizing Subtle, Long-Term Threats" and "Responding to Long-Term Threats".)

It would be a very serious mistake for alternative educators to think that they can protect their own separate sphere of education and do not need to worry about what happens in the public schools. Among the reasons this would be a mistake are:

- The general public expects, and compulsory school attendance laws require, that children attend some kind of school. As our society's general definition of education changes, the expectations and limitations which are put on alternative education will inevitably change. In other words, people may be willing to accept the idea of *alternative* education, but it has to fall within their idea of what constitutes *education*. The more public schools are required to use standardized tests or other standardized assessments, which in turn dictate curriculum, and to meet state requirements rather than being subject to local control, the more limitations will be inevitably and indirectly placed on alternative educators.

- Attempts are being made to strengthen the connections between conventional public schooling and employment. For example, proposals are being made to increase the emphasis that schools place on preparing students for employment, including testing tenth graders to determine who will take vocational education or "tech-prep" courses and who will take college preparatory courses. Other proposals would make passing a skills assessment, and earning a certificate of employability, requirements for graduation. If these proposals are adopted, students of alternative schools will be handicapped in finding employment. (Some alternative educators may argue that employment will not be a problem as long as students from alternative schools can show that they are at least as qualified and well-prepared as public school students who have earned certificates. But how can an alternative school be alternative in any meaningful sense of the word if it has to meet the standards and expectations of a conventional public school education?) It is especially important to note that alternative educators can lose their flexibility, responsibilities, and rights in this way without anyone even considering policies that would directly increase regulation of private education.
- Attempts are being made to increase the amount of time a child spends in school. They include increasing the emphasis on early childhood education, lengthening the school day and/or the school year, and extending the number of years covered by the compulsory school attendance law. Any of these will increase the time that parents interested in alternative education have to be considering, planning, and documenting (formally or informally) a clearly recognizable education for their children. Even parents who define education in a very free and unstructured way will still be answerable to the state (through the compulsory school attendance law at the very least) for a longer period of time.
- The more tightly the forces of business and professional self-interest groups control public schools, and the greater the differences between conventional schools and alternative schools, the more alternative education will be perceived as a threat that must be stopped, controlled, or better still, forced to become like public education. This is one of the key reasons why

homeschooling causes so much distress among professional educators and policymakers, despite the fact that homeschooling clearly works well as a way of educating children and its numbers are likely to remain small. Alternative education will simply not be allowed to go its merry way, making its own independent decisions regardless of what is happening in public education. Alternative education is far too powerful an idea, far too dangerous to "the system" for the protectors of that system to allow this.

- In a more general sense, public schools exert a strong influence on our whole society. Assumptions made by public schools and values taught by them strongly influence the children (and parents) who are involved with them. Thus the lives of the majority of American citizens are strongly shaped by public education. The fact that many people do not appear to be concerned is no excuse for those of us involved in alternative education not to be. Alternative education simply does not exist in a vacuum, and cannot afford to act as if it did.

If alternative education is to continue, alternative educators/parents need to be aware of both direct and indirect threats, and they need to act to counter these threats. Each of these will now be discussed in some detail.

Recognizing Direct, Short-term Threats

The rights and responsibilities of alternative educators/parents may be compromised in a number of ways, including the following:

- New legislation may increase the regulation of alternative education by requiring increased reporting and/or testing or other forms of assessment. At this point private education is governed and controlled by state laws. However, the federal government is increasing its involvement in education through America 2000, plans for national standards in education and national assessments, and other such programs. Therefore, alternative educators need to concentrate on state legislation, but be prepared for the possibility of federal legislation as well.
- Some legislation grants a government agency not only authority to administer the law but also authority to make rules that carry the weight of law and further determine how the law will be enforced. In states in which the department of education has such authority in matters concerning private education, ed-

ucational policy and regulations that are considered to have the force of law can be established by the agency without the approval of the legislature or the signature of the governor. (Sometimes public hearings are required, but they generally receive less press and are taken less seriously than legislative hearings.) Alternative educators in such states need to be alert for possible rule changes by the state department of education. To determine whether the department of education in your state has rule making authority in matters relating to private education, begin by asking other alternative educators. If they do not know, call the person in the department of education who works with private schools. Also ask a state legislator, either one of your own or the chairperson of one of the education committees. If such rule making authority exists in your state, request that you be notified when additions to or changes in the rules are being considered and especially when hearings are scheduled by the department and the legislature. Then check periodically with the department of education and with legislators to see if any changes are being contemplated or have been proposed, since government agencies sometimes "forget" to notify concerned citizens about their activities.

• Bureaucracies have a built-in tendency to try to expand and increase their power and influence. State bureaucrats and local school officials may, deliberately or inadvertently, exceed their lawful authority in the demands that they make of alternative educators for reporting or other actions. These illegal demands may set precedents that then become widespread unless alternative educators are well informed about what the laws and regulations actually require, have interpreted these laws and regulations themselves, and counter the officials' actions.

• Some alternative educators may attempt to get themselves out of a difficult or threatening situation by agreeing to give bureaucrats or school officials more information than is legally required, by agreeing to have their curriculum approved or their students tested or assessed, by demonstrating that they have credentials that exceed those required by law, or similar actions. Such actions may set dangerous precedents as the officials continue to require them of the individuals involved and begin requiring them of other alternative educators.

Minimizing And Responding To Short-term Threats

Understand the legal foundations of the rights of alternative educators/parents.

As alternative educators/parents, it is essential that we understand our fundamental responsibilities and rights. Not only will such understanding provide us the basic factual information needed to think, speak, and act effectively; it will also give us much greater confidence as we work to protect our responsibilities and rights and to respond to threats to alternative education. Also, remember that, important as it is to protect alternative education, this is not enough. We must also be aware of developments in education as a whole, because these will strongly affect us as well. We cannot afford simply to retreat to a protected spot and say, "We don't care what happens to conventional education; we are safely protected by our right to a private education."

An understanding of the foundation of individual rights in education in America today begins with the realization that the U.S. Constitution does not specifically mention education. Laws that govern education are based on other provisions of the Constitution not directly related to education. For example, compulsory school attendance laws are based on the policing powers given to the states by the U. S. Constitution. Laws governing education exist only because people have consented to them. This means that if the people withdraw their consent, the laws can be changed, which gives us some basis for hope. However, once consent has been given, withdrawing it is very difficult, so we need to be very careful about the educational laws to which we give our consent.

One of the foundations of individual rights in education is the fact that compulsory school attendance laws require attendance, not education. This is a very important distinction. The law can and does require that children attend an educational program, and children can and do comply. This can be demonstrated and enforced. But the U. S. Constitution does not authorize the state to prescribe a specific educational program or dictate the outcome. Also, there is no general agreement on what it means to be "educated" or on how one demonstrates that one is "educated." Any attempt to set definitions and requirements would quickly violate individual rights and freedoms. Courts have ruled that schools cannot be held accountable if children attending them fail to become educated. Therefore, laws which require education (rather than simply attendance) could be challenged on constitutional grounds. The fact that the U. S. Constitution does not grant the states the authority to require education has important ramifications, beginning with strong limitations on the state's ability to dictate curriculums or the content of educational programs.

However, the important distinction between attendance and education is currently being seriously blurred and threatened by proposals that emphasize "outcome based education." Both students and schools would be judged (and often financially rewarded) on the basis of scores from "performance based assessments" (tests that claim to measure what students have learned and how well prepared they are for employment or college). Since requiring outcome-based education is not a power granted to the state by the Constitution, it can only be required if the people give their consent through legislation. However, if such proposals (including proposals for national standards in education and a national testing program) are not stopped, the people will in effect be giving their consent to the idea that the state can require education (rather than just attendance), it will be very difficult for the people to withdraw this consent, and a very important educational right and a basic freedom will be lost.

Parents' rights in education are also strongly supported by U.S. Supreme Court cases such as *Pierce v. Society of Sisters* (268 U.S. 510 [1925]) and *Farrington v Tokushige* (273 U.S. 284 [1927]). The court has ruled that parents have a right to secure for their children an education consistent with their principles and beliefs and that the state may not have a monopoly in education. Recent rulings by courts in various states have reaffirmed this.

An old legal maxim that alternative educators have used very effectively in arguing against state regulation is, "Hard cases make bad law." In other words, a law designed to take care of the worst possible hypothetical case is almost certain to be long, difficult to enforce, and more likely to prevent good people from doing good than bad people from doing bad. It is unfair and solves nothing to punish conscientious alternative educators by passing an unnecessarily restrictive law that does not solve problems of "high risk" children or families anyway. Such a law would also damage the effectiveness of good alternative schools.

For more information on the legal foundations of rights in education, see Resources Notes at the end of this chapter.

Read and interpret the laws in your state that apply to alternative education.

Find out how the laws in your state affect alternative education by getting copies of the laws. Look them up yourself, ask a librarian for help, or contact your state legislators. Read and interpret these laws yourself and discuss them with other alternative educators. Do not rely on information and interpretations you get from local school officials or the state department of education. Find out how the laws are generally interpreted by the courts, how strictly they are enforced, and by whom. For more information, see Resources Notes at the end of this chapter.

Exercise your rights and responsibilities and respond to short-term threats.

For reasons discussed above, many people who are committed to conventional education feel that alternative education is a threat which must be carefully controlled so it gradually becomes like conventional education. Therefore, alternative educators must be constantly alert for threats to their rights and freedoms. New policies and regulations need to be examined to determine whether they violate basic rights, and protests need to be lodged and pursued if they do. Proposed legislation needs to be carefully monitored to determine how it will affect alternative education. Attempts by school officials and other bureaucrats to exceed their statutory authority need to be countered by pointing out the discrepancy between what the law requires and what is being demanded and by refusing to comply with the excessive requests. Care needs to be taken not to set precedents that will handicap other alternative educators even if they do provide a short-term solution for one alternative educator.

Beware of trying to solve problems through new legislation or court cases.

Finally, mention should be made of two responses that generally do not work. First, attempts to have legislation passed that will supposedly protect alternative education have serious drawbacks because:

- It is naive to think that a mere law could provide enough protection, since the opposition to alternative education is expressed in many ways and on many fronts. General tolerance and acceptance of alternative education by the community is necessary for alternative education to be secure.

- It is very difficult for a small minority which lacks power and money to get a bill passed. (Since less than 25% of the adult population in the United States has children of school age, alternative educators will be a small minority until demographics change significantly.) Minorities are much more successful in legislatures when they are defending themselves from unreasonable attack and can draw on the support Americans tend to give beleaguered underdogs.

- Any legislation can easily be amended. Therefore, introducing a bill opens the door for all sorts of unreasonable and unworkable provisions to be passed against alternative education. Although each situation must be carefully evaluated individually, it is generally much wiser for alternative educators to live with laws that are workable, even though they do not give clear protection to alternative education, have a few undesirable provisions, and/or are ambiguous, than to risk introducing new legislation.

Another approach that generally does not work is trying to resolve problems through court cases (for example, taking a case to court in an attempt to have a law or policy overturned or declared unconstitutional). In the first place, court decisions are likely to be bound by ideas and approaches that are widely accepted in the dominant culture, so that people (such as alternative educators) who are arguing for principles and practices that differ from those of the dominant culture may find that rulings tend to go against them. Second, a court case can force a definite pronouncement on a law or rule when alternative educators would be in a much better position if the law or rule were left ambiguous and applied to individual situations as needed. Third, a court case forces the court to make a judgment about alternative education before there has been enough time for this approach to education to be tried, shown to be effective, and accepted by the larger community.

Recognizing Subtle, Long-term Threats

In addition to direct, short-term threats, alternative education is being challenged by changes that are occurring in conventional education that could virtually end the possibility of meaningful alternatives in education. To understand the subtle and long-term threats, it is important that alternative educators/parents understand these changes.

What is happening in American education today?
Among the important developments in American education
during the twentieth century:
- Conventional schools have increasingly adopted the factory
  model and tried to produce educated citizens in the same way
  that objects are produced on an assembly line, using so-called
  "economies of scale." Curriculums, textbooks, and tests have
  been standardized. Expectations and requirements are now
  linked to children's ages, rather than being based on their
  strengths and needs. Schools are run by huge bureaucracies
  that work to increase their own power and are seldom respon-
  sive to needs and initiatives of individual students, teachers,
  schools, or districts.

The concept of economy of scale has resulted in the consolida-
tion of schools and school districts. In the long run this has been
much more expensive in monetary terms because of transportation expenses, the costs of school administration and bureaucracies to run large schools and districts, etc. The cost in human
terms has been even greater as communities have lost local control, children have been further removed from their homes and
families, schools have ceased to function as neighborhood gathering places, and specialized classes for so called "learning disabled"
students have led to increased labeling of children.

- Education itself has become a big business. Over $1 billion is
  spent on education in the United States every day. There are
  strong vested interests in education, and decisions are often
  made on the basis of dollars rather than on the basis of what
  would be best for children and their families.
- Increasingly schools are serving as institutions of social control
  in the United States today, despite the rhetoric about this being
  a land of freedom and opportunity. The insistence of those in
  power that children be raised so that they will become willing
  participants in the American consumer economy has led to increasing reliance on schools to instill the necessary thoughts,
  beliefs, and values in children. The goal of a conventional
  school is increasingly to prepare children to serve the needs of
  the state and the economy.

A distressing manifestation of this increase in social control can
be seen in the legislative proposals masquerading as "educational
reform" that in reality would change the fundamental nature of
schools and education as they are defined in this country. As was

shown under the heading "Understand the legal foundations of the rights of alternative educators/parents" above, the state historically has required attendance but not education. However, increasingly educational bureaucracies have been trying to expand the role of the state in education and move from simply compulsory attendance to compulsory education. The spread of standardized testing has been one giant step in this direction. In 1972, only one state required such tests; by 1990, all 50 states did. These tests dictate curriculum since teachers must prepare students for the tests. Proposals are now being made to replace standardized tests with "outcome-based assessments" and to make a diploma contingent on passing competency tests, perhaps in areas such as work skills and social ability as well as academic subjects. With such significant changes in the works, alternative educators cannot afford to stand by and watch, feeling we can take refuge in laws that protect private schools. These changes will affect all of education, not just public schools.

- A civil religion has developed in America, based on economic success and economic security. Its beliefs include the idea that the economy is more important than the family, freedom of religion, or independent thought. For example, the tax structure favors businesses over individuals, workers are expected to be willing to move away from their extended families and communities if their relocation is more convenient for their employers, and increasingly two incomes are required to maintain the standard of living achieved with one income in 1970. In a religion like this, the role of schools is to serve the state and the economy.

This civil religion has operated for the benefit of a few at the expense of many. During the 1960's and 1970's, problems with this approach became increasingly clear. The 60's witnessed a rejection by youth of reliance on experts, authority, and accumulation of wealth as the way to personal salvation. During the 70's, a variety of alternative movements in health, diet, education, and spirituality appeared. During the 80's, a growing number of people chose voluntary simplicity rather than greater wealth. Also during the last 30 years many people have lost ground economically and/or have increasingly realized that there are not good paying jobs awaiting high school or college graduates.

Many people can see that this civil religion is not working for them and are unwilling to cooperate voluntarily with the system. More repressive measures are being instituted to force people to comply with an unfair and unjust system. For example, a number of states have enacted one or more of the following truancy measures: revocation of driver's licenses, revocation of work permits, placement of students in detention centers, and reducing a parent's monthly AFDC payment if her children are truant. America 2000 is currently the main proposal to remedy this breakdown of the civil religion. (A discussion of America 2000 may be found below.)

- Pressure on schools from business is also increasing. For example, in June, 1991, the U.S. Department of Labor issued a SCANS (the Secretary's Commission on Achieving Necessary Skills) report entitled *What Work Requires of Schools*. One representative quote:

As the Secretary of Education has said, "America 2000 is not a program but a crusade." If that crusade is to succeed, education must effectively be linked to work. Employers and labor leaders, therefore, must participate in decisions about what future American schools will look like, what kinds of skills and knowledge they will teach, and what kinds of certificates of competence will accompany the high school diploma. (p. 30)

- Increasingly schools have been looked to as the solution to an incredible range of social problems that have nothing to do with education in the traditional sense of the word, problems from racial inequality and tension to teen pregnancy, drug abuse, and the spread of AIDS. These are certainly serious problems deserving our concerted efforts to solve or at least mitigate them. But their causes are complex and outside the control of schools, and their solutions are so controversial and beyond the realm of schools that it is totally unrealistic to expect schools to solve them. But the really dangerous fall-out from this notion that schools can solve social problems is that it plays right into the hands of those who would increase the power and control of the schools for other ends, such as to serve as instruments of social control and the economy. The idea of schools as saviors is too convenient a rationale for increasing the power of schools, generally at the expense of families and the individual.
- Schools are increasingly taking over many of the traditional functions of the family, weakening families and increasing the role that the state has in raising children. This can be seen in

the emphasis on sending children to school at earlier ages, teaching morals and values as clearly identified subjects within curriculums, providing day care in public schools, and using schools to teach parents what the school or social services wants parents to know about parenting skills.

- Large, powerful, and well-financed professional organizations of educators have been developed to protect and promote the self-interests of their members. Teachers unions and associations of school district administrators and of school boards now strongly influence educational policy and legislation through paid professional lobbyists. However, significant differences often exist between the ideas and goals of the leadership of these organizations (which tends to focus on protecting the self-interests of the organization and the group it represents) and many individual members (who really care about children and families and want to work in or with schools that are directed toward meeting the needs of individuals and their local community). Also, few if any of these organizations are balanced by organizations working to promote the needs and interests of children and their families. Increasingly, the voices of children and families are not being heard or considered as conventional education is controlled by bureaucracies, professional organizations, and big business.

All this means it is a mistake for parents to assume that conventional schools are institutions that are designed to help children learn what interests them and what will be most valuable to them as they lead productive, meaningful lives; to help children develop their own unique talents and abilities; to help children learn in ways that suit them best and according to their own timetable; to support parents as they make basic decisions and carry out their responsibilities for raising their children; and to contribute to their local community by bringing people together and working to meet the educational needs of the community.

To be sure, many parents and some teachers, administrators, and school board members view schools in this way. But many people both inside and outside schools have very different agendas for schools. For them, schools are seen as expanding job markets, places through which large profits are to be made, and means of solving a whole host of social problems totally unrelated to education. And since these forces are much more powerful and much better organized than the voices speaking for the interests of children, parents, and families, they increasingly are controlling the schools and their futures.

This is not a pretty picture and is certainly not what most parents want to hear about schools. But it is such a strong reality that it is a serious mistake to try to work in any part of education in America today without at least a basic awareness of what one is up against.

How does conventional schooling manage to wield so much power in our society?

The main power brokers want schools to be instruments of social control. As an example of this, school officials often say directly to corporations, "Tell us what kind of product you want, and we will produce it." The educational establishment and big business do not trust what families or individuals would do if given more money and power or less indoctrination through the schools.

An enormous public relations effort is put into telling falsehoods about the importance of schooling to surviving in a high-tech world, to getting a job, and to America's remaining competitive with other industrialized countries.

Education has long been viewed by most Americans as the way to become somebody, to improve one's lot in life, to pull oneself up by one's boot straps. Schooling has been put on a pedestal and is difficult to criticize.

Conventional schools also enjoy a certain immunity from criticism because many people contend that, "I went to conventional schools, and I've turned out all right, so why should I worry about the schools?" Others, less charitable, even say, "I had to suffer through the trials of conventional schools, and it toughened me-- kids today should have to go through this, too."

There are few checks and balances within the American system of public education. For example, courts have consistently ruled that parents cannot hold a school responsible for failing to educate their child. Because of the fundamental nature of education, there is no effective way to determine whether a school is doing a good job. It is very difficult to have teachers or administrators removed from their positions. Public schools face no competition unless parents are willing to make the financial sacrifices necessary to obtain a private education. The only consistent and meaningful political opposition public schools face is from business interests and taxpayers who want to keep the costs of education low. Even so, businesses generally appreciate the social control role schools play and seldom challenge the educational methods schools employ.

If the goals of America 2000 were realized, how would they affect education and our society?

Many of the worst current proposals for so-called "reform" of education are articulated with frightening clarity and force in the six goals of America 2000, the Bush administration's educational plan, and the state and local 2000 programs it has spawned. (Note: Even if Bush is no longer President and the 2000 plan has been scraped by the time you are reading this, rest assured that the thrust of this plan is probably being pursued under some other banner.) Here are the 6 goals of America 2000 and brief comments on each.

1. All children in America will start school ready to learn.

Comments: This goal overlooks two very important realities: First, children are born ready to learn, in their own ways and their own time. Second, any child who has reached "school age" has already learned a breath-taking amount, including the highly complex skills of walking and verbal communication, at home, with the help and support of his or her parents and others. And yet this misguided goal could be used to justify all kinds of powerful early childhood education programs, governmental intervention in homes of children who have not yet begun school, programs for testing and keeping portfolios on children who have not yet entered school, etc.

To be sure, young children need proper love, care, support, nutrition, and medical care. Certainly there are children (and other people) in our society who need help meeting these basic needs. But trying to solve complex social problems under the guise of preparing children for school shifts the emphasis from support for families to a justification for outside intervention, the merging of social services with educational services, a move toward state-controlled education, and a strengthening of the idea that the role of children is to serve the schools and the state.

2. The high school graduation rate will increase to at least 90 percent.

Comments: This goal denies the fact that for many young people, better alternatives exist than continuing to attend a school that does not make sense for their lives, driving them toward a diploma that will not even solve their economic problems because a reasonable job is difficult to find even with a diploma. This goal justifies tracking students in either vocational education or college preparatory programs, thus perhaps increasing the likelihood of graduation but often not serving the needs or interests of the students. Also, this goal could be used to justify a myriad of punitive truancy measures.

3. *American students will leave grades four, eight, and twelve having demonstrated competency in challenging subject matter including English, mathematics, science, history, and geography; and every school in America will ensure that all students learn to use their minds well, so they may be prepared for responsible citizenship, further learning, and productive employment in our modern economy.*

Comments: Here is the rationale for all kinds of standardized testing and assessment, possibly a uniform, standardized national testing program. Since tests dictate curriculum (because students have to prepare for what the tests cover), this could lead to a standardized national curriculum. Having schools "ensure that all students learn to use their minds well" is a frightening idea incompatible with a free society. Making schools responsible for preparing people for "productive employment" opens the door for business to require all kinds of vocational training, employment skills, etc. Schools cease to be places where children can learn and demonstrate individual initiative and ability and instead become places where workers are mass produced.

4. *U. S. students will be first in the world in science and mathematics achievement.*

Comments: Here is a blatant statement that schools are to serve the state and the economy rather than the needs of students, their families, and their communities. Goals such as this can lead to unbalanced curriculums and unreasonable rewards for students who happen to have technical ability. Misleading claims about other countries (most commonly Japan and Germany) are increasingly used to justify longer school days and years, testing, and other such proposals.

5. *Every adult American will be literate and will possess the knowledge and skills necessary to compete in a global economy and exercise the rights and responsibilities of citizenship.*

Comments: This opens the door for schools to extend their authority to adults. Everyone would have to serve the economy, demonstrate competence in required skills, and live up to a definition of "citizenship" devised by those in power.

6. Every school in America will be free of drugs and violence and will offer a disciplined environment conducive to learning.

Comments: It is mind-boggling to think of ways this goal could be used to justify severe, punitive, unreasonable, unworkable disciplinary and truancy measures. Civil liberties could be lost as strict behavior codes, drug testing, and search and seizures are instituted or strengthened.

In general, these goals are based on using education and schools as the primary if not the sole basis for solving much larger problems in our society such as unemployment, poverty, inadequate health care, and nutrition. When these are labeled "education goals," education and schools are identified as the problem, education and schools can become even more repressive in their role as agents of social control, and larger underlying problems that do not relate directly to education are neither articulated nor addressed.

To read for yourself what the government is saying through America 2000, call 1-800-USA-LEARN for information and a free newsletter.

Responding To Long-term Threats

Seek out accurate information.

It is essential to obtain accurate information about what is happening in and to conventional schools, what public policy is being made and by whom, what trends are developing, what proposals are likely to be made in the near future and how they would affect education. This information cannot be obtained from the mass media, because the media is too much a part of the establishment and its values. Also, the media often strives to keep advertisers happy and to present what most people want to hear.

Therefore alternative sources of information are needed. First-hand information is best, based on our own observations from visiting a conventional school or attending a school board meeting and from conversations we have with key participants (such as children we know, teachers, administrators, policymakers, business people, and bureaucrats). Few of us have the time or resources to cover this topic thoroughly, build and maintain networks of contacts, listen enough, and fit the pieces together into a coherent whole. But we can be as alert as possible and then supplement our own observations by discussing them with as many people as possible and reading a variety of alternative publications. It is great to find a publication that agrees with our perspective, biases, beliefs, perspectives, goals, but any alternative publication (well, within reason) will help readers break out of the mind-set of the dominant culture and think more clearly for themselves. And take heart, such interpretive work is really easier than it may sound--once you understand some of the key assumptions, trends, and developments (for example, you may want to use some of those discussed above as starting places), you can interpret for yourself the "facts" you encounter in the media, find examples that reinforce or modify your understanding, and make sense of developments that heretofore were puzzling.

Examine your own assumptions about education.

Parents who decide to explore alternatives in education often find that they need to re-examine their own school experiences and their assumptions about education. Many of us have been so thoroughly indoctrinated by our own school experiences and the attitudes that pervade our whole culture that it can be very difficult to realize that many of our ideas about education are assumptions and not "fundamental truths." It can be even more challenging to let go of them. Many parents find that only gradually, as they gain more experience with alternative education, and as they observe their children and are helped by them, do they really begin to understand what education can mean and how exciting and freeing it can be. In the long run, many parents find they learn as much or more from their family's involvement in alternative education than their children. They finally learn how to think for themselves. One of the reasons that alternative education is so important and powerful is that it offers hope for the adults as well as the children who are involved.

Perhaps the most widely-held and destructive assumption about education in our culture is that neither adults nor children can be trusted to learn what they need to know simply because such knowledge is available and will be useful to them, because they want to learn, and because they are capable of learning. This undercutting lack of trust informs the way in which schools are organized and how they treat children. It is the basis of the assumption that material must be selected for children and taught to them; that they must be tested; that anyone who makes a mistake must be punished, humiliated, or at least corrected; that competition must be used as a motivator; and that the principal work of a school is to control children.

Choose alternative approaches to education for yourself and your children.

Anyone, of any age, who chooses alternative education is making an important contribution to education in America today, because she or he is keeping alive, strengthening, and spreading the ideals of free education, of individualized learning, of people taking responsibility for their own lives and their own families.

A typical curriculum for adults in America today is something like: rely on information you get from the mass media; believe what the government tells you; get a job, learn what you are told there, and obey orders; put your job ahead of your family; make as much money as possible regardless of the costs to you, your family, your community, or the environment; rely on material objects for meaning and salvation; and distrust others since you are competing with them for material wealth and power. However, alternative education for adults could include thinking for yourself, questioning authority, finding meaningful work even if it is outside a conventional career track and pays less than other jobs, choosing voluntary simplicity, respecting other people including children, and developing your creativity. The choice is ours.

Does this mean that we think that no constructive learning takes place in conventional schools? No. Occasionally some positive learning takes place, thanks to strongly committed individual teachers and stubborn, independent, responsible students. But unfortunately most children learn much that is destructive in conventional schools, like how to do others in through competition, how to unquestioningly follow authority, how to be greedy consumers. Conventional schools can be dangerous places. Does this mean that one should never take a class in a conventional school? There may be times when a given course will appropriately serve a worthy end, but taking a few carefully selected courses with one's own clear goals in mind is a far cry from sending three, four, or five year olds to conventional schools and letting the dominant culture raise them.

Inform others about what is going on in education today.

Share with others your insights and understanding of what alternative education can mean to both adults and children and of how it is being threatened by changes in conventional education today. Since education affects everyone, everyone should be informed. But such information is not readily available. We need to work on a grassroots level to spread this information, discuss it, and act on it. Share these ideas with as many people as possible, including friends, relatives, neighbors, co-workers, members of organizations to which you belong, and teachers in conventional schools.

Find allies and work on the grassroots level.
Look for potential allies. Be as broadminded as possible; "worthy causes" often bring together strange bedfellows, who may then end up learning a great deal from each other. Remember that the only way we can protect our own rights and responsibilities is by protecting the rights and responsibilities of parents to choose the education they want for their children, whether or not their choice is the same as the alternative we would choose.

Conclusion

The more we alternative educators/parents understand current developments in American education, the more we realize the importance of our decisions about alternative education to children, ourselves, and our whole society, the better able we are to make wise decisions about education. As citizens, we have a moral obligation to contribute to the building of a positive approach to education in this country. As alternative educators/parents, we need to be aware of and respond to direct and indirect threats to alternative education and to our basic way of life. Let us unite to work to protect the rights and responsibilities of alternative education and to help shape a positive future for education in America.

A Conversation with John Taylor Gatto

A teacher for 26 years in the New York City Public Schools, John Taylor Gatto was three consecutive times named New York City Teacher of the Year, and in 1991 was named New York State Teacher of the Year. His success has been hailed in hundreds of media articles and interviews, and he has been commended for his work by four U.S. Presidents. Gatto is the author of *Dumbing Us Down: The Hidden Curriculum of Compulsory Schooling* (New Society Publishers, 1991), the subject of many videos, and a popular speaker at educational conferences around the country. This interview, by Mark and Helen Hegener, appeared in the November/December, 1991 issue of *Home Education Magazine*.

Can you begin by telling us a bit about yourself, John?

Well, I'm a 55-year-old ex-western Pennsylvanian from the Monongahela Valley, I think that's an important part of who I am, it's not just a regional identification. I've been a school teacher in New York City for 26 1/2 years, about half that time teaching very prosperous children, overwhelmingly white, the sons and daughters of the media aristocracy in the United States, and for about half that time teaching kids from Harlem and Spanish Harlem. My school district has found me for many years an indigestible lump, so they moved me from school to school, I guess to encourage me to quit, or at least to tone down what I do.

And what I do is bend the bars of the factory school cage. I operate on different assumptions than systematic schooling does. I assume that childhood is an imaginary state, that in fact very, very early in life we are fully gifted. I would reject most of the theories of child development as being artifacts of the way we do things rather than some inevitable biological destiny.

So I assume that kids are competent, that they are anxious to develop and be powerful people, I assume that talent is very, very widely distributed, not distributed on a pyramidal pattern in any way, that that too is an artifact of the way we do things. Using those assumptions, my kids have created a record of accomplishment, even though their standardized test scores, their skin color, their social class, and their economic class says they can't do these things... my kids have created a record of accomplishment over the past 15 years in New York City that's quite unbelievable and very, very dangerous, since, if a teacher operating without assistance can apparently do these things, then the system itself comes under challenge, even though I never directly challenged it, or haven't until recent years.

Obviously, you and I know, I don't do these things for kids. They do them for themselves. What I do through a variety of stratagems is get out of kids' way, and let them be who they are, or find out who they are, and the byproduct of that is good performance, or great performance.

Can you tell us about your family?

I've been married for 30 years this December, we have two children, Briseis, who is now 28, and Raven, who was 23 in September, and both of them were National Merit Scholars. And I'm ashamed to say that, to tell you the truth, because I am now such an implacable opponent of any form of standardized testing and ranking, that I'm sorry my kids did so well.

Many people have earned that distinction, but now have to wonder about all the effort.

Yes. It's chasing a prize that really isn't worth having, because it tends to lead to another chase, to another prize that isn't worth having, and if you're really successful at capitalizing on your National Merit Scholarship, you've condemned yourself to an endless life of chasing prizes that aren't worth having, and an inevitable situation that you'll find yourself in eventually, where you lose these battles, and other people, who run faster, will pass you by.

In your speeches and your writing, you draw a tremendous amount on history. What does history tell us is going to happen?

First of all, there is no present. It's an instant, the summary of all the pasts. So without tracing the past, it's quite impossible to know who you are in the present. You can be a good engineer, that is, you can solve instrumental problems, but all the political problems that really determine what values you hold, or are allowed to hold, and what the ramifications of those are, can't be handled without understanding history.

Now why you have to go as far back as you possibly can, is that the pattern is much clearer when the smoke of political conflict has cleared away. It's very, very easy to see that in 330 B.C., when Plato wrote *The Republic*, in Book Five he says the family must be destroyed. If you want the kind of state that operates in a rational, predictable fashion, then you must destroy the family. Actually Socrates said that. And of course everybody reads *The Republic*, it's compulsory reading in every elite college in the Western world, and has been even in the early medieval era. The whole Christian religion, universal Christianity that comes through St. Augustine, is based on Plato's conception, our idea of heaven and hell - it's straight out of, I think it's Book Ten of *The Republic*, that's where it occurs for the first time, and that's how it's transmitted, it's Plato's thought.

Nevertheless, to back up, when Plato lays down a blueprint for an organized, sane, rational, predictable state, he says that this state cannot take place while the family exists. That the family is independent and feudal and various and that what you want is central control. So you have to eliminate the dialectic. What nobody notices is that back in Book Two of *The Republic* Socrates says that this isn't a state worth having, that the ideal is a life built around the logic of family and knowing how to do one thing well. He says, so you're proud of your work, and you come home to your family and your children, and you drink a little wine, and you play games, he actually says that, I mean, it's a slight interpretation, but not much.

But these two rich kids, Glaucon and Adamantis, say to Plato, "But that's a state for pigs, a city for pigs. We want a place where some people can lay around on couches and eat grapes." And I believe that's literal, too. I haven't read *The Republic* for a decade, but he says, "Alright, if you want the feverish state, I'm going to begin to describe how to bring it about, but you will not like what I have to say." And then *The Republic* unfolds.   Well, for most average, bright Americans, when they hear Plato and they hear *The Republic*, you're talking about ancient history, and you might even among a literate set be talking about a brilliant writer and a brilliant thinker, but I don't think anybody, or very, very few people, realize that Plato's *Republic* is a canonical text, like the *New Testament* is for Christianity, or like *The Torah* and *The Talmud* are for Judaism. They're texts that don't change no matter what the circumstances are from era to era, they say the same thing, in the same way, so that eventually over time what they do is to create an institutional pattern, and that pattern imposes itself on our behavior and on our choices. And that has been done. Plato's *Repub-*

lic was magnified and multiplied and refined by St. Augustine in about 380 A.D., I think, in *City of God*. And *City of God* becomes the blueprint for the universal Christian church, which remains uniform until the early sixteenth century when Martin Luther, and a little bit later John Calvin, reformed that church. Now that reformation, if you study it very, very closely, is simply - and I mean this absolutely - is simply the reintroduction of Scandinavian pagan values, a religion called the Old Norse Religion. The ethics of that religion emerge intact in Luther, and much more intact in Calvin, because Calvin was trained as a lawyer and he wrote it down to institute the Christian religion. It's a way to look at child-rearing, and a way to look at the choices you make in life.

If you know these things, it's very, very easy to understand the anomalies that seem to appear in American schooling. For example, when people say "I don't understand why this is happening, when everybody knows it's the wrong thing to do."

Well, that's if you deal with things on a logical basis. But if you're dealing with them on a theological basis, you have a much, much different rationale for why things happen. And I absolutely believe that what we're involved in here is a religious manifestation, although not tied to any particular manifestation. Although if I had to do that, I would tie it to Congregationalism and probably Presbyterianism, and to some extent to the Methodist phenomenon, which is a very late development and not theological at all, it was a way to control people living in outlying settlements who could not be held in check by Anglicanism. So what we're doing is training kids to a world that certain religious visions thought was the world we ought to be living in.

We're bypassing the family.

Yes. And that is the single universal continuity from Plato down to now, every major Western thinker - by the way, at least 95% of those people have been childless men. That's fascinating, it took me three years to realize what my research had turned up. I'd fill these file cards out and throw them in a pile like everybody else does who writes, and I'd note their family status, so here I'm getting... Francis Bacon: childless, married very late in life and then only for political reasons; Descartes: childless; Rousseau: childless because he gave his children away; Augustine: childless; Plato: childless; Erasmus, who is a big figure here who's hardly ever considered: childless; Hobbes, who writes *The Leviathan*, the justification for government bigness and centralization, very, very important text: a childless man. Virtually all of them childless. Fascinating.

Do you have any ideas about why people accept the ideas of these kinds of men?

Oh, absolutely, I can tell you why. It took me again about seven years of thinking to figure it out. If you live in a material universe where acquiring things is very important to you, then family is an absolute deterrent to maintaining that sort of a world, because family involves values like affection, and sympathy, and passion, and types of pleasure that lead nowhere in a material sense.

Furthermore, families are impossible to regiment. If you have an army going into battle, and it's a well-familied army, the army's simply not going to fight as well, because each person doesn't think that victory in the battle is as important as his wife and his kids. We have a classic example of that from the very first novel ever written, *The Odyssey*. Odysseus, or Ulysses in the Roman version, goes off to war, and he fights for ten years. During that time he amasses an enormous treasure, he's very rich, and he rises to the very top of the status pyramid, he's powerful, women throw themselves at his feet, and furthermore in his travels he's offered immortality by this good-looking goddess. But at some point it dawns on him that all of this is nonsense, that the only thing that matters is his wife and his kids, who he left behind, and he spends ten years fighting his way back to them, only to discover that his wife has acquired, I believe it's 107 boyfriends, and it's not going to be so easy, and furthermore, his son's a little bit ticked off that dad stayed away from home for twenty years.

How is it, that that is the very first extended story that's been preserved in the history of Western mankind, and that it's certainly as popular and potent a story today as it was 28 centuries ago when it was written?

Familied peoples, of the nature of good families, do not organize very well, because to organize is to abandon your own family as the central locus of meaning in your life. If people don't organize very well they can do very well on a local basis, but as soon as you transcend the precincts of a small town or a farm, they don't do very well in comparison to people who treat other people like units or cells that can be mustered toward some centralized mission.

Let me give you the best example that I've found. The Spanish armies, which dominated Europe for several centuries, were superbly well trained. But because of the logic of the Mediterranean - and partly because of the logic of Catholicism, which celebrates the local, even though it's a universal religion - the Spanish army had a code that when a man was hurt in battle his friends and buddies would rally around him and they'd fight to preserve his life and they'd carry him off to safety.

The English armies, which eventually prevailed over the Spanish armies, were no better trained, in many ways they were inferior armies, but they had this one idea, that if a man was hurt, God wanted him hurt and for you to race to the aid of your friend - which would mean take active people out of combat - was flying in the face of God's will. Now you can quickly see that mathematically, two evenly matched armies in combat, one having Philosophy A and one having Philosophy B, which one would prevail?

So getting to the heart of the Old Norse ethic, the Viking ethic that dominated Europe from 600 to 900, maybe even up to 1100, because you want to consider that the invasion of England by William the Conqueror was really the invasion of Scandinavia - that wasn't from France, that was from Normandy, the land of the Norsemen. Normandy had been given to the Vikings in order to attempt to calm them, to pay them off for not slaughtering the Celtic population of France, the Teutonic population.

Anyway, tell me where I was.

You were giving us an example of why family...

Oh, why the family? Yeah, had I figured out why? So, sure, what you can produce materially depends to a great extent how much you can concentrate on your purpose, how much you can cut out extraneous and detracting demands on your time. So someone who believes that the acquisition of power, or money, or status, or whatever is the central purpose of life, will do much, much better than someone who would like to make a buck so that he can go fishing with his kids on the weekend, or so that the family can go on a picnic, or so that his wife could stay home and make a sanctuary for the family - there's just no comparison.

Now I'll give you an irony on that before it slips my mind. In the organization of western corporations, above the mid-level of management, not to have a family is absolutely not to get promoted. If you look at the CEO's of American corporations, as I did -

my information's coming to you from about 1987 - you'll find that virtually every one of them has a wife and family. And if you'll look down through the corporate hierarchy, to the controllers and the other top positions, executive vice president, you'll find that virtually all of them have wives and families. It only when you get to middle management, and the rookies, and that section in-between, that you find single men. Very fascinating. Beyond the middle management ranks someone without a family can't be trusted, because they have no hostages to fortune. They have nothing that would bind their loyalty, nothing that would slow them from constantly looking out for number one. And so either such a system has evolved or, and I would say much more likely, on the most rarefied levels of business theory for many centuries this fact has been known, and acted upon.

In spite of that, what I'm hearing is that the family's really at cross pur-poses with the leadership of this great nation in areas such as the current push for a global economy...

First of all, there is no global economy. That's a flat piece of non-sense. I'm often, when I'm speaking, say, I want you to imagine a country that has such abundant supplies of food that it feeds half the world. A country that has such abundant supplies of energy that it has a choice of which energy to use and that it can avoid us-ing inexpensive technologies or can put them in reserve, in abey-ance, because it has such an overwhelming amount of fossil fuel available to it. Imagine a country that has unlimited quantities of metal, of wood, of fiber to make clothing from. Now such a coun-try has the capacity to, inside it's national boundaries, make a uto-pia for everybody in local economies, in what sense can such a country be said to be dependent on international favor or competi-tion for anything at all?

But that's one of the lines for the current education reform. We'll be number one with our global economy. I keep hearing that over and over...

A little bit of that's sinister, but I think most of that's because as a schooled nation, we have been deliberately taught not to think. In fact, Bertrand Russell noted that in 1926. Russell was looking in his lordly fashion at the Russian Revolution, and he said that more radical than the Russian Revolution is the American experi-ment in compulsory schooling, which he said has for the first time in Western history, deprived even it's potential ruling classes of the ability to think dialectically, which is of course the ability to challenge the given wisdom. And he said that in his opinion, it was the most radical experiment in human history.

Doing this, to operate on the assumption that people were interchangeable cells, or components in some large machine, I hope some of your readers are hearing echoes from Calvin's great work, *Institutes of the Christian Religion*, which will be available in every large library in the country, and is very well worth reading. Calvin lays down that what we are involved in is a vast cosmic machine in which everything is predestinated, including who's going to win and who's going to lose.

Can you help us see what challenges might lie ahead?

I think that you're going to get some form of choice almost immediately. It will probably come state by state. But the federal government, under Lamar Alexander as Secretary of Education, has really laid a radical proposal on the table, and I have not seen a press interpretation that understands how radical it is. It simply says that they're going to underwrite one school experiment in each one of the 535 congressional districts, no two of these being alike, all of them growing out of the competitive process where people in a congressional district - not through their congressman, but through a body in Washington headed up by Tom Kane, the former governor of New Jersey - will decide which one in District A and which in District B wins, and they'll get a million dollars and probably an awful lot of help to establish a demonstration school that reflects the locality.

Well I can absolutely guarantee you that if that ever came to pass, and we had 535 model schools reflecting the needs and the feelings of the people in a congressional district, that there would be rumbling and erosion among the centralized schools from that alone. We have in addition to that men like Chris Whittle, who I had dinner with a couple of weeks ago, and talked to for four hours, who are committing, I think Whittle is committing three billion dollars, to open 20 schools in 1996 - that's tomorrow, isn't it? - and 1,000 by the year 2000, but of course obviously the larger number is contingent on the success of the smaller number. But what Whittle has committed himself to is setting aside 60 million dollars of his own money and hiring 100 people to sit around for three years in Knoxville and come up with a blueprint for a different kind of schooling. And what I said to him was that coming up with a blueprint is simply to reproduce in miniature the wrong direction that public schooling is already taken. And of course you and I know, Mark, that most private schools are simply cosmetic imitations of public schools. They're not based on the way that human beings learn and grow and develop.

What you're going to get is a profusion of small entrepreneurial school enterprises, what I hope you'll get is churches and corporations and farms and foundations all saying hey, we want a chance to do that too, we have our own version. And what I think could happen is inadvertently we could recreate the schooling situation that we had in the United States before 1848 when the Boston School Committee passed its compulsory school law. We'd still have state schools, but they would be now fighting for their lives in competition. As a consequence, I think, everyone would be better served.

Now comes the other shoe falling. If that kind of decentralization is followed by a very efficient imposition of national testing and a national curriculum, and government punitive action against those independent members that can't compete successfully, then what we will have is the worst of all possible worlds. That is, we will be decentralized so there will be no longer any way for the whole country to lament what's happening to those kids, and yet the government will now be able to broadcast centrally to all these hundreds of thousands of independent divisions.

So we're really walking a tightwire here. I think we absolutely have to support any move to diversify.

In your acceptance speech for the New York City Teacher of the Year you said that "We live in a time of great social crisis and we seem to have lost our national identity." Can you discuss that idea?

This is also historical, but it's very interesting. I think we tried to short circuit the process of turning a country or a state into a nation. It takes hundreds, perhaps a thousand years before a state, some geographical territory that's held together by the baron or by some power, to actually get a sense of mutual identity, like we're all cousins in some way. And we tried to short circuit that, by in the middle of the 19th century, seizing the control of the information mechanism and the other forms of regulation and imposing from a center one central idea of what our nation should be. It didn't work from the beginning, but ideologically, there was im-

mense support for short circuiting the process by the rising industrial giant that we were becoming. Our brilliant insight led to developing internal communications within the country, building
road systems and railroads, and to supporting any form of technology that enhanced the swift movement from place to place. By
doing that, we released abundant quantities of energy that no other nation in the world had ever released, and by doing that we
quickly rose to a dominant position in world markets.

In order to maximize the profits from the new industrial system,
and from this brilliant insight that by augmenting the transportation system we would be able to do that better than any other
country in the world, by doing that we created a proletariat, and
now our schools found it necessary to maintain a proletariat, and
to do that the teaching of critical thinking had to be removed.

It's funny, but nobody has to take my word for that. Just grab a
bunch of textbooks that were printed in the 1830's and 40's, before
compulsory schooling, and you will see what kids in fourth and
fifth grade schools were learning then. And I can guarantee you
that only in American elite colleges is the same sort of diet offered
to the constituency - it was offered to the average American fifth
grader in 1830! It's just fascinating. I have a fifth grade textbook
from upstate New York which is such a systematic and rigorous
analysis of the Greek use of rhetoric to create powerful citizens -
and it's meant for eleven-year-olds! I have no doubt, by the way,
considering the history of American demagoguery, that in fact
they learned it! They learned it because it immediately led to power, to be able to persuade, to overcome objections.

We're farther from being a nation today, even though what we
have is central myths that come to us from television. We have
very little regional loyalty any longer, I mean, it's still there, but
it's much diminished. We have almost no local loyalty. Someone
might sing *I Left My Heart in San Francisco*, but they'll leave it there
and go to Atlanta or New York or Boston, and we've promulgated
this idea that that's a better life, and everyone knows behaviorally
that it isn't. Our families are falling apart, our lives are falling
apart, our physical health is falling apart. We're really in an awful
lot of trouble, much, much worse than I think the press has begun
to touch. But all of us know that, in our gut, we've lost faith in the
solutions, and that's why you get this hysteria about enlarging the
school day and enlarging the school year, and then it'll work, and
you and I know it'll work worse!

Have we lost that faith, or has it been taken away from us?

Once you arrange schooling to be comprehensive, and once you
have a piece of technology like television which functions in exactly the same way that central schooling functions, and you dovetail
the two, you butt those two pieces together so that it preempts all
the time available to grow up, what's been taken away is the possibility that we ever could have faith in anything! It never got a
chance to develop, so in that sense you're right, it was never lost,
because we're turning out generations that don't believe in anything at all.

*It seems like at some point people would begin to realize what's going on,
what's happening.*

But where would they reach then, for a solution? Write to the
newspaper? That's part of the problem. Write to their congressman? He's part of the problem. The problem's economic, at bottom, and of course, in my at bottom it's theological, but let's leave
Calvin and Luther and St. Augustine out of this for a minute.

I think the only problem we have is nobody knows how to
make this abundant economy actually deliver its goods to all the
varieties of human beings there are, and so a system has evolved
in which there is a justification for some people getting eighty or
ninety times what other people get. And once this emerges as a social reality, then there's absolutely a vested interest in keeping it
that way. It doesn't have to be guys with their collars turned up in
secret meetings saying, "and now we'll do this to keep the kids
down." It's just to everybody's advantage to do that.

Let's just talk for a moment about destroying kids' lives. It's an
exceedingly profitable thing to do. If we did not turn out hideous-
ly dependent young men and women every year, what on earth
would happen to all the counseling professions? What on earth
would happen to the substantial numbers of people who operate
our criminal justice system, or our colleges that teach these various roles to our criminal lawyers, I mean, we could really spend a
week on this. A huge part of our economy, that is how people
make their living, is taking care of other people who don't know
how to take care of themselves. If you were suddenly install a system - and I believe it is possible to suddenly install a system - that
would turn out strong, independent, clear-eyed, confident young
people, what would you do with them? Where would they go?

Where would they get jobs? Who would want them around?

A vast majority of the parents who come to homeschooling, are unfortunately so well educated, that they're wrestling with feeling competent themselves.

And that's good, isn't it? To wrestle? To ever feel that you've arrived, it seems to me, is to die at that moment. I think some of the things that we should be doing for each other, though, is buoying each other up, and saying that you're doing okay.

The simple reaching out of a hand, a little pat on the back, the circulation of truth and reality versus these insane myths that have been codified in the writings of - who's that Swiss lunatic, Piaget? - and others, that somehow or other there is an absolutely well-known, scientific body of knowledge that says we move from a to b to c to d... In fact, what really underpins all the speakers of the Piaget type is the real theological belief that there is a right way and it can be discovered. And he's gotten closer than the last guy and the next guy will get closer than him. And in order to combat that, the medicine we need is these waves of information, and also we need to teach each other what questions to ask.

We really have to teach people how to challenge assumptions, and what larger assumptions gave them those assumptions. Where is the evidence that somebody without a college degree doesn't do well, other than those fields where by definition you have to have a college degree?

So with all of our assumptions, and our dependence on experts and degrees, are we just merrily going down the road to societal collapse?

I'm not, either professionally or in an amateur sense, an ecologist, but the fact that we are jeopardizing the basis of life on Earth in order to run this kind of economy is just electrifying. And the reason that it's happening, is that there is no we, there is no community here, this is not a nation, it's a state. There's a huge difference, nation coming from the root, nativity, we have some commonality, but we don't have. So our state function is always irrational. It's psychopathic, and I use that word surgically, not promiscuously. We are a psychopathic society because we operate on a series of bottom line calculations given to us by a university intelligentsia who says you can rationalize your work place, for example, by not hiring women because there's a one in two chance that they'll become pregnant in the first three point nine years and then you'll - you know what I mean, there are millions of these things that have been computerized by now. It all came out of the Harvard Business School in the middle sixties, that the bottom line that any sort of social alteration is justified if you could increase the profits you got as measured by cash flow.

Well, the minute you do that, you have a psychopathic institution, because it has no conscience. An individual in the institution can have a good conscience, in fact every individual in the institution can have a conscience, but if ultimately what you have to do is serve the bottom line directive, then what you're going to get is a compassionate Mark Hegener, looking at me and saying John, we don't want to lay you off, and yes, it's true that we could afford to keep you, and yes, your family then wouldn't have to go on welfare and break up, and we know that, and we're very, very sorry, but you can see that if we did that for everybody, well, we'd only break even this year. We can't do it, John. I'd lose my job, even if I wanted to do it, John, it would show up and the accountants would scrutinize my decision and say, this man's lost his mind. So systematically, we have created all of our institutions after a psychopathic model, the school premier among those, because it takes the largest amount of our national treasure, other than our defense establishment.

And we're all set up by the schools to serve these institutions.

Sure! Or it couldn't work! If we taught the dialectic - period - none of these institutions could function. No matter how much we try to correct ourselves, and I include myself in this, people who were themselves well-schooled can never see very clearly, we see imperfectly. Now I've fought and struggled with myself for 25 years to rip out the programming, and I still find large clumps of wires beaming a message into me when I think I've made it, I mean every few years I think now I've made it, now I can see clearly, and then another installation reveals itself. So we're going to have to do it by stages.

It seems as though our whole business is doing that, helping parents rip out the wires.

Yes, rip out the wires, but you can't rip out the wires, you can't do it efficiently unless you can first get people to accept that they're full of wires, and that they have to be ripped out. And that only they will know where those wires are. If they've had any association with newspapers, magazines, television, or schools, count on the fact that 80 or 90% of what they think they think, someone else thought for them.

You know the real trouble, if we can just for a moment become philosophical, is this ancient combat between the idea that all human life is machined and predestinated, and the idea that there's free will. What Immanuel Kant finally determined was that all human life is predestinated, but it has a capacity for free will that doesn't come easily. It comes painfully, through struggle, through making hard decisions, through always generating your own lines of meaning in life, and always verifying anything that you've been told. Never accepting anything on faith or trust that you don't hold provisionally. I mean, you might have to do that in order to function. But once you understand how other people infect your mind, colonize your mind as my daughter says. Once you understand that, then I think that you can be much more efficient at screening out this information before it takes hold inside of yourself, and then you can transmit much better with your behavior with your children how a genuinely liberty loving world would function, and also I think begin to evolve a theory of schooling, or theory of human life, because for us to treat schooling as a separate institution is convenient for a discussion like this, but it itself is a false myth. Learning is, as you people say over and over again - and correctly - learning is quite as natural as breathing - there isn't any way to stop it. All you can do is pervert it, so that you have huge amounts of life wasted on learning that really has no value.

I keep asking myself how we got into this mess, and in listening to your explanation I wonder if we might have gotten here simply because it was the easy path. As people moved to avoid that struggle you speak of, they simply allowed themselves to be told what to do and what to think because it was the easiest thing to do.

Where would you get the courage to know how to struggle, unless you had seen such courage modelled for you? I believe that it's innate in all of us, but for it to develop from a seed without watering or fertilizer, is possible but I don't think it's something we should expect to happen very often. Oddly enough, and this is interesting, what you do see is more and more and more among older people, is that seed becoming self-watered and nurtured, almost when - I don't believe what I'm going to say now - but when it's too late people begin to come into themselves. By too late I mean when the commercial culture freezes them out and says we no longer want you to work for us and we're not going to give you any status and we don't care that your pension isn't inflation adjusted, when the world turns its back on old people, I've seen huge numbers of them slowly but very effectively liberate themselves from these confining myths that minimize their own spirits.

Then are we just struggling to play the game with the deck stacked against us?

Well, the deck's stacked against you. You're not struggling, though, to play a meaningless game, because struggle's the name of the game. Without struggle I don't think you can become fully human, so in a real sense that's what the dialectic is all about. The easiest thing is to accept what other people tell you. And what the dialectic teaches, and Aristotle, and I'm sure he didn't invent the dialectic, but as far as I can trace, he's the first clear understanding of how essential the dialectic is, and he expatiates on it in several of his own writings.

The dialectic requires you to do something totally unnatural, and that is to say that anything that seems to be absolutely true, cannot be true at all. I mean, it's an amazing contradiction of our natural predilection. It says that anything that seems to be totally and unmistakably true, has been arranged that way because it's useful to someone else for you to think that way. And therefore I would start on the operational premise that it's totally false.

I'll give you a specific example. If I say that your life will be ruined if you don't go to school, anyone that's been trained to think dialectically says then my life will be ruined if I do go to school. Well, now that you've established the opposite pole, the antithesis, as it's called in logical thinking, now you begin to work backwards toward the original statement, using your own eyes, ears, and primary evidence to figure out - not which is correct, because neither will be correct, in no case will the thesis school is necessary be correct, or the thesis school will ruin you be correct - but it will be somewhere on the line in between, whether it's closer to the original thesis, or closer to the antithesis, you can't know until you invest your own eyes and ears and experience and test the premise. Now if you do that with every major line of thought in your head, of course it's very easy, if you're trained to do that the way aristocratic kids were trained to do, throughout human history, in all cultures, and the way they're still trained in a very, very few super elite schools, to do, then it's extremely easy to do, and you come to this great clarity and confidence and ability to do anything.

Notice how awful that is - and put quotations around "awful" - for parents if your kid is taught to think dialectically, because nothing that you ask him to do will he not challenge! At the dinner table he'll want you to justify why this is proportioned this way and that that way. And that sounds a lot worse than it is...

With our kids we live with that everyday!

Yes, and of course what comes with it is the compassion and affection not to abuse that. It's to understand that there are so many right ways, that what you're really doing by this give and take at the dinner table or anywhere else, is stretching your own imagination. You're not looking to win by beating your parents or by beating your kids, saying well, I've won nineteen of the last thirty-six arguments...

Okay, so struggle is what Helen said. And struggle is not futile, struggle is the core of a good life, I'm certain of that. Even though all of our utopian visions are people in white robes standing at the seashore listening to harp music, I don't think that that really is where human destiny is at. It's in stretching and enlarging the you that you were given, and obviously to do that has to be painful, and it has to involve what the Greeks called agony - the agon - wrestling, wrestling with yourself. Competition, of course, is a false path, that seems to pay off for struggling, but it pays off in the wrong coin. It pays off in material things, and what you use the material things for is to buy the freedom from struggle. There's a marvelous irony there, I mean there *must* be some kind of a divine force to have such a marvelous irony bred into us!

Conversation with Seth Rockmuller and Katharine Houk

Seth Rockmuller and Katharine Houk are actively involved in education in many different ways, and at many different levels. As founders and directors of the Alliance for Parental Involvement in Education (ALLPIE), Seth and Katharine work with a wide variety of issues in education on a daily basis, and encourage parents to familiarize themselves with the options and then to select the method or combination which will work best for their family. Seth and Katharine are the parents of three children, Tahra, 22, Benjamin, 12, and Emily, 9. They make their home in the rolling countryside near East Chatham, New York. This interview, by Mark and Helen Hegener, appeared in the January/February 1992 issue of *Home Education Magazine*.

Mark: Can you start out by telling us about ALLPIE?

Seth: A couple of years ago we sat down together and decided what we would like to do with our lives. We looked at what we had been doing, and at what we would like to continue to do, to see if there was some way to put together the things I had been doing and the things Katharine had been doing in a way that we thought would be helpful to us and to other people.

I had been working for ten years with the State Education Department here in New York State and had a lot of background through that with education generally and education law, primarily in public education. Our private lives had been growing away from that. Our daughter had been in public school, a Waldorf school, and eventually in home education. In the course of that process we'd thought a lot about education, and what we wanted in the way of education for our kids. The idea was to merge what we had been doing -- what I had been doing professionally and what we had been doing personally.

What we came up with was the idea that we'd been moving toward, parental involvement in all education. We wanted to see if there was some way that we could get together resources that would be helpful to people, put people in touch with each other, and provide a place they could get information and contact other people.

Mark: How has it played out?

Katharine: Well, that's been very interesting. I got a letter from a woman a couple of days ago who was just absolutely thrilled to find that there may be people in the universe who did not condemn her for combining public education and home education. She had found no support in the public schools, and she was rejected by homeschoolers for being a traitor because she sent her kids to public school part time. To think that there was an organization that said, "Yes, whatever works for you, go for it. Whatever you feel is best for your children, to help them grow, that's what you should go after!"

We've been finding that there are people coming out of the woodwork who want to be able to combine these alternatives, who don't want to be known as "I am a homeschooler, period." or "I believe in public education. Period." In order for things to happen these artificial divisions are blurring. So consequently we're seeing more and more people who want to start learning centers, or alternative schools, or that sort of thing. I don't know that we had thought about those kinds of things when we started out.

And then of course there's the whole political interest in parental involvement from educational institutions.

Seth: The relationship between the large institutions and parental involvement is a very tricky thing now. There are all sorts of ambivalent feelings, on my part at least. It seems that for parental involvement to work in any sort of education, whether it's public schools or private schools or at home, it has to come from the families.

It's interesting, and gratifying, to see the recognition by large institutions (federal, state, union, whatever) of the importance of parental involvement. Yet there's a certain misgiving I have about having them make this an issue. They can't make it an issue for parents. Parents have to come to it themselves, or it will just be co-opted. That's my fear. Once it becomes a mandated component of education that parents be involved, it provides a framework by which the system can sort of take it over and make it part of the system, instead of parents and families remaining an outside voice calling for changes, calling for meaningful input, calling for a voice in the way things are actually run.

I think Katharine's exactly right: when we first started ALLPIE, and it was only a couple of years ago, there was hardly any talk about parental involvement at the governmental level, at least not very much that was getting through, and that has come a long way in the last couple years. But it's come a long way in such a way that I don't know that the final outcome will be positive. I like the recognition of the issue, but I have concerns about what will happen to parental involvement if it is institutionalized.

Mark: If we allow some of these programs, such as the Parents as Teachers programs in Missouri, which are still voluntary, to be instituted and made mandatory... boy, the implications are pretty scary.

Seth: That's sort of what they're talking about doing in New York State, although I'm not sure what the specifics are at this point. Some kind of mandate that every school district has to involve parents, that they have to set up a procedure for involving parents. When it comes from the state telling the schools, the schools telling the parents, it becomes something other than a grassroots vehicle for change. There's a big buzzword in New York state for their educational reform, it's really a buzz phrase: "top down support for bottom up reform." I see the danger in this becoming top down support for top down parent involvement.

Mark: But can institutions really function any differently?

Seth: I guess my feeling is that in many ways that's not our concern. I think that parents need to act independently, regardless of what the institutions are going to do, and the message I get from it is don't depend on the institutions. And it's hard. It's very hard for us to do it from the outside because we're used to relying on institutions in many ways.

Katharine: Our entire schooling has taught us that the institution knows best, and that the expert knows best, so it's very difficult for parents to step outside the institutions and start their own parent groups, independently. And when they do it's hard for them to keep them going. But also when they do, it opens their eyes to their own personal power, that they probably haven't experienced since they were three and four years old and hadn't been taught that they didn't know how to learn, and that they didn't know how to take control of their lives.

Mark: Can you talk a little bit more about how you two got to where you are, that whole process?

Katharine: I think for me, it was learning from my children, who have shown me, and continue to show me again and again, what learning can be when it's not imposed and coerced. We were helped tremendously on our journey by having a very strong-willed first child, who would not put up with being told what to learn and when to learn it! That really opened our eyes. When we became home educators it was almost against our will. We were very insecure about it, but we could see no other way. I really feel that we learned a tremendous amount from our children. Our children have led the way into the work that we ended up doing.

Seth: From my perspective, when you work for a large institution, like the State of New York, you don't always see the implications of what you're doing. You're dealing with a lot of people within the institution that you know more or less personally, and they're real people. They're all trying to do a good job, they all take their jobs seriously, and you sort of relate to it all on that level. Maybe there are some people who aren't doing what they're supposed to do, but for the most part it's made up of well-meaning people.

But as we got more and more into looking at the education of our own kids and what was relevant to them I began to disconnect what I was doing at work and what I was seeing at home as the outcome of that work. You could have thousands of people who were doing their jobs, and doing a decent job of it, and when that got filtered through the layers of institution that they were dealing with, the effect on people was not beneficial. All that good effort was essentially perpetuating the institution, and was not really a force for positive change on a "my kid" level.

Since leaving the state, and working on the outside, I see that even more strongly. Although I don't have the personal contact I had before with the people within, I can see from the outside much more clearly what happens. Working with the parent group at the high school, and with the teachers and the administration there, I see what the state does, and I see the effect it has on what teachers do day to day, and how what the teachers do affects what the students do day to day.

It's not like the institution is either equal to or greater than the sum of the parts—it's totally different. The sum of the parts has absolutely nothing to do with what comes out of the educational bureaucracy. What comes out is more driven by the very existence of an institution like that than by everybody's individual efforts.

That's not to say that every once in a while the institution doesn't do something good and beneficial for somebody, or doesn't fit somebody's needs in some way, or isn't damaging to them in some way. But overall, it's no longer where I really wanted to put my efforts, in perpetuating that system, when there was so much to be done in getting people to overcome their reliance on that system.

Mark: Your work through ALLPIE must be helping people with these kinds of efforts...

Katharine: When people say "This school doesn't work, that school doesn't work, there aren't any other schools, and I'm sure that I can't handle homeschooling all by myself!" ALLPIE can say, "Okay, here are the ways that some other families have handled it, and we can put you in touch with these individuals, and they can empathize with you, and offer you the resources that they have used in a similar situation." It's giving people the gift that we wish we'd had when we were asking those kinds of questions years ago. And yet we would not be here if we had not learned from our children, what it is that they need and how to help them find it.

Seth: I think in many ways the most wonderful thing about the existence of home education is that it frees you to create all sorts of other educational alternatives. You can use home education as a base and build anything from it. My hope is that there will be a whole continuum of different types of programs, from a straight home education program all the way to more organized school. We know some people locally who've recently started a learning center. What those people wanted was a place to get together two or three times a week with some regular programs and some opportunity for the parents and for the kids to share things. When some other people came to ALLPIE and said that they wanted something that was sort of a school but very small, and they didn't want to start a school, we could look at that model of a learning center and say, "Well, why don't you do a learning center? But it doesn't have to be the same learning center, it doesn't have to be structured the same way. It could be much more organized. You could meet much more regularly. You could have a regular teacher instead of all volunteers."

ALLPIE wants to help families discover all those little niches where people feel comfortable. Some other people wanted to create something very much like a school, but they didn't want to go through all the hassles of opening a school, and they wanted to support home educators, set up a program that was fairly regular, with very interesting classes... I love to see all these things developing, with people on very local levels, very small scale saying this is what we want, this is what this group of people wants, that is what that group of people wants, and saying "Hey, we can do it! We don't need to settle for what's out there!"

Katharine: What that requires is people being able to look at themselves and their own families, and to look in a very clear way at their children and to listen to what their children are saying to them. I think it helps people tremendously to get together with other people who are struggling with these same issues. Not so that--as in Missouri--we can teach parents to be parents, but rather so that parents can learn from each other, without being told how they should be relating to their children.

Seth: In a way it's to rebuild some of the networks that have been broken down by the disintegration of extended families. I think people learned an awful lot from those environments in the past, and to a large extent they don't exist any more. So people are in some ways having to build their own networks to do some of that work that the family did in the past, sharing all that wisdom about childrearing, about helping children to become capable people functioning in the world.

Mark: You mentioned that ALLPIE recently had a Board meeting. Can you tell us what kinds of directions ALLPIE is headed in?

Katharine: We are expanding our Board, preparing for the growth that is happening, setting up ways to bring in more volunteers to help out, because there are so many requests for information and that sort of thing that we now need more help, but also to develop more materials to help parents. The Board is ready to make this commitment to grow.

Seth: I'm sure that anyone who's worked with any kind of non-profit volunteer group like this probably has learned, as we've learned, that it's wonderful to put all your time into developing programs and materials, talking to people and doing these things that you get involved in that program to do, but we've come to that point where we realize that ALLPIE needs to have some kind of a financial base in order to continue to do that. A very important part of any organization is to make sure that the organization is going to have the means to do the work that it wants to do. So that was certainly a part of the discussion at the Board meeting, what kind of commitment can we get from people to work toward making sure that those means are available. And as well as having people say "Yeah, we really want to develop these programs and policies," they also undertook the commitment to see that the organization could afford to do that. Real world existence issues are easy to ignore, but you can't ignore them if you're planning to be around for a long time.

Helen: Do you get a lot of interest in your work from other areas of the country?

Katharine: Most of it falls within the northeast, so we get a lot of people from New York State, but also Massachusetts, Connecticut, New Jersey, Pennsylvania... We also will have intense activity with people in California all of a sudden, or a pocket of people in Florida, so it really varies. Recently a school district in South Carolina became very interested, and ALLPIE provided that district with lots of materials for its parents' center.

Seth: ALLPIE has supporters all over the country and receives contacts from other countries as well. I think a lot of our activities are in the northeast now because that's what we can afford to do, but what we hear from other parts of the country is that many people would like something local along the lines of ALLPIE. We can send the newsletter and provide some resources, but we're just not in a position to be able to travel all over the country at ths point. That is one future goal that ALLPIE has, to encourage this kind of activity to grow and be centered in different areas, or maybe decentered is the word--it doesn't all have to come from one source. We are interested in networking with other organizations that are doing this kind of work or parts of it, like a parent group in a public school or home education groups that are interested in the types of work we're doing, or private school associations. Not everything has to span the whole spectrum as ALLPIE does. I think it would be wonderful if there were more groups that did, because I think that parents have an awful lot in common in dealing with all these educational issues.

Helen: If someone wanted to work with ALLPIE, or to start an organization like ALLPIE, is there a source for information on how to go about it?

Katharine: We have set up what we call ALLPIE partnership groups. If a group of parents gets together and wants to form an advocacy group of any kind, homeschooling, alternative involvement, whatever, we offer information on how to set up such a group, things they might want to consider: a newsletter, how to get the word out, this sort of thing. We have materials that we send to them, and we offer them ongoing support. Although we haven't widely publicized this yet, we do have several groups which have taken us up on it and we supply them with what they ask for, but we will need more funding and more workers on this end before we can further develop the partnership group idea.

Seth: If anyone is interested in setting up something like ALLPIE, or working with ALLPIE regionally, we're certainly interested in talking with them about it.

Mark: Are there any other comments you'd like to make before we close this?

Seth: I'd just like to repeat that there's a real danger now that parent involvement is going to be co-opted by large institutions, by the federal and state governments, parent involvement is in danger of being defined in a particular way, put into a cubbyhole, and packed and dispatched in a way which is inoffensive to those institutions. I think it's really important that grassroots parents' efforts not allow that to happen.

The State Education Department in New York, as part of its New Compact for Learning, has said that it's going to adopt a regulation which mandates parental involvement in all school districts in the state. That means that it's not going to be coming from the parents. There's a great danger that parents will be selected in some ostensibly equitable way, which doesn't really give everybody a say in how it's done. And there's a distinct danger that it will become more of a vehicle for preserving the status quo than for changing anything.

I would urge parents, wherever they see this, not to let it happen, but to insist that any group that be set up really come from outside the system, because it really needs to do that to advocate effectively.

Helen: Do you see a need for homeschooling parents to get involved in those kinds of changes? I know the attitude of many parents is "my kids don't go to school anyway, so why should I get involved?"

Seth: It's a real individual thing. When New York State home educators were trying to change the homeschooling regulation last year, homeschoolers from all over the state went to see their local Regents, the Board of Regents being the governing body for policy making and approving regulations with respect to education.

Those homeschooling parents who went and spoke with the Regents had a major effect on them, not only their thoughts about home education. What the Regents heard from home educators fit very well into what they were thinking about, at least on the policy level of educational reform in New York State. So I'm convinced that home educators have an awful lot to contribute to a discussion of education, what learning is, what should take place in a learning environment, and what takes place in their learning environments. I know that it was very well received by the Regents; they were very impressed, and they said so publicly. I don't see any reason why that can't work also at the local level for any parent who wants to undertake to do that.

It's more difficult, I suppose, to want to do that when you're not doing it with respect to the system of education that your child's participating in. But when home educators do participate at the local level they have the ability to stand back a little. Because their child isn't in the system, they have the ability to see things a little differently, and I think that contributes to the discussion of education generally. While it's important that parents be in there advocating for their children, it's also important that they not lose faith in what happens in the long run either, so it's useful to have some people who have a different perspective, and who are not just concerned about one particular issue at one particular time.

Helen: That would seem to go hand in hand with your ideas about bringing education back into the community. If that's really going to work everyone's going to have to get involved with it.

Katharine: There are people who wonder why home educators would join a public school committee, but so far nobody has said "go away." So far the ideas have been welcome. I see that as a very encouraging sign.

Vouchers And Alternative Education

—— Larry and Susan Kaseman ——————————————————

Vouchers. Here is a concept that is being strongly promoted as a way to strengthen and reform America's school system, save enormous amounts on the costs of education, and give parents choice in their children's educations. Perhaps a voucher system could be designed that would accomplish these ends. But the approach that is being pushed today would instead increase the control and authority that the state, the educational establishment, and big business have over education; reduce the choices that are available to parents; and seriously damage alternative education.

What are vouchers? The basic idea behind vouchers is that parents should be able to use their share of the tax money that is collected for education to send their children to a school that they choose. Since parents will choose the best schools, the reasoning runs, these schools will receive the resources and financial rewards they need to continue. Weaker schools will be strongly encouraged to improve, competition will strengthen all schools, and costs will be lower because schools that are competing for students will become more efficient. In theory and as originally formulated, a voucher system would have given money for education directly to parents who would then have decided what was best for their children. Such a voucher system is not such a bad idea; in fact, it might be a good idea. However, *in reality*, the voucher system as it is developing in this country will cause many more problems than it will solve and will seriously damage both conventional and alternative approaches to education.

What is wrong with the current proposals for a voucher system?

A voucher plan has been forecast in America 2000, in proposals the Bush administration has made to Congress, and in the Milwaukee pilot choice program. This approach has been designed so that parents will not receive vouchers themselves. Instead money will be sent directly from the government to schools that parents choose. At first glance this may not seem like a significant change, but it is. It means that the government, not parents, will have control over the schools that receive money. This approach allows the government to decide which schools are qualified to receive public funds. In fact, it has been strongly argued that the government must protect citizens by regulating the schools which receive vouchers. Otherwise, this inaccurate argument runs, public money will be flowing to private institutions which the government does not hold accountable, and, this inaccurate argument continues, this action would be illegal and unconstitutional.

Yet, such a voucher plan would be like the government telling people they could have dinner at a restaurant at government expense, then saying that the only "qualified" restaurants are McDonalds but everyone should appreciate the fact that they can choose whichever McDonalds they want. Such a meal program would also greatly weaken home cooking, because many people could not afford to pass up a free meal and buy their own ingredients.

Therefore, not only would vouchers not give control to parents, vouchers would instead increase the control that government, the educational establishment, and big business have over education. To determine which schools qualify to receive vouchers, the government would set standards that schools must meet. This obviously would give the government an enormous amount of power and control over the educational system. Also, big business is playing an increasing role in setting educational policy in an attempt to ensure that schools will produce workers who can keep the American economy competitive in the world market. (See the chapter "Becoming Involved in the Politics of Alternative Education," especially the information on America 2000.) So much for the idea that the purpose of education is to help children learn and develop their unique strengths and abilities!

The method the government appears to be choosing for determining which schools will qualify for vouchers will do an incredible amount of damage to American education. Results of standardized tests and assessments would be used to show which schools can be trusted and are being held accountable. They will allegedly protect the public from unscrupulous educators. The use of tests and assessments is troublesome for two very important reasons.

First, tests and assessments dictate curriculum. Students must be prepared to take tests and, hopefully, perform well on them. Therefore, the curriculum must focus on the skills and information required by the tests, and teachers must teach to the tests. By deciding which schools will qualify for vouchers on the basis of standardized test results, the government will be controlling the curriculum in these schools.

Second, focusing on the outcome of education changes the fundamental nature of education in this country from that of providing a service to help parents help their children learn, to that of requiring that children learn certain skills, values, beliefs, and approaches to life. It switches the focus of education from the *process* of providing opportunities for children to learn and encouraging them to do so to the *outcome* of their learning. When the outcomes of education are emphasized, the government has strong control over people's very lives. Of course this is in addition to all the other negative aspects of standardized tests, including their being biased, unfair, and inaccurate; their interference with children's learning; their destructive effect on a child's confidence and self-esteem; their potential for misuse in labeling children and placing them in special education classes, etc.

By emphasizing outcomes, current voucher plans will enable the state to move from requiring attendance to requiring education. Since the U.S. Constitution does not mention education, laws governing education have to be based on other constitutional provisions or must receive the consent of the people. Compulsory school attendance laws are based on the policing power granted to the state by the Constitution. But compulsory school attendance laws only require that children attend school; they do not prescribe a specific educational program or dictate the outcome. However, in focusing on standardized test scores and on the outcome of attendance, vouchers would strengthen the move toward compulsory education. The government would have much greater control over what students were taught and through standardized tests and assessments would supposedly measure whether or not they had learned.

Vouchers would give the government control over private education. The toll on alternative education would be serious. Vouchers would indirectly provide parents the money they need to send their children to schools that qualified for vouchers according to the government's standards. Therefore, more parents would be able to afford private schools. But because these schools would have to meet the government's requirements, there would really be no choice. Private schools receiving vouchers could not provide an alternative education. And schools that chose to sacrifice vouchers so that they could provide true alternatives in education would have a much harder time getting money that they do now, because vouchers would give some parents the illusion of choice and would draw many potential alternative school students to voucher-supported private schools.

It is incredible that without passing a single law or formulating a single policy directly regulating private education, the government could gain so much control over alternative education simply by instituting a voucher system. Rather than supporting and encouraging a wide range of alternative approaches to education, vouchers would become a way that educational bureaucracies, big business, and the state could control alternative education and make it like conventional education. This, in effect, would spell the end of alternative education in any meaningful sense of the word.

Given the fact that our schools are in trouble, if vouchers won't work, what will?

A better way to reform education would be to let parents decide how to spend their education dollars by allowing families to keep their money and/or issuing tax credits. Since parents are widely recognized as the primary educators of their children, we should be supporting families and children rather than trying to solve problems through institutions.

What can opponents of vouchers do?

Realize that it will not be easy to overcome the strong effort that is being made to promote vouchers as one of the solutions to problems facing American schools today, especially since the fundamental idea that parents should be able to choose an education for their children has strong appeal (and rightly so--the problem is that vouchers will undercut rather than make possible that choice).

Share your concerns about the risks of vouchers with other alternative educators/parents and help them to see that despite the way vouchers are being promoted, they would seriously damage if not eliminate alternative education.

Share your concerns with parents who are not involved in alternative education but who should realize that vouchers would be a serious threat to freedom of education and ultimately freedom of thought.

Discuss these issues with teachers you know, to help them realize how much they would lose through vouchers and how unwise it would be for them to rely solely on the opposition to vouchers being presented by teachers unions.

Be alert for legislation in your state which would pave the way for vouchers. For example, in addition to the many other reasons for opposing state-mandated standardized tests and assessments, such instruments are the key to establishing vouchers. Legislation to increase testing or assessment and/or make it more uniform by requiring that schools begin using only tests developed by the state department of education could easily be a giant step toward vouchers. This is also a reason to be concerned about the national standards and national testing program that is currently being pushed by the Federal government.

Conclusion

A careful look at the voucher system as it is developing in this country reveals that it would not give parents choice in education. Instead it would increase the control that the government, the educational establishment, and big business have over education. It would seriously damage our educational system by emphasizing the outcome of education and using standardized tests and assessments to measure that outcome. It would also increase control over alternative education by the government and make it much more difficult for alternative education to exist in any meaningful sense of the word. Alternative educators/parents and other concerned citizens need to consider this carefully and take action.

For Further Information

ORGANIZATIONS and PUBLICATIONS

The AERO-Gramme
The Alternative Education Resource
Organization
417 Roslyn Road
Roslyn Heights, New York 11577
516-621-2195

Options in Learning
The Alliance for Parental Involvement in
Education
Post Office Box 59
East Chatham, New York 12060-0059
518-392-6900

National Coalition News
National Coalition of Alternative
Community Schools
58 Schoolhouse Road
Summertown, Tennessee 38483
615-964-3670

SKOLE
72 Philip Street
Albany, New York 12202
518-432-1578

The GATE Newsletter
The Global Alliance for Transforming
Education
4202 Ashwoody Trail
Atlanta, Georgia 30319
404-458-5678

Changing Schools
c/o Colorado Options in Education
98 North Wadsworth Blvd. #127, Box 191
Lakewood, CO 80226
303-331-9352

Holistic Education Review
39 Pearl Street
Brandon, Vermont 05733-1007
802-247-8312

Rethinking Schools
1001 E. Keefe Avenue
Milwaukee, WI 53212
414-964-9646

BOOKS

Arons, Stephen *Compelling Belief: The Culture
of American Schooling* (McGraw-Hill, 1983)
Copperman, Paul *The Literacy Hoax*
(Morrow Quill, 1978)
atto, John Taylor *Dumbing Us Down: The
Hidden Curriculum of Compulsory Schooling*
(New Society Publishers, 1991)
Kaseman, Larry and Susan *Taking Charge
Through Homeschooling: Personal and
Political Empowerment* (Koshkonong Press,
1990)
Holt, John *Freedom and Beyond* (E. P. Dutton,
1972)
Holt, John *Escape From Childhood* (E. P.
Dutton, 1974)
Holt, John *Instead of Education* (E.P. Dutton,
1976)
Illich, Ivan *Deschooling Society* (Harper &
Row, 1970)
Miller, Ron *What Are Schools For: Holistic
Education in American Culture* (Holistic
Education Press, 1990)
Ravitch, Diane *The Troubled Crusade:
American Education 1945-1980* (Basic
Books, 1983)
Spring, Joel *The Sorting Machine: National
Education Policy Since 1945* (McKay, 1976)
Spring, Joel *The American School: 1642-1985*

RESOURCE NOTES:

For more information on the foundations
of parental responsibilities in education, see
John Holt's *Teach Your Own: A Hopeful Path
for Education* (NY: Delacorte, 1981), pp.
271-324 and John W. Whitehead and
Wendell R. Bird's *Home Education and
Constitutional Liberties: The Historical and
Constitutional Arguments in Support of Home
Instruction* (Westchester, IL: Crossway,
1984). Although both these focus on
homeschooling laws and their foundations,
much of the information applies to
alternative education in general, and the
way in which legal questions are discussed
provides a helpful model for
non-homeschoolers.

Two helpful books on locating and
reading laws are Stephen Elias's *Legal
Research: How to Find and Understand the
Law* (Berkeley, CA: Nolo Press, 1982) and
Using a Law Library, published in 1983 by
HALT, Inc., An Organization of Americans
for Legal Reform, 1319 F Street NW,
Washington, DC 20004.

CHAPTER THREE

Alternative Educators

Alternative Educators:
A Different View of Learning

"A teacher affects eternity:
He can never tell where his
influence stops."
    –Henry Brooks Adams

Throughout the centuries education has been one of the great endeavors of mankind. The accumulation and refining of knowledge, the selection and distribution of what is to be known, the never-ending manipulation of facts and figures to achieve social and political ends characterize an enterprise unequalled in history. Knowledge is power, and those in power have always determined how knowledge will be dispensed among the citizenry.

For almost as long as education has been controlled by those in power, there have been voices protesting that control. In his book *What Are Schools For?* (Holistic Education Press, 1990) Ron Miller, Ph.D., founder and former editor of *Holistic Education Review*, includes a chapter on the pioneers of what he terms holistic education. He notes that "the roots of holistic education are far deeper than the human potential movement or the 1960's counterculture; they extend back over two centuries through the work of several dissident, innovative educators."

Among these early educators are French philosopher Jean-Jacques Rousseau, Swiss educational reformer Johann Pestalozzi, founder of the modern-day kindergarten Friedrich Froebel, pioneer American educator Amos Bronson Alcott, the highly influential John Dewey, and many others. (Maria Montessori and Rudolf Steiner also contributed greatly to these early roots, but they are both discussed in a separate chapter.)

Miller notes that these early educators have never been considered a cohesive philosophical movement, but rather they have, for the most part, been a radical fringe element, speaking out against the increasingly materialistic, overly rigid intellectualization of education, yet only sporadically having any real effect on the development of schools and schooling methods.

"If we taught children to speak, they'd never learn."
–William Hull

Even today, while we as a society are undergoing tremendous political and academic turmoil, "there is virtually no serious questioning of the fundamental assumptions and purposes that underlie contemporary educational practices. It is simply assumed that 'education' means imparting certain facts and skills to those students smart enough (and disciplined enough) to learn them. It is simply assumed that the primary purpose of education is to enhance the economic and technological capacity of the nation so that we can compete with other nations and ultimately defeat them. And it is further assumed that there is a direct connection between these first two assumptions: once we impart enough facts and skills to our youth, our nation will not only prosper, but prevail over all others."

In his book, Miller challenges these assumptions about the purposes of mainstream American education, and argues that we, as a society, must reexamine and redefine our models of education. He's not alone in issuing this challenge. Many educators and authors, several of whom are also profiled in this chapter, have sounded the alarm about the real purposes of American education.

"The question I have been trying to answer for many years is 'Why *don't* they learn what we teach them?' The answer I have come to boils down to this: Because we teach them–that is, try to control the contents of their minds."

–John Holt
How Children Fail

In *The Night is Dark and I Am Far from Home* (1975, revised edition 1990) Jonathan Kozol wrote, "The first goal and primary function of the U.S. public school is not to educate good people, but good citizens. It is the function which we call–in enemy nations–'state indoctrination.'"

In *Teaching as a Subversive Activity* (1969) Neil Postman and Charles Weingartner opened their first chapter with these words: "...one of the tenets of a democratic society is that men be allowed to think and express themselves freely on any subject, even to the point of speaking out against the idea of a democratic society. To the extent that our schools are instruments of such a society, they must develop in the young not only an awareness of this freedom but a will to exercise it, and the intellectual power and perspective to do so effectively. So goes the theory."

In reality, substantive questioning of authority is discouraged. Schools are places where children learn how to submit to authority, to bury their yearnings for free expression and to submit to regimen and disciplined monotony. This process often entails the outright destruction of a child's intellectual capabilities; people who know too much are not likely to be submissive and willing to conform when it goes against reason and common sense, as much of what happens in school does. Knowledge is power, and those who hold the power are not always willing to share all of the knowledge.

Education as we know it today is an articifial edifice raised to provide a platform for social change. Educator and author James Herndon noted, "The purpose of schools is not teaching. The purpose of schools is to separate sheep from goats."

Ron Miller stated it well when he wrote, "Radical educators argued passionately that a bureaucratic, hierarchical society is wrong--not abstractly and ideologically, but profoundly and humanly wrong. To control and sort young people for the sake of institutional efficiency is to crush the human spirit."

So why do we continue in this mad headlong rush? Because we, as a society, have been led to believe that schools, whether public schools, traditional private schools, or alternative schools in their many forms, are necessary to the learning process. In fact, they are only necessary to the social and political processes.

And yet, because as a society we have embraced this definition of education, have accepted almost unquestioningly the idea that learning must happen separately from the rest of life, we will not in the near future abandon the idea of school as the proper training ground for our young. The overriding belief that the purpose of schooling is simply to teach reading, writing, and arithmetic ensures that schools will be with us for quite a long time. And so long as we have schools, we will continue to have those who speak out against their misguided application.

In this chapter we'll meet a few educators who have spoken out for change. Four equally notable educators, Maria Montessori, Rudolf Steiner, A. S. Neill, and John Holt, are profiled in later chapters.

"Our society institutionalizes learning, tries to direct and control it, and thereby distorts and sometimes even ruins it."
    –Larry and Susan Kaseman
Taking Charge Through Homeschooling: Personal and Political Empowerment

Jean-Jacques Rousseau   (1712-1778)

Born in Geneva, Switzerland in 1712, French philosopher Jean-Jacques Rousseau was an enigmatic, yet profoundly influential author and exponent of democracy and romanticism. His *La Nouvelle Heloise* (1761) was the most popular novel of his century, and Rousseau's political philosophy influenced the development of the French Revolution.

Leaving home at the age of 16, Rousseau wandered and worked at what was available, eventually making his way to Paris. He lived most of his life with an illiterate servant girl, having five children with her and sending them all to the Foundling Hospital in Paris, where few children were known to survive. He was called a hypocrite and a writer of paradoxes for condemning the arts while writing literary and musical works himself, and for his treatise on raising children after abandoning his own.

Nevertheless, his writings, done in eloquent, epigrammatic, and personal style, expressing belief in the goodness and worth of man, and emphasizing the deep need in human nature for emotional insight, were quite popular and influential. His sensibility, pedagogical ideas, and concepts of popular sovereignty both expressed and influenced the age of romanticism and revolution. He praised the simple, virtuous pleasures of family life and portrayed nature in the serenity of lakes, woods, and hills. He believed that education must be natural self-activity, and wrote in *Emile* that "the first impulses of nature are always right; there is no original sin in the human heart."

And yet Rousseau maintained in *La Nouvelle Heloise* and in *Emile* that it was not enough for men to obey the laws. Their minds and their wills must also be captured, and all individual rights must be given up. By deceptive devices and conditioning, the child must be formed in the desired model, under control while believing himself free. Rousseau held that a return to nature was neither possible nor desirable, he favored the creation of a moral and just state, reorganizing society into communities in which all persons would be completely controlled by the use of training, guidance, state-controlled propaganda and censorship, and the reduction of privacy to eliminate special interest groups and to control ideas. The state or community would become the center of power, spying would be a necessary part of life, and a "civil religion" would be embraced, with violators being expelled or put to death. He even invented a system for behavioral control which presaged some modern theories of psychological conditioning.

In *Emile* Rousseau wrote that children should be taught with sympathy and by appealing to their interests, rather than through discipline and with strict lessons. But he also felt that the thoughts and behavior of children should be carefully controlled. The many paradoxes presented by Rousseau and his writings are still being argued by today's scholars.

Johann Heinrich Pestalozzi   (1746-1827)

Johann Heinrich Pestalozzi was a Swiss educational reformer, a pioneer in what he termed "psychologizing education," whose theories laid the foundation of modern elementary education. Born in Zurich, educated at the University of Zurich, Pestalozzi studied for the ministry, began pursuing a legal career, but eventually turned his attention to education. He tried implementing Rousseau's theories in the education of his own child, but found them impracticable, and from that experience he decided to study children and education for himself. A particular interest of his was the education of the poor and working classes, and he gave his home for the care and training of a group of neglected children. Aided by the competent but illiterate peasant woman Elizabeth Naef--the model for Gertrude in his later writings--Pestalozzi gave the children an education quite different from what was standard in his day, focusing on love and understanding rather than rote learning and harsh discipline. The school was discontinued in 1779 for lack of funding, but it had laid the foundation for his later work.

Pestalozzi wrote from 1779 to 1798. One of his primary works of this time was *Leonard and Gertrude* (1781), the tale of a humble but devoted peasant woman whose devotion and lofty purpose transform her entire village. This was one of a number of works which profoundly influenced the evolution of modern pedagogy.

In 1798 Pestalozzi was appointed head of a school of orphans at Stans, and in 1799 he became teacher at an elementary school in Bergdorf. Joined by other progressive teachers, Pestalozzi organized an institute for training teachers in his successful methods. In 1801 he wrote the influential *How Gertrude Teaches Her Children*, which has been called one of the great classics on education. The institute moved in 1804 to Munchenbuchsee, then in 1805 to Yverdon on Lake Neuchatel. Pestalozzi's ideas and influence spread,

and he contributed greatly to educational practice and theory, primarily through educators from Europe and the U.S. who came to
Switzerland to study with him at the institute. For the next 20
years, until his death in 1827, Pestalozzi continued his experiments in education and developed his theories.

Pestalozzi believed that social reform could be brought about
through the intellectual and moral development of the individual
child, rather than by political revolution. He placed great emphasis on moral instruction, believing that moral virtue was vital to
the constructive role of the individual in society. An important byproduct of Pestalozzi's reforms was the acceptance of his ideas by
the state and the gradual transfer of schools from church domina-
tion to government-supported institutions for the training of its
future citizens.

Friedrich Wilhelm August Froebel   (1782-1852)

Friedrich Wilhelm August Froebel endured an unhappy childhood and very little formal schooling, educating himself through
wide reading and close contact with nature. After studying with
Pestalozzi for two years, Froebel served in the army, then started a
school for boys in 1816 called the Universal German Educational
Institute, near Griesheim (moved to Kielhau in 1817), where other
teachers came to study his methods. He completed his most important work,*The Education of Man*, in 1826, writing, "Education
consists of leading man, as a thinking, intelligent being, growing
into self-consciousness, to a pure, unsullied, conscious and free
representation of the inner law of Divine Unity, and in teaching
him means thereto."

In 1836 he moved to Switzerland because of allegations of his
radicalism. In theory and practice he showed evidence of mysti-
cism through the use of balls and circles, which he believed the
child would recognize intuitively as symbols of the unity of the
universe. Froebel continued his work in education, returned to
Germany and decided to dedicate himself to the education of very
young children.

In 1837 he opened an institution for preschool children at Blan-
kenburg, Thuringia, naming it the Kindergarten in 1840. The idea
was accepted, and several kindergartens were founded in Germany. Continued suspicion of Froebel's unorthodox beliefs and
methods hampered the growth of his movement, and in 1851 the

Prussian Minister of Education brought a ban on kindergartens. Froebel died in 1852. When the ban on kindergartens was lifted in 1860, the movement resumed its rapid growth in Germany and elsewhere.

Froebel's educational system was based on a belief in the underlying unity of nature, and religious training was a fundamental principle, but Froebel rejected the idea of inherited sin. The importance of self-activity in the development of the child was stressed, and the role of the teacher was not to instill or indoctrinate the child, but rather to encourage the child's self-development.

Amos Bronson Alcott   (1799-1888)

Amos Bronson Alcott was a pioneer in the development of child-centered education, and has been called the precursor of John Dewey. An American trancendentalist philosopher, educator and author, Alcott began teaching school in rural Connecticut in 1825. His innovations, inspired primarily by the Swiss educational reformer Pestalozzi, centered on the physical, emotional, and intellectual well-being of the child, rather than on the conventional rote teaching of facts, and this approach quickly drew widespread attention.

In 1828 he moved to Boston and opened a school, from 1830 to 1834 he conducted an experimental school in Philadelphia, and in 1835 returned to Boston to establish his famous experiment, the Temple School. Elizabeth Peabody's *Record of a School* (1835), detailing his methods of instruction, aroused widespread interest in his work, but in 1836 and 1837 he published his two volume *Conversations with Children on the Gospels*, transcribing classroom dialogues, which was denounced as blasphemous and obscene, and he was eventually forced to close the school.

Friends with Emerson and Thoreau, and known as a dreamer and a visionary, Alcott was involved with the founding of "Fruitlands," a cooperative, intellectual, vegetarian community. He was also a member of the religious and intellectual Brook Farm Association, a communistic experiment participated in by some of the most prominent New England writers of the time.

While Superintendent of Schools in Concord, Massachusetts from 1859 to 1865, Alcott issued a series of annual reports on his advanced methods of education which received wide circulation. In 1879 he started the Concord School of Philosophy and Literature. By this time his daughter, Louisa May Alcott, had achieved fame and recognition for her writing, and assumed the support of the family. Amos Bronson Alcott died in Boston in 1888.

Jean Piaget (1896-1980)

Jean Piaget, a Swiss biologist turned psychologist and educator, developed a theory of child development known as genetic episte-mology, defined as the study of how a child acquires and modifies abstract ideas, such as the concepts of causality, space, time, force, and morality. In more than thirty books, published in several lan-guages, Piaget and his associates elaborated a study of cognitive growth and development in childhood that was comparable in it's significant influence to Freud's achievements in the field of emo-tions.

Born in 1896 in Neuchatel, Switzerland, Piaget published his first scholarly papers (on mollusks) while still in high school. In 1918 he took a doctorate in natural science at the University of Neuchatel, then became interested in the development of thought in children. He taught at various universities in Switzerland and France, and in 1921 began to do research in child psychology at the Institute J. J. Rousseau in Geneva, serving as its co-director from 1933 to 1971. In 1955 Piaget founded the Center for the Study of Genetic Epistemology, an organization which studies thought processes. He was Director of the International Bureau of Educa-tion from 1929 to 1967, and a professor of psychology at the Uni-versity of Geneva from 1929 until his death in 1980.

Piaget's findings stressed not heredity or environment, but the interaction of various factors as the child constructs and recon-structs his or her own model of reality in several successive stages. As a biologist, Piaget felt that psychology had erred by starting with the adult human and working backward to understand the child. He wrote that the end product of a biological organism is not the best place to start if you wanted to understand that organ-ism, for the biases and viewpoints of a mature logic were carried into the research.

Piaget wrote that one must start his research at the beginning of life and let the being itself show how it grows. He found that the child had to build his or her own intellectual knowledge for inter-preting and physically responding to the world, and he found that the child goes through clear developmental stages in this growth of intelligence, much like the stages of physical development. According to Piaget, the child's brain system and structure of knowledge undergo specific transitions, or shifts of logic, in a specific sequence, at each of several genetically predetermined age levels.

His more important writings include *The Language and Thought of the Child* (1926), *Judgement and Reasoning in the Child* (1928), *The Psychology of Intelligence* (1950), *An Introduction to Genetic Epistemology*, in three volumes (1950), *Science of Education and the Psychology of the Child* (1969), and *Biology and Knowledge* (1971).

Francis Wayland Parker (1837-1902)

An American educator and leader in the progressive education movement, Francis Wayland Parker advocated informal methods of instruction and a relaxed social atmosphere in the classroom at a time when the normal teacher held strict authoritarian rule over the classroom, employing rigid teaching techniques and enforcing an inflexible discipline and regimentation on the students.

Born in Bedford, New Hampshire on October 9, 1837, Parker began to teach at the age of 16. He served in the Union Army during the Civil War, rising to the rank of Colonel, and after the war he returned to teaching until 1872.

In that year he travelled to Germany, where he studied the new teaching methods being advocated by educators such as Pestalozzi and Froebel. Upon his return to the United States Parker served as Superintendent of Schools in Quincy, Massachusetts, and began applying his progressive ideas, which became known as "the Quincy system." Parker pioneered the introduction of science courses, developed strong programs of geography in the elementary schools, urged that classrooms be free of corporal punishment, and proposed that the child be made the center of the educative process.

In 1889 Parker founded and was the first principal of his own school, The Chicago Institute. When this school became the University of Chicago's Department of Education Parker became the Department's first director.

Parker's most well-known book, *Talks on Pedagogics* (1894) discussed the inequity and injustice of the domineering, authoritative teaching methods and the passive, powerless role of the student. On corporal punishment he wrote, "Corporal punishment has for its basis the working hypothesis that children are bad by birth, by nature, and by tendency, and that this badness must be suppressed; that children do not like education or educative work; that it is necessary to discipline the mind through fear..."

Parker heartily disliked the use of rewards, grades, rankings and the like as a means of control: "Bought at home, bought at school, with merits, percents, and prizes, bought in college and university with the offer of high places, the young man with a finished education stands in the world's market-place and cries, 'I'm for sale, what will you give for me?' The cultivation of the reward system in our schools is the cultivation of inordinate ambition, the sinking of every other motive into the one of personal success."

Francis Wayland Parker died on March 2, 1902, but not before he had exerted great influence on modern educational practice. In his book, *What Are Schools For?* (1990) Ron Miller writes, "Like most mainstream reformers, Parker was most disturbed by the moral failure of Americans to achieve their ideals." Miller then quotes from *Talks on Pedagogics*: "Why is it that the sordid nature of man is so highly developed in our country? Why is it that man looks upon his fellow man as a means to his own selfish ends? Why is it that we doubt almost every man who seeks for office--doubt whether he loves his country more than he does himself?"

Miller continues, "Parker's answer was that selfishness is cultivated in the old-fashioned methods of the schools; once we institute a science of education, he implied, all will be well. There is not even a hint in this book that 'looking upon his fellow man as a means to his own selfish ends' may be fostered by a materialistic, capitalist worldview."

John Dewey (1859-1952)

John Dewey was an American educator and philosopher, born near Burlington, Vermont in 1859. Generally regarded as the "father of Progressive Education," and one of the most influential thinkers of his time, Dewey's writing and teaching affected not only philosophy and education, but also psychology, law, art, and political science.

After graduating from the University of Vermont in 1879, Dewey spent three years teaching, during which time he published his first philosophical articles. He went on to a distinguished career in teaching at several universities. As an educator he believed that education should not only be concerned with the mind but should also develop the student's manual skills. He declared that education must include a student's physical and moral well-being as well as his intellectual development.

Dewey was an eloquent advocate of what is called liberal education, feeling that it was the most useful of all types of learning. Dewey summed up his position in his "Pedagogic Creed" of 1897. He wrote, "I believe that all education proceeds by the participation of the individual in the social consciousness of the race... Through this unconscious education the individual gradually comes to share in the intellectual and moral resources which humanity has succeeded in getting together... The most formal and technical education in the world cannot safely depart from this general process. It can only organize it or differentiate it in some particular direction."

Dewey argued against perceiving education as merely test scores, achievement standards, discipline and order in the school classroom. He believed that education is not simply a kind of preparation for a life which begins after graduation, but rather, that education is itself an integral part of life, and should be treated as such.

Dewey's ideas were adopted by the "progressive education" movement, which is distinguished by its emphasis on socialization rather than on academics, and which has been criticized as the production of "well-adjusted citizens," rather than to impart any particular skills. In protest of the misuse of his ideas by this movement Dewey wrote *Experience and Education* (1938), in which he states, "The belief that all genuine education comes about through experience does not mean that all experiences are genuinely or equally educative. Experience and education cannot be related to each other. For some experiences are mis-educative."

In an address delivered at Ann Arbor, Michigan and later printed in the November, 1936 issue of *Education Digest*, Dewey, then Professor Emeritus of Philosophy, stated, "There is a conflict in education between two supposed ideals, one being the acquisition of information and certain useful skills, and the other being the development of the capacity to think, the power of judgement. The first of these two ends was established when the sphere of available knowledge was limited and within the bounds of human compass; but its influence in the school was greatly increased by the part that accumulation and acquisition have played in American life. The schools have set out to have their pupils accumulate knowledge in much the same way that their elders were striving to accumulate property.

"That there is a conflict between these two aims running through our whole educational scheme seems to me undeniable. The purpose of accumulation is historically older and more ingrained. The development of intelligence is a more recent aim both in education and in society generally."

Dewey's suggestion was to provide a sense of direction for American education. In the foreword to Dewey's *Education Today* (1940), Joseph Ratner wrote, "Some educators, in recent years, have asked whether the school dare build a new social order. Dewey's answer to this basic question the reader will find written throughout *Education Today*. It is that no social order, least of all the democratic, can be securely built unless the school is an active participant in the building of it."

John Dewey died in New York City on June 1, 1952. While hailed by many as one of the greatest educators America has seen, there are many others who attribute the problems of our present school system to his influence. His many books, spanning over 60 years, include *Psychology* (1887), *The Ethics of Democracy* (1888), *Applied Psychology: An Introduction to the Principles and Practice of Education* (1889), *My Pedagogic Creed* (1897), *Ethical Principles Underlying Education* (1897), *The School and Society* (1899), *The Child and the Curriculum* (1902), *Moral Principles in Education* (1909), *Democracy and Education* (1916), *The Public and Its Problems* (1927), *Characters and Events* (1929), *Experience and Education* (1938), *Education Today* (1940).

Ivan Illich (1926-)

Born in Vienna, Austria in 1926, Ivan Illich came to the United States in 1951, subsequently becoming a U.S. citizen. Educated at the University of Florence, the University of Rome, and the University of Munich, among others, Ilich was ordained a Roman Catholic Priest in 1951, became Monsignor in 1956, and left the priesthood in 1969.

Illich, who has been described as a multi-faceted genius, founded the controversial Intercultural Center of Documentation (CIDOC) in Cuernavaca, Mexico in 1961. At that time a Roman Catholic monsignor, Illich founded CIDOC as an orientation school for missionaries, technical assistants, and other volunteers, but when Illich's radical vision of a de-politicized, de-bureaucratized church of the future began to appear in magazines in 1967, CIDOC became the center of a bitter ecclesiastical controversy. To avoid embarrassment to the church, Illich severed CIDOC's denominational ties in 1968 and resigned his priestly duties in 1969.

Ivan Illich has since described CIDOC as a "free-thinking university," and Illich himself has been described as "an amazingly brilliant man who likes to have bright people around him..". In his 1970 book, *Deschooling Society*, Illich wrote, "The very existence of obligatory schools divides any society into two realms: some time spans and processes and treatments and professions are 'academic' or 'pedagogic,' and others are not. The power of school thus to divide social reality has no boundaries: education becomes unworldly and the world becomes noneducational."

Illich compared the school's function to the role of the powerful churches of history and noted that it is one of the modern institutions whose primary purpose is the shaping of our vision of reality. He wrote, "School teaches us that instruction produces learning. The existence of schools produces the demand for schooling. Once we have learned to need school, all our activities tend to take the shape of client relationships to other specialized institutions. Once the self-taught man or woman has been discredited, all nonprofessional activity is rendered suspect. In school we are taught that valuable learning is the result of attendance; that the value of learning increases with the amount of input; and, finally, that this value can be measured and documented by grades and certificates."

In an article for the magazine *Utne Reader* (November/December, 1987), Illich discusses his book, *Deschooling Society*: "It attracted a great deal of attention, but its central point, that compulsory education is a modern tool, or technology, that serves to ritualize 'progress', was missed entirely." According to Illich, modern definitions of "progress," with their accompanying destruction of ecological balance, can only be redefined with a change in our methods of education. He writes, "[No one] can free themselves from progressive consumption until they free themselves from obligatory school."

In an article for the *Miami Herald* (1975) John Dorchner wrote "Ivan Illich has an uncanny ability to uncover, and then attack, the most sacred cows of Western civilization. He advocates abolishing compulsory education, because he thinks school systems encourage ignorance, not knowledge. He wants medical services drastically reduced, because he believes doctors are responsible for more sickness than for health. He thinks people would save time if transportation were limited to the speed of a bicycle." Peter L. Berger noted in a piece for the *New York Times Book Review* (1983), "It is impossible to agree completely with Mr. Illich. It is also impossible to ignore him."

His more important books include *Celebration of Awareness:A Call for Institutional Awareness* (1970), *De-Schooling Society* (1971), *Retooling Society* (1973), *Medical Nemesis: the Expropriation of Health* (1976), *Shadow Work* (1981).

Jonathan Kozol (1936-)

Born in Boston, Massachusetts in 1936, Jonathan Kozol graduated from Harvard University with a B.A. (summa cum laude) in 1958, and did graduate study at Oxford in 1958-59. Kozol was hired as a substitute teacher for the Boston Public School System in 1964 and 1965, at the height of the civil rights problems. With no training in education and with no experience as a teacher, he was sent to teach in a segregated classroom in the Boston Public Schools. In 1965 Kozol was fired from his fourth grade teaching position for refusing to restrict his reading and reference materials to the list of approved publications.

From that experience he wrote the critically acclaimed *Death at an Early Age* (1967), which received the National Book Award in 1968. The book documented the repressive teaching methods used by Kozol's colleagues, techniques he believed were designed to reinforce a system that would keep the black children separate and unequal. Kozol also analyzed the irrelevant and often racist curriculum materials, discussed the widespread practice of punishing disobedient children with rattan whips, and unflinchingly decribes the dirty and unsafe conditions of the schools.

In 1966 Kozol, with several others, founded one of the very first free schools in America, in Roxbury, a black district of Boston, and from that experience his second book, *Free Schools* (1972), was written, in which he noted, "The obedient teacher in the public school, no matter what his personal bias or political position, is compelled by law to serve the interests and the purposes of the flag that hangs beside the door. The teacher in the Free School does not need to feel compelled to serve the interests of that banner. He does, however, need to serve some interests. His allegiance is not to nothing, it is to something."

Kozol was sharply critical of the tendency of many free schools to leave children's learning to their own whims, and he wrote in *Free Schools*, "In the face of many intelligent and respected statements, writings, essays on the subject of 'spontaneous' and 'ecstatic' education, it is simple truth that you do not learn calculus, biochemistry, physics, mathematical logic, constitutional law, brain surgery or hydraulic engineering in the same spontaneous and organic fashion that you learn to walk and talk and breathe and make love. Hours and seasons, months and years of long, involved and - let us be quite honest - sometimes non-utopian labor in the acquisition of a single unit of complex and intricate attainment go into the expertise that makes for power in this nation."

In 1975 Kozol wrote what would become an underground classic, titled *The Night is Dark and I Am Far from Home*, an examination of the values and goals of American middle-class education. Earning Kozol the disfavor of the powerful mainstream press, the book, which further examined the idea that schools are effective primarily as centers of national indoctrination, found a readership in colleges and universities, "not in schools of education, but in political science, sociology, and literature classes." By 1987, when the book was officially out of print, students were reading illegally photocopied printings, assigned by their teachers. Part of the reason for this can be found in the book's compelling opening paragraphs, which echo with the ring of truth even today: "U.S. education is by no means an inept, disordered misconstruction. It is an ice-cold and superb machine. It does the job: not mine, not yours perhaps, but that for which it was originally conceived. The first goal and primary function of the U.S. public school is not to educate good people, but good citizens. It is the function which we call—in enemy nations—'state indoctrination.'"

The Night Is Dark and I Am Far from Home was released in a new revised edition in 1990. Kozol's other books include *On Being A Teacher* (1981), *Illiterate America* (1985), *Rachel and Her Children: Homeless Families in America* (1989).

Herbert Kohl (1937-)

Born in 1937 in Bronx, New York, Herbert Kohl graduated from Harvard University, A.B. (magna cum laude) 1958, did graduate study at University College, Oxford 1958-59, received an M.A. from Columbia University in 1962, and did additional graduate study 1965-66.

Herbert Kohl has taught, administered, and written extensively about public alternative education, and has consistently called for a redefinition and reformation of public education. Author of several acclaimed books, including *36 Children* (1967), and *The Open Classroom* (1969), Kohl has written that education's first goal should be to "develop informed, thoughtful, and sensitive citizens." He writes that this can be accomplished by teaching six basic skills: "the ability to use language well and thoughtfully; the ability to think through problems and experiment with solutions; the ability to understand scientific and technical ideas and use tools; to use imagination and to participate in and appreciate personal and group expression; to understand how people function in groups; learning how to learn through life and to contribute to the nurturance of others."

Discussing his book *36 Children*, Kohl says that he was "able to take children who had experienced failure and self-hatred in school and enable them to flower emotionally and intellectually. This involved my throwing out the standard curriculum , reworking the schedule of the day, and most of all, listening and learning from my students and building a curriculum that used the strengths in their lives."

In *The Question is College* (1989), Kohl examines what our present society calls meaningful work and discusses options to going from high school directly into college. Writing from the position that doing work which one enjoys and finds rewarding is essential to real happiness, Kohl presents several answers to the ever-present questions about what a young person should do with his or her life.

Herbert Kohl now lives with his family in Point Arena, California, where he is Director of the Costal Ridge Research and Educational Center, which he established in 1978. His many books include *The Age of Complexity* (1965), *36 Children* (1967), *The Open Classroom* (1969), *Reading: How To* (1973), *On Teaching* (1976), and *The Question is College* (1989).

For Further Information

PUBLICATIONS:

Holistic Education Review
39 Pearl Street
Brandon, Vermont 05733-1007
802-247-8312

SKOLE
20 Elm Street
Albany, New York 12202

BOOKS

Dewey, John *Education Today* (Putnam, 1940)
Illich, Ivan *Deschooling Society* (Harper & Row, 1970)
Kohl, Herbert *36 Children* (The New American Library, 1967)
Kohl, Herbert *The Open Classroom* (New York Review of Books, 1969)
Kohl, Herbert *The Question is College* (Times Books/Random House, 1989)
Kozol, Jonathan *Death at an Early Age* (Houghton Mifflin, 1967)
Kozol, Jonathan *Free Schools* (Houghton Mifflin, 1972)
Kozol, Jonathan *The Night is Dark and I Am Far From Home* (Simon and Schuster, 1975, 1990)
Piaget, Jean *To Understand Is To Invent* (Grossman Publishers, 1973)
Rousseau, Jean-Jacques (Trans. by Allen Bloom) *Emile* or *On Education* (Basic Books, 1979)

CHAPTER FOUR

Homeschooling

A Bold Approach to Learning

"I think it is up to each of us, as parents and learners, to be able to say, 'This is what I think is worth learning, this is what I think we need to know.' We should be allowed to make these decisions on the basis of family and community, and not on the basis of what some far-off expert says we must do."

–David Colfax

What is homeschooling? What do parents do with their children at home all day? How do they find the materials, the resources, the time? Don't children who are kept at home miss meeting and playing with other children? How can a parent possibly hope to meet all the needs of several lively children at the same time? How can a parent be qualified to teach?

Homeschooling is making the news these days. People are talking about it. Parents are wondering what it's all about, and whether or not it might work for their own families. Who chooses to homeschool their children? One might as well ask who chooses to drive Fords, or buy computers, or keep cats. Cut a cross section of American life, and chances are good that you'll find several homeschooling families.

Homeschooling has been a remarkably successful grass roots movement, with newspaper and magazine articles, radio and television programs, and hundreds of conferences and seminars spreading the latest news and information each year. But there is still confusion about just what homeschooling is.

People ask where to find "the homeschool curriculum," how many hours per day they should teach their children, or how they will know when their child is ready to be taught. Having been educated in our highly structured and controlled school systems (both public and private), it is difficult for most people to imagine another way for children to learn. Homeschooling can be as simple as families being together, the younger ones learning from the older ones how to grow and be... or is it the other way around?

There are many ways to homeschool. How do you choose the method best suited for your family? Ask yourselves what kind of teaching/learning program you would feel comfortable with. Does your family prefer a structured routine, with daily lessons defining the learning? Or would a more relaxed approach to education suit your family better? Most homeschooling parents begin to relax their expectations as they come to realize that children can and will learn without constant coercion. Learning becomes a part of what happens every day, and "teachable moments" - those special times when a child might be receptive to an explanation of photosynthesis or a discussion of the political history of Europe - become a part of everyday life.

Experiment with several different methods until you find one that seems right for you and your children. Let your learning program change as time goes by. Most families find their ideas about teaching and learning to be constantly changing as they discover and apply new methods, or as capabilities expand and grow. Many families might start out with a formal, structured program and learn to relax as the child's abilities blossom. Other families will begin with a relaxed approach, letting the child discover on his own, and then gradually build into a formalized learning program when the child shows a

"I wonder if people are becoming easier to manipulate. Once upon a time there was more room for independent farmers, low budget inventors, experimenters, eccentrics, and nonconformists of every kind. Now great institutions, powerful economic forces, and the relatively new idea of compulsory public education tend to force us into more clearly defined, manageable groups. Home education encourages people to be more unpredictable and creative in how they look at themselves. I think without homeschoolers and lots of others who question authority and who question institutions we're in great danger of losing all our dreams to a society which, and I don't mean to be dramatic, but a society which is a little more Orwellian than we might care to have."

–Earl Stevens

readiness for (and interest in) structured lessons.

If your family has decided to try homeschooling you might be asking at this point, "How do we get started? Where can we find more information on what we need to do?"

The best place to begin is by familiarizing yourself with the subject. Get a good book on the topic, or take out a subscription to a homeschooling publication. If you'd like to learn about homeschooling first hand - if you want to actually talk to someone who's doing it - a local homeschooling support group can help.

Homeschooling is much more than education -- it's a completely different way of looking at things. It's refusing to march to the tune that most people hear... it's creating your own music instead. Homeschooling is a departure from the accepted norm, a decisive step in assuming personal responsibility for your family's future.

When parents make the decision to teach their children at home it often opens the doors to a whole new world, a world in which the parents, as well as the children, will be learning and exploring and discovering new ideas.

"Our children become less mysterious to us when they are not gone for eight to ten hours per day. The small patterns and rhythms of their lives, and ours, can be seen and understood. When our children are with us the cycles and the seasons become more apparent as we watch them growing and learning. Small discoveries can be shared, and more important triumphs can be seen in their true context. Our children become as small apprentices, learning from us the daily skills, taking our wisdom as their own."

–Mark and Helen Hegener

Won't They Be "Different?"

—— Becky Olson ——————————————————————————

"Aren't you doing your kids a disservice by homeschooling? I mean, how will they fit into the real world if they haven't been schooled like everyone else? Won't they be different?"

"I sure hope so!" I wanted to say. "I really want my children to be different!" Her question was honest enough. She was concerned about my kids' futures. I don't think she would have ever understood if I'd tried to explain to her why different is good. So I just smiled and said, "Well, they seem to fit in most everywhere," as I glanced past her shoulder at my youngest daughter scooping up her baby and the rest pairing off, already finding common interests.

Our society pays great lip service to "being your own person." Several years ago a TV commercial applauded the individual who took the last exit off the freeway in search of his uniqueness. we still idolize the Horatio Alger ideals of fortitude, hard work, and the concept that "anyone can work their way to the top." Chances are now that one of those fictional boys would have difficulty getting a job, because in reality independent thinking and self taught skills are not valued.

Yes, those of us that have opted to homeschool are working to help increase the value of being able to think through a problem and find the solution, either independently or in a team. When you watch a young child that has bonded well with his parents and the world around, that has been encouraged to use explorative powers, the child doesn't sit down in defeat when he comes to an obstacle in the path. This free thinking individual puzzles out a way to overcome, or use the barrier instead of fighting it. In fact if it is indeed an insurmountable obstacle, the child may just sit down and explore it. The child may choose, too, to accept the obstacle as a quest too big to conquer today. He may turn his back and leave this for another time. Or the child may call to a larger person - parent, friend, or sibling - to help move the obstruction.

This same child, in later years, if left to use his own creativity, will face all challenges the same way. Speaking, reading, arithmetic, roller skating and calculus will all be looked upon as a conquerable challenge, if not today, then perhaps tomorrow, next week, or next year.

One of the amazing attributes I see in homeschooling people is they don't take their validation from their "book larnin'." My own children have given up trying to convince adults that knowing the multiplication tables or the capital of South Dakota is not an indication of their learning abilities. Data is not valuable in and of itself, but rather is gathered and stored to be used later on. Whether the use is to answer a trivia question, solve a math problem or write a letter, each is an equally respectable reason for using the information.

As my oldest becomes a teenager, she doesn't feel a need to give in to peer pressure if it makes her uncomfortable. All her life *she* has decided what is the upper limit of her involvement with anything—from sleep, to reading, to multiplication tables, to jumping into the deep end of a swimming pool. If she wasn't comfortable with it or didn't see a valuable reason for doing it, she wouldn't do it. These skills are a great help to her in making the decisions teens must make daily. Peer pressure is a factor in her life, but not *the* deciding factor.

Children that are home most of their young life learn to get along with people of all ages. Homeschooled kids make great baby-sitters, because they enjoy being with people. I'm always amazed at how patient these kids are with little ones as well as adults. These baby-sitters seem to innately understand the value of play, and enjoy sitting down to simple board games, or more complex computer games, with the child they are taking care of. Because self-esteem is high, the younger child often teaches the older one the rules of the board game and the tricks of the computer game. Information is shared equally.

These same kids seldom get impatient with a well meaning adult who talks down to them in a store or rushes over to prevent them from touching a breakable object. They smile, step back, and still look at the beautiful item. Sometimes they ask questions about the item, or call me over to share the view. If I sense a real need for the child to touch it, I'll hold it and let the child explore it gently with their fingers. Often the clerk will comment on how gentle the child is with fragile items.

Children that don't find their days cut up into blocks of time have the healthy ability to go with the flow. Having been allowed to explore things until they are finished, they have a higher frustration limit. Most often they understand that the project will be waiting for them when they return. I rarely find homeschool parents complaining about the lack of attention span their children have. More often than not, the parents are frustrated by the child's need to follow a course of study to the very end, along with several detours into other disciplines that contributed to the original project.

One young woman's fascination with cats led her and her mother on many an exploratory search through the public library, encompassing ancient and medieval history, genetics, animal husbandry, biology, literature, archeology, anthropology, and a half dozen more subjects. Once she started, every contributing discipline had to be methodically explored. Some books were read to answer one specific question, others were explored cover to cover, and many of these led off to other studies. By the time the fascination has become a glowing ember instead of a blazing need, an amazing amount of information had been covered, as well as the satisfaction of following a project from beginning to end. Skills had been learned to facilitate the search for information: use of the library card catalog, reading and note taking skills improved, and so on, but these were tools to help answer questions. There was no written report to enable someone else to decide whether the work had been worthwhile, or had been done correctly, or had followed arbitrary parameters set by an authority figure. The girl was pleased with what she had learned and that was the only validation she needed.

For many years the buzz word in big business has been "team work." This has been a difficult concept for Americans to take to heart. From preschool on children are taught that when the final countdown comes, winning is why the game is played. Although adults admonish children to share, sharing the credit for an accomplishment at the office can spell doom. The driving force of America is competition, one-up-manship, winning.

As I watch homeschooled kids interact, so many times the challenge of the game seems far more important than winning. When they choose up sides for a ball game, little ones are just as valued as big players. When winning isn't the answer, it's not necessary to degrade the lack of skills one player may have.

My son and his friend were competing with each other on a computer game. After it was all done, their satisfaction was defined as a comparison. "I'm almost as good as Stephen in this game, and he is as good as I am in the other game." Neither of these two boys' self esteem rested on beating the other, only upon improving skill levels.

The problem solving skills that these children are learning in their independent exploration of the world will, indeed, make them different. Being different is always a challenging path. With challenge comes growth and independent thinking. Above all of that comes happiness. Those of us involved in helping nurture a "different" person are different, too. When we, like the toddler, stop fighting the obstacle in our path, and accept and explore it, we find happiness in our peace. This is the gift we pass on to our "different" children.

The Way We Learn

—— Catherine Johns ————————————————————————

Life is interesting. And perhaps the most fascinating part of it is the way we change and grow, discovering new ideas and parts of ourselves which we never knew existed while discarding worn out habits and belief systems. In my efforts to learn and to grow, both as a mother and as a person, I have found my perceptions about education changing as I come to understand more about myself and my children.

We started home schooling three years ago with a very structured curriculum. Our children had always done very well - academically - in school, and while we were excited about the idea of teaching them at home we could see no reason to change the way they were being taught. So we enrolled them in an accredited correspondence course. We set aside several hours each day for "learning" and I buckled down to assume the schoolteacher's role in the education of our children.

At first the novelty and the newness of it all kept us going. I loved playing teacher, instructing my very own miniature classroom, and the kids loved not having to go to school any more. Curiously, they never once mentioned a longing for their old classmates, even though they had seemingly been quite close with some of them. Socialization has never been an issue - the kids play with their friends when the latter aren't in school and it seems to be enough.

The structure of the curriculum made my job simple. Just read the directions and teach. Easy as "add water and stir." But after about six months I had to admit that we were really having trouble. The children never wanted to finish their lessons, they were bored with the repetition and busywork, and they balked at most of their assignments. With the more advanced subjects I found myself losing patience... explaining basic math concepts was just not as much fun as I'd imagined it would be, especially when I found myself explaining them for the fourth time to the same kid!

So we gradually loosened up our schedule. I quit "going by the book" (in this case the "teacher's manual"), and we started improvising, seeing what we could substitute for the coursework that would be more interesting and yet still get the lesson across. At first we had trouble keeping to the specific subject, which I felt was "necessary" because at the end of each month we had to send in a test "proving" that we had completed the assignments. I found myself "teaching to the test" and resenting it. But the kids seemed to enjoy skimming over the workbooks, doing a few problems on each page. It was encouraging to see them doing their work with enthusiasm again, instead of with little black clouds hanging over their heads! I was still worried about their progress, and sometimes I arbitrarily insisted that they complete workbook pages they could probably just as well have left unfinished, but on the whole we were all enjoying what we were doing much more than before.

The next fall we made our biggest decision -- we simply didn't re-enroll in the course. With some of the several hundred dollars we saved on tuition we went on a wonderful "educational shopping spree" and purchased books on all sorts of interesting subjects, dozens of grade level workbooks in every subject imaginable, a much-longed-for set of encyclopedias, a big beautiful world globe, a high-power microscope, science kits, lots of interesting charts and maps and posters, puzzles, games, models, arts and crafts supplies, and several educational programs for our computer!

Then we built a special "learning room" in the garage. We made it bright and fun, with lots of murals and posters on the walls, bookcases full of interesting books and things to see and do and study, shelves piled high with projects to do, two big desks, a large work table, and a couple of comfortable easy chairs.

We also now have a program we call Integrated Learning. Instead of pages and pages of worksheet math problems, we do math in our heads on the way to the store. I let the kids add up my grocery bill and balance the checkbook (which they find terribly exciting!), and we halve and double recipes. Instead of boring essays and compositions we write letters to friends and family, write away for free samples and interesting offers (the kids love to get the mail), and they write in their own journals.

When they want to know something about electricity, or dinosaurs, or the civil war, they know where and how to find the information - with or without my assistance. And of course we all enjoy excursions to museums and libraries and historical sites and the zoo.

My husband and I have finally quit worrying about whether or not our children are learning "enough." When we took them out of school it was in the hopes of being able to really share in their lives, to develop a friendship with them that just didn't seem possible with them gone for all but a few hours each day. We had seen our friends' kids become gradually more and more distant as school and sports and extra curricular activities pulled them away – and we didn't want that to happen to our family. But had we stuck to the structured coursework, I think we would have had a far more serious problem of resentments bottled up inside us all for various reasons. We ask enough of our children in their daily chores, and expecting them to learn the many things that children should learn. The added burden of sticking to some far-off school's expectations for our children was one that none of us needed.

The changes we've made in the way we teach our children have penetrated into our lifestyle. I find myself being more patient, more willing to listen. We take every opportunity to make field trips and educational excursions, and have found that they invariably bring us all closer, giving us the shared experiences that families need to grow with each other. And instead of trying to do all the housework myself so that it gets done "right," I let the kids do their share - not by assigning tasks or chores, but by helping them to see that running a home is a family affair.

The kids seem to somehow understand that learning is their responsibility. It's rare when a week goes by without their initiating a project to learn something new - and surprisingly, it will be something like multiplying fractions as often as it's something like baking a souffle!

Life is indeed interesting. And with children, it can also be immensely rewarding.

John Holt (1923-1985)

"One of the main differences between a free country and a police state, I always thought, was that in a free country, as long as you obeyed the law, you could believe whatever you liked. Your beliefs were none of the government's business. Far less was it any of the government's business to say that one set of ideas was good and another set bad, or that (compulsory) schools should promote the good and stamp out the bad. Have we given up these principles?"

The author and radical alternative educator John Holt was a noted asker of questions, and, at times, his questions rankled the establishment mentality.

John Holt was born in New York City, April 14, 1923, the son of a wealthy insurance broker. Educated at such elite private schools as Le Rosey in Switzerland and Phillips Exeter, his education proved to be the discouraging experience that he later came to believe it is for many children. In an interview for *The Mother Earth News* magazine (July/August,1980) Holt stated that he "knew how to 'play the game,' so I never had any difficulty with school." But Holt grew bored with it as he grew older, and admitted that by the time he reached high school he would not read a book unless it had been assigned.

In later years John Holt became increasingly blunt when asked about his education, replying "I have come to believe that a person's education is as much a part of his private business as his politics or religion, and no one should be required to answer questions about it. May I say instead that most of what I know I did not learn in school, or even in what most people would call learning situations."

After graduating from Yale University in 1943 with a degree in industrial engineering, Holt entered the U. S. Navy and served on the submarine *U.S.S. Barbero*. When World War II ended, he moved to New York City, and from 1946 to 1952 worked with the World Federalists, a group advocating world government as the best way to prevent nuclear war. After traveling in Europe in 1952 and 1953, He returned to Colorado to work for room and board at a private high school, eventually moving into a teaching position. Becuase he had no prior training as a teacher he later noted that "I didn't know all the alibis that conventionally trained instructors use, excuses which imply that something's wrong with students who don't learn."

In 1957 Holt moved to Cambridge, Massachusetts and began teaching fifth grade in the Shady Hill School, a select private school, was dismissed for his unconventional teaching methods, and went on to the Lesley Ellis School in Cambridge, where he taught fifth grade, worked with beginning readers, and developed a mathematics curricula for grades one through six.

In 1964, at the suggestion of a friend, Holt wrote *How Children Fail*, drawing on letters, notes, and journals kept during his teaching experiences. Meeting both criticism and critical acclaim, the book explored Holt's observations that much of what goes on in schools is confusing, boring, humiliating, frightening, demeaning and oppressive for children. His second book, *How Children Learn* (1967), focused less on school than on children's activities in general, their games, sports, conversations, and activities in daily life, and presented Holt's view that children want to learn, and are good at it when not interfered with by adults and schooling.

In 1977, deciding after many years that the school system was hopelessly mired in its own bureaucracy, Holt founded a newsletter for parents and others who might want to explore alternatives to public and private schooling. *Growing Without Schooling*, distributed almost exclusively by mail, became a forum for people who were searching for ways to remove their children from school, and for new ways to help children learn. In issue #2, Holt wrote, "...When learning happens, the school takes the credit; when it doesn't, the student gets the blame. In the old days the schools said the kids were stupid, bad, lazy, or crazy. Now they say they have mysterious diseases like 'minimal brain dysfunction' or 'learning disabilities.' Under whatever name, these remain what they always were - excuses for the schools and teachers not being able to do their job."

Holt's small newsletter touched a raw nerve. By the fourth issue it had close to 500 subscribers, and by the seventh issue John Holt had appeared on Phil Donohue's television show and had a publisher interested in a book on homeschooling. By the tenth issue, over 10,000 letters had poured into the *Growing Without Schooling* office, evidence that parents were indeed looking for new ways to teach their children.

But beyond his crusade to help children and their parents learn and grow, John Holt offered another, deeper message. In *Freedom and Beyond* (1972), he wrote, "A large part of our problem is that few of us really believe in freedom. As a slogan, it is fine. But we don't understand it as a process or mechanism with which or within which people can work or live. We have had in our own lives so little experience of freedom, except in the most trivial situations, that we can hardly imagine how it might work."

Holt did not believe in perfect freedom. He said that those who saw freedom as the absence of limits simply misunderstood the term. But he was ever quick to defend the freedoms of children. He insisted that school was not simply a good idea gone bad, but "a bad idea from the word go. It's a nutty idea to believe that we can have a place where nothing but learning happens, cut off from the rest of life."

Holt advocated the development of facilities which would empower people, and enable them to assume some control over their lives: facilities such as libraries, storefront reading centers, and the widespread use of cassette tapes.

Personally, John Holt has been described as "eccentric." In an article for *Yankee* magazine (December, 1981), Holt is quoted as saying: "My actions sometimes are on the edges of some kind of normal distribution curve, and I guess that's what eccentric means. But they're not queer or nutty. My actions are eminently sensible."

John Holt was interested in conserving natural resources, the ecology movement, and especially in the development of renewable forms of energy. A lifelong learner, he took up many new pursuits in his later years, interesting but unusual activities such as the cello, downhill and water skiing, and horseback riding.

In September, 1985, John Holt died of cancer. When informed of the disease, he had refused radiation or chemotherapy, believing from his own research that the methods did more harm than good. His work, and the publication of his magazine, *Growing Without Schooling*, has been continued by his associates. A collection of his letters has been published as *A Life Worth Living: Selected Letters of John Holt* (1990), compiled and edited by Susannah Sheffer, editor of *Growing Without Schooling*.

It seems a strange quirk of fate that Holt's early books on education, classics such as *How Children Fail* (1964) and *How Children Learn* (1967), should still be hailed as suggested reading for teachers in training, while one of his last books, *Teach Your Own* (1981), became the handbook for hundreds of thousands of parents who were taking their children out of the public and private school systems to teach them at home.

John Holt's last book, an insightful exploration of the ways in which young children learn, was published after his death as *Learning All the Time* (1989). In that book he summed up much of his philosophy in the last chapter: "We can best help children learn, not by deciding what we think they should learn and thinking of ingenious ways to teach it to them, but by making the

world, as far as we can, accessible to them, paying serious attention to what they do, answering their questions--if they have any--
and helping them explore the things they are most interested in.
The ways we can do this are simple and easily understood by parents and other people who like children and will take the trouble
to pay some attention to what they do and think about what it
may mean. In short, what we need to know to help children learn
is not obscure, technical, or complicated, and the materials we can
use to help them lie ready at hand all around us."

Learning Free

—— Craig Conley ——————————————————————

Although it is commonly perceived as a social stigma and vast
sums of money and man hours are devoted to its prevention and
cure, dropping out of school is not necessarily a terminal condition. Every summer, most of the students I know start talking
about how they would like to put off returning to school. Once I
put it off for two years. After attending high school for a year and
a half I put it off permanently.

I really had little part in the initial decision to leave school. My
parents were dissatisfied with the alternatives to public school in
the town in which we lived. They thought they could do a better
job teaching my brother and me at home and decided to give it a
try.

I spent two years out of public school, pursuing my education
through correspondence study and travel. It was surprisingly easy
to get permission from the local school authorities. My parents
took a friendly approach and refrained from criticizing the school
system, and I am sure that helped.

For a family contemplating homeschooling it is more important
to understand what it is not than what it is. At least for us and for
the homeschooling families we know, it is not an escape from
what is wrong with your family or your child or your public
school. In our experience, good situations became better and bad
situations became worse with homeschooling.

Probably the most important knowledge I gained in my years of
home study was that it is impossible to separate living from learning. Everything is a learning experience. I found that learning
does not take place just six hours a day in a formal classroom, but

rather, all the time, everywhere.

My classroom varied from my father's woodworking shop where I measured and practiced fractions, to the public library where I read biographies of famous people. Through homeschooling I gained the freedom to explore my own interests at leisure. These included reading, music, drama, and travel.

When we traveled, my brother and I plotted the route to where we were going and kept track of the gas mileage. We spent time in Washington, D.C. and explored along the East Coast. We also visited the space centers in Houston and Cape Canaveral and Kitt Peak, Arizona. Perhaps the most interesting time was that spent in museums. Our favorites were the Smithsonian and the Chicago Art Institute.

At home I had time to read alone and with my family. I was also able to take lessons in creative dramatics, tap dancing, art and piano. These are things that were not offered in the schools in our town. My brother and I, according to our interests, were able to participate in classes that would not have been available to us had we been in school. In most communities, classes and activities are designed to segregate by age. A young person in school is denied the opportunity to participate in many instances simply by virtue of his school schedule. The assumption is made almost universally that young people have no interest in learning unless they are coerced or compelled to do so. Nearly every YMCA or YWCA, community center or church organization in this country, and certainly every "school" organization, separates classes into adults and children.

I was able to spend more time with my parents and their friends. When I attended public school I spent most of each day in a classroom with people exactly my own age. In the course of my home study experiences I got to know families all over the United States who were also actively trying to learn in non-traditional ways. Common interests - rather than age - formed the basis of our friendships. Having the time and the opportunity to get to know adults of all ages as individual people with different interests and aptitudes, whose abilities were not determined by age, helped me see myself as such a person.

I realized that my education is my own responsibility and had the confidence I needed to pursue knowledge independent of a school atmosphere. Coming to this realization helped me in my decision to leave high school early and enter college.

Being an unschooler gives you an uncommon perspective.

Without the categorization that school imposes upon you, anything is possible for you. You could be teacher or student, friend of an 80-year-old or a baby. Your time is open for you and you can choose.

When you are out of school, not only do your parents teach you, but you also teach your parents. You learn what they don't know as well as what they do. Learning is a cooperative effort. By working with my parents, I discovered how they think. When you work together, you learn about each other as people, not just parent and child.

Staying out of school wouldn't be a good thing to try unless your family believes that learning is a human process that happens as naturally as breathing. It requires a kind of optimism, curiosity and excitement about the world and the belief that the "natural" way to learn is the best. In this situation you need to like and trust each other a lot. Sometimes it takes a lot of patience to work closely with your family.

One comment I frequently hear is "homeschooling works for you, but it would not work for most families because the parents would not be qualified or capable." Homeschooling requires no special education or training. On the contrary, the only requirement is the desire to do it.

Over the years the opportunity to learn at home has meant different things to me. Initially, it gave me the time, space and freedom to develop my interests and personality with a minimum number of restrictions imposed by a school structure. Now, having left school and entered college at 16, I view the importance of this experience differently. I have participated on a state level politically in fighting for laws that would permit parents the freedom to teach their children at home. Talking to legislators and hearing objections when I, along with other homeschoolers, testified before the Louisiana House Education Committee, I realized how integral a part of freedom - in the broadest sense - education is.

If citizens are not permitted the freedom to learn as they choose, they cannot in fact exercise any freedom. What began for me as a child as an experiment in alternative schooling has become central to my philosophy as a man. Learning free is living free.

A Conversation with Pat Montgomery, Ph.D.

Pat Montgomery, a widely respected author and alternative educator, is a founding member and past president of the National Coalition of Alternative Community Schools, a Council member of the National Homeschool Association, and the founder and Director of Clonlara School in Ann Arbor, Michigan. This interview by Mark and Helen Hegener appeared in the September/October, 1990 issue of *Home Education Magazine.*

Pat, as Director of Clonlara School, what do you do each day?

I answer a lot of mail, talk a lot on the telephone, and over the period of twelve years, the substance of what I do through the mail and on the telephone has changed. At first, I'd say in 1980, '81, '82, I think I was a fire extinguisher--maybe I was even the whole fire department--putting out fires that were started by the principal of a school, the superintendent of a school, the state Department of Education people... and this was anywhere, in any state, as soon as they discovered someone was home educating, or as soon as someone requested information about home education, then the fire would be ignited, and I would have to put it out: "That's okay, these people are not crazy; yep, they're fine, they haven't changed into monsters over the summer period; yes, it is legal; yes, your own law says that..." and so a lot of what I was doing, in those early years, was snuffing such flames. In the latter years, that's not so. It's a known entity now. I spend a lot of time now talking to principals, superintendents, truant officers, judges, and lawyers about home education. And in the case of school people it's frequently to inform them precisely what our families are going to do to comply, because that's so tricky in various states. School officals tend to want more than the law requires, and I have to point that out to them frequently. Another thing that I do more and more with my time is advise lawyers, especially in divorce and child custody cases where homeschooling is an issue.

What am I telling the families? I'm telling the families a lot of how to--and by that I don't mean how do you homeschool, because there is no one answer to that, but how to do it in the framework of what the family has told me. "My child is..." and then fill in the blanks: "perceived to be learning disabled by the schools, or my child is so far ahead and isn't getting challenged elsewhere, or my child is one of ten and I think she needs x-y-z..."

So I'm doing a lot of what I like to call handholding. Going forward together with the family, exploring different ways of attacking an issue important to them, and then of course applying it to what our program can offer that family.

What kind of paths are home educators exploring right now?

The new ones that I see are, in some cases, retreading old ones. For example, people who home educate in an innovative way rely a lot on their intuition, and that is so rewarding to me because I find that institutionalizing anything stomps out a reliance upon intuition.

Can you define institutionalizing?

Well, institutionalizing in my scheme of things, and from what I've observed over many years, is packaging something. Getting the why and the wherefore and the how to--that's the critical part, the how to--and then assuming that this model is sufficient, is average enough, to fit everybody, and then putting it in place and saying "There, that's it. And that's how you do it."

That is not totally negative, because there are lots of things in our lives--mechanical things--that ought to be institutionalized. We ought to find simpler ways of doing them, and historically, we've done this. We've institutionalized a lot of things, to the betterment of humanity. Unfortunately, we've used the same model in education. And I say that's unfortunate because it lets people become lazy, and it lets them assume, well, it's being done according to that public school model or that private school model or whatever, and therefore it's being done the best it can and don't question it, take it for granted, and don't have any part in it. It includes having the experts tell you what to do, having a hierarchy, a stratification: these are the ones who do it every day, these are the ones who think about it, so they know more about it than anybody else.

In going back to our path, relying upon oneself, getting up one's antennae, and saying ah, well why do this? How come? For what? How could it be done in a different way? That, then, starts to question these institutions that are packaged deals. And that in my book is very, very good. That's what I think needs to happen all the time.

Do you see Clonlara's role as facilitating the exchange of information between home educators and those who deal with larger numbers of students?

I do. Even though at this point there is no one here whose time is dedicated just to research. But we are ourselves encouraging and helping other folks who are doing research. Our findings in dealing with families are available to people who are doing master's research work and doctoral degree search work here at the University of Michigan and at Eastern Michigan, which isn't very far away. And we encourage our families, for example, when they're contacted by researchers, after finding out certain things, to either participate in the project, or not, depending on their own best likes, and by that I mean, more and more people relate to us, "Well, there's this research project going on and they're approached me, Jane Homeschooler, should I get involved in it?" And we have some questions available to our families that they can ask themselves: Who's doing the research? What's the purpose behind it? What good will it serve? Who will it serve ultimately? Will I have access to the results of it? And after examining those issues, and coming up with some conclusions, then deciding either yes, I will use my time this way, or no, I won't. Basically, if it serves homeschoolers well, then we say yeah, it might be worth an hour or two of your time. So we do give that kind of guidance and that kind of encouragement.

Can we discuss some of the specific learning styles or problems that your families are dealing with?

It comes to my mind that one of the most often asked questions is "My child has been labeled learning disabled, or whatever. There are so many initials nowadays--EMI, EI, MBD, MI, ADB-- that somewhere along the line somebody has been shunted into one of these initials, and then the family has questions like, "That being the case will I be able to really help this child?"
So there's a feeling of some deficiency there. "I'm not an expert, I don't know these initials, I don't know what to do about my child given this declaration." What I try to work out first of all is who labelled the child, why was the child labelled, do you yourself as a parent perceive any significant needs of your child? And sometimes they'll say, "Why, no, I disagree totally, I don't think he has a

deficiency in attention at all, because he'll spend hours here, working at his Legos, or building projects, and he doesn't seem to have a deficiency at all."

So in some cases you'll be able to point out that the deficiency lies in some classroom approach or some system approach like having to go to school and having to be distracted by these other kids most of the time, or having to perform. Children don't fit too well into the closed classroom pattern. We force them to, and when we force them to, then we come up with these so-called deficiencies: EMI, MI and all that alphabet soup of problems. So if in fact there isn't much of a problem outside of the learning disabilities classroom, then we have one direction that we can go.

If the parents say, "Yes, I do perceive that he does have a lot of trouble staying with a project," then we have to examine what projects they are. Helping his dad, or reading to you, or what are they? So then we examine some of that. And again, depending on that examination we go one way or another.

Now we come to a parent who says, "Oh, yes, no question about it, I am in total agreement, there is some kind of an impediment here, to my child being able to—maybe it's read, maybe it's count—whatever." Now then we can explore a lot of different avenues, where can I get help. And what does the problem exactly look like? Then we'll go through those. And sure, there is a lot of help available, there are people who have had children like this before. And what I'd like to accentuate with families is—time is on your side. You've come up to this point where you agree that a child has this or that impediment to this or that skill. Time is on your side. If you can find a good way to work with your child in developing this or that skill, that's the best you can do. That's the only thing that anybody can do. Any expert anywhere... that's what they're going to try to do. And they don't have the answers—they're going to do a trial and error, if they're good—and that's what you will do as a parent.

However, a big question then becomes why do it? If it's a matter of "Well, he has to learn to read," well, okay, I'll buy that. Ultimately, it's very important to have that skill.

"Well, he has to learn to count." Okay, I'll buy that. It's important to have that skill—on some level. But if it's anything else: "He has to learn this scientific inquiry method..." or "He has to learn all about this social studies stuff..." or "He has to pass this or that test..." no, I don't agree with that. I think you're concentrating too much on what a child cannot do instead of accentuating what he can do, and that's much, much more important, and that's going to take us down the more positive trail, and so ultimately, one has to get to that point, where you sort out why you're doing what you're doing with any given child, and work with the positive.

We have a lot of individual teachers who are helping families. Yet we obviously still have a lot of people comfortable saying this is what you do and this is how you do it. Here is potential conflict...

Well, I think probably the biggest area of conflict here is in a person feeling lack of self-confidence, deficient himself. It's so much more comfortable to be able to say, well, I took my child over to the clinic and they said this and this and this and now it's all fixed up. Well, I sent my child to public school and they did this and that's the right way, he graduated magna cum laude. There. See? That's how you do it.

So much more comfortable to give the responsibility to someone else and when it's done well, hooray, hooray and when it's not, to blame them, or to say, see? See, they don't know what they're doing! Even the experts don't know. I think when you boil it all down, no matter who you are, this human being here, with the title of expert, or teacher, or student, or parent, has to take the responsibility for herself. And that's very difficult. It's easier to give it away, and then point the finger. Or join elbows and say hooray, hooray we did it! Either way, it's easier.

But I think that what home educators are showing us now is that more and more people are willing to say, okay, these are my children, I gave birth to them and I'm responsible for them, and I will shoulder the responsibility for better or for worse. And yes, I will make many mistakes, but I'll be responsible for them. And yes, I will have many victories, and I'll be responsible for them. And there's the difficult thing. In institutions the most common thing to do is to accept the responsibility to a point, and then say, "Oh, well, it was the principal's fault. The principal had this policy and I had to follow it. I'm only the teacher so I can get out of it. It's not my responsibility. Look, the parents sent me this child, and I had to deal with him, et cetera, et cetera." Always with the finger going, and institutions are great for that, and that's a very human thing, we all do it, but in institutions you get to do it for a fare-thee-well, and nobody calls you on it, necessarily. But here in my home school, with just us responsible, well, it can get a little scary, and there's where you start getting on the tender ground.

But I find that very exhilarating ground! Because what am I doing when I take this responsibility and I say "Okay, for better or for worse, I'm doing it, I'm responsible, I'm calling the shots, and when I need this resource of so-called expert I'll go get it, but I'll take the responsibility for getting it and I'm not going to blame that person, because I might not even buy what she tells me hook, line and sinker." What am I doing? I am passing this information, this ability, this character strength down to my children... and they are then much more apt to follow my lead and say, "Yes, I'm responsible here." And we then grow up a whole bunch of people who become responsible people, responsible for their own growth and development, to a large extent, responsible for those around them, willing to shoulder a load, willing to say "I made a mistake, it's my fault--I'll better it." Willing to be good human beings, and I find in that one of the real strengths of home educating. And again, I call that a lot intuition, relying on one's intuition, and not being afraid to take the risk. Sure, it's scary ground, and one of the major things that happens in the Home Based Education Program with Clonlara School is that kind of going forward together that we are able to do with our families. It marks a big difference between saying "Do what Clonlara School does because it's the right way," we don't do that--there is no right way. There are a lot of right ways, and together we might be able to find them.

All these new paths, all of these lessons learned, are really rather messy as compared to the institutional approach. What do we do with that?

Well, I think we have some precedence in that. What about when there was no institutional school? That's a relatively new phenomenon, not even 200 years of what you and I know as schooling as an institution. What about before that? I think we can point to many, many people in history, inventors, authors, artists, and say goodness gracious, look how old Van Gogh was before he first started to paint! I think he was in his fifties! And John Holt was fifty before he took up the cello! And Buckminster Fuller said that the problem that he saw with human beings developing to their fullest extent was specialization. Somebody told them "You gotta go to school and you gotta learn to be an engineer." And "You gotta go to school and you gotta learn to be first violin in a symphony." And when you specialize to that extent you close out all the other avenues that will make you a well-rounded, educated person. I find that we have deviated from the course of having well-rounded, educated individuals, developed individuals, by the institution of schools.

How do we deal with this?

I think we use it to our advantage. I think home educated folks use the institutions to their advantage. They exist, and if we need them, they're there. But I'm the one who's going to determine my path. And that means that there will be a lot of changes made in my lifetime. And I'm not afraid of those changes. Change is always a fearful thing, going into the unknown, setting our foot on the shaky path, it's pretty scary. But home educated students will accept it all during their lives, and they will also say, "An institution's over there, I'll go use it for a while." And I think that's a real intelligent thing to do.

What about those who oppose home education?

I find that when there are those who oppose home educating-- and there still are, sad to say--they do so from two directions. They do so because they feel it's a threat to their jobs. If, in fact, home education is successful, then we won't need as many administrators in schools, the school population will decline, I'll be without a job if I'm a truant officer or a principal or a superintendent or whatever. So money is what it boils down to. Fear for themselves and fear for their kind.

The other aspect that they come from is power. Unfortunately, they are of the mind that they own students and families. Unfortunately, there is a proprietary attitude on the part of school people far too often toward those they serve. They are of the mistaken mind that kids exist for the school instead of the other way around. So it's from this position of having been given too much power by us that they say, "Well, wait a minute, you can't do this, I'm the professional, you don't know what you're doing, you don't even have a certificate."

Those are the two directions from which they come. Both of those have to be addressed, and I find that a good portion of my job is to address them. I'm in the position where I have the paraphernalia of the system, I have the degrees behind my name, and one of the first questions I get from this group of people is "Wait a minute, if you're an educator, how can you support these home educators that don't know what they're doing--who don't have what you have? And if you took all the trouble to get it why are you throwing it away on these home educators?"

The power thing is also a pride of purpose, and I don't want to diminish that, I don't want to underrate that. If you were a superintendent you would have this pride of purpose, I would, too. I'd say, "Look, I built this school district up to such and so and I'm so proud of it," and then I would perceive that somebody over there doesn't appreciate what I've done here, and my pride would show.

I'd like to go back to a statement you made: "They have been given too much power by us..."

Yes! That's just one of the things that happens when you have this bowing down and acceptance of institutions. Bowing down and accepting without question does very bad things for individuals. It causes them to think that the doctor always says the right thing. And that when he doesn't reveal to me the nature of my illness that's his prerogative. I don't have the right to know. And when he says the baby has to be delivered in the labor room of the hospital, I believe him. And I accept trends as they come down and I start forgetting about my roots. Where are babies born in Peru, for example? Out in the fields, when people are busy with hoeing. I forget all that, and I buy into this institution.

And that's what we've done with schooling. We've given them far too much power, and we're quaking, we're fearful people, and we say, "Well, they must know how to do it, they've been doing it longer than I have."

I'm not talking about an unwillingness to share. That's okay. And to keep the institutions honest--and the people in them, and to keep questioning them, and to use them. That's fine. But to sell out to them, that's unfortunately what has happened. And that's what home education as a movement is addressing.

Can we talk about legislation and regulations?

Yes. There are four ways in which regulations get handed down to Jane and John Homeschooler. And it's done in various states in any one of these four ways.

One of them is by a direct action of the legislature. A law passed. And then the regulations arise from the basis of the law.

The second is Department of Education, or Public Instruction, whatever it's called in a given state, will sit down and examine the regulations that exist, or do not exist, as the case may be, and then develop some. Doesn't necessarily ever get to the legislature of that state, it's done right on the Department level.

The third way is that there will be court action. Somebody will take something to court, and because of the court action a decision will be handed down, and that becomes the way things are. In Illinois this happened. In Massachusetts this happened. In Pennsylvania, to some extent, this happened.

The fourth way is that an Attorney General in a given state is asked for his opinion by the Department of Education, or by anyone in the bureaucracy, and then the Attorney General gives his opinion and says, "Yes, home education is okay if you do such and such..." and then that becomes the regulation that people are asked to follow.

That fourth one does not have the weight of law for Jane and John Citizen. They think, "Well the Attorney General said it, I have to do it." But no, you don't. If it's reasonable I encourage them to do it. If not I tell them that it doesn't have the weight of law. The regulations done by the Department of Education do not have the weight of law either. That's why a lot of people say, "Well, we have to go to the legislature in our state, because we do want something that has the weight of law." I disagree with that.

There are hurdles for every one of those four ways of regulating. Legislation is no panacea. And unfortunately they don't see it. "But there'll be a law. And we'll be protected by the law, you see." But it will be amended when nobody's looking. That's one of the hurdles. Laws sometimes are not fair in their application. That's one of the big hurdles.

So I would say that no matter from which direction the regulations arise in a given state, they have advantages and disadvantages for home schoolers. Now of course you and I know that there are many states where home educating is easily done, and fairly done, and people are not fearful. In fact, in most states that's the case now. We have the odd few like North Dakota, and Iowa, and Michigan, where people are harassed, and taken to court, and in some cases to jail, even, because of very restrictive home education regulations.

A lot of people will ask before they make a move to any state, "My work is carrying me to X state, what are the home school regulations like in that state?" The unfortunate thing about that question is there's no one source for the answer. People think there is.

Oh, you want the answer? Contact the Department of Education in any state and find it out--ha, ha, ha! Not true! In the state of Michigan here the Department of Education gives you a different answer. They say the way they'd like it to be and not the way it is. And they do that across the board, no matter who asks. And that's true in other states as well.

So you can't cite one source and say your question has been answered. The Home School Legal Defense Association has a binder that they sell and it lists all the states and the regulations in it. And I have discovered that in some instances what people are being told in the binder is not necessarily the way home educators need to comply with the regulations.

Would it be helpful to review situations in which your families find themselves relative to rules and regulations of individual states?

Yes, I think that would be interesting. Here in assembling our binders that get sent to the families enrolling we have a first few segments devoted to regulations in your state. And the pages in there are blue pages... so we can talk about the blue pages, simply because we want to differentiate--most of the pages in our binder are white.

To call attention to these regulation pages we have ""Your State Regulations, Clonlara, and You." That's the title of the blue pages. And they point out all the things I told you: that your state regulation comes from an Attorney General's opinion, or yours come from the Department of Education, or yours come from....

That's the first portion, your state regulations as we see them. Then, down in the second portion of the blue pages is what does Clonlara do with you and for you, to comply with what we just said above. And there's the difference between us and anyone not enrolled in our program. We have some in-house jokes here. We say, "Oh, I hope the family's not from Pennsylvania... or New York... or Ohio..." Because of all the states those are the three that require us to put in blue pages followed by yellow pages followed by pink pages followed by beige! And the more colors we use, the more steps have to be taken to comply with the regulations. I'm not saying they're the worst states in which to home educate, no, no, no, no---they're just the ones that require the most steps, on our part and on the family's part, to comply.

Now there are other states that require certain things, like Arizona requires testing. Florida requires testing and submission of the test results at the end of the year. So does Virginia. California has some choices that you can make: do I fill out an affidavit, do I join with an independent study program, do I enroll in an out of state school, and there are other choices.

There are the really easy states, like Washington, for example. We say, "Oh, I hope all the new enrollees are from Washington! I hope they're all from Illinois, or Indiana, or Oklahoma, or Missouri..." Because those states require practically nothing, on the part of the enrolling family, and on our part, to comply with the regulations.

Notice I do not say laws. Because laws mean--most people say laws when they talk about home schooling--laws mean it was an act of the legislature. In most states they were never enacted. Take Pennsylvania. It's interesting. The reason why we don't like Pennsylvania is because of all the stuff you have to go through--parents have to go through.

There was a case in Pennsylvania, and the judge, in deciding the case, said that the family could continue to homeschool and the state had better get it's act together. As a matter of fact, by the end of that given year, by December 31, the legislature should have passed a law, and if the legislature did not pass a law the judge said, "I will. I will make a ruling that will become law." And that was a threat to the establishment, because they pretty much got the message that the judge wouldn't rule in their favor.

So the state did, then, go through the legislative process. And I think they only had a few months to do it--maybe from July to December. And on December 31 of that year, at that eleventh hour, the legislature did pass a law. And it's very complicated, and that's why it's not one of our favorite states. You gotta do this, and you gotta do that, and I'm afraid people were not interested in the ease of home educating and freedom of choice for home educators and the right to home educate--these were not primary in the minds of the folks that got this enacted.

It's not unlivable, no, there is no unlivable state, actually--not even Michigan. Some people think it is, because if you read in certain descriptions of how to homeschool in Michigan, Michigan is always last on the line, because we require certified teachers, but what's not being told is Clonlara, in Michigan, filed suit against the state and got that requirement greatly modified for all homeschoolers, not just the people enrolled with us. And that's not put out by the Department, and that's not put out by HSLDA, for example, and unfortunately a lot of people don't know that.

Do you have any questions you want to ask of the homeschoolers ?

Well, I would like to ask them how often they raise their eyes from the most important thing--their family--in their day-to-day. How often they raise their eyes, and look beyond to what they're doing, and what they're accomplishing, in the broad scheme of things. To examine that briefly--and they don't have a whole lot of time to spend ruminating, I know--but how often do they do that? The exercise might impress upon them the significance of this home education movement.

I encourage them to realize where what they're doing, their simple choices, where that fits in the broad scheme of resurrecting the family as a pillar of society, strengthening those fundamental units in our society, toward building a better world, toward peopling it with individuals: their children, and their children's children.

I'd like to ask them, in conjunction with that, what role do they see themselves playing in the lives of all those who will never home educate or be home educated? What is their contribution? I can think of a lot of answers to those questions. The answers to those are the reasons why I do what I do.

Providing a Learning Continuum

—— Susan Nelson ——————————————————————

Educating young children at home begins at birth and includes every subject and method imaginable. All parents educate their children, although most do not consider themselves educators. Human children are not born with much in the way of instinctual behavior. The job of human parents is therefore twofold: they must first care for and protect their offspring, and concurrently teach them what they need to know to survive -- eventually without the parents' care and protection. By the time a child is school age, around five or six, parents have given instruction in communication skills, social behavior, ecology and the environment, nutrition, literature, health and safety, genealogy, history, anatomy and physiology, mathematics, art, music, physical education, and much, much more.

If the child is lucky, most of this instruction has been given to him on an individual basis at a time when he has shown an interest in the subject taught. Assisting his parents with these many activities and discussions are friends, relatives, neighbors, associates, and sometimes total strangers.

Then, at a time determined by local custom, this educational process is for the most part supplanted by another -- known as school. The child begins to spend from three to six hours each day in a room with twenty or thirty other children. He or she is, for much of this time, expected to sit quietly, stand in line, talk in turn, and eat, rest, and use the bathroom on a predetermined schedule. He or she is also introduced to the world of paper work at this tender age. Most of the paperwork done by young children in schools is a matter of filling in blanks (worksheets) or filling in spaces (coloring). Usually, all of the children are directed to do their paperwork in precisely the same way. There are penalties for finding alternate uses for the paper or for not filling in the blanks or spaces according to the directions. Doing the work too quickly or too slowly is also frowned upon. My rather dim view of school paperwork is derived from my belief that it is neither a healthy nor a productive activity for children.

If parents who are looking for a good school find one in which children are for the majority of the day singing, talking, dancing, running, painting, drawing (not coloring), playing games, becoming involved in dramatic activities, listening to stories, building, gardening, sewing, etc., it is certainly a program worthy of further investigation. It is partly because such programs are difficult to find that many parents are teaching their own children and foregoing formal education. *describes Waldorf*

Parents face several hurdles in taking on -- or rather, continuing -- the task of educating their own school age children. The most obvious are the legal and logistic questions. Is this allowable under the law and how do I go about getting set up? These questions are slowly being answered as parents in many states have set in motion precedents for homeschooling.

The second set of hurdles is more a matter of confidence and finding ways to synthesize ideas and resources. Often, parents are intimidated by the prospect of designing a program, choosing a curriculum, assuming the role of teacher. Like many fears, these are unfounded. These seeming obstacles exist because parents often assume that they must create a school within their home. On the contrary, in order to continue the education which has taken place during the first years of a child's life it is not necessary or even desirable to radically alter your teaching methods. For young children, it is best that the parent serve as the model for the teacher, and not the reverse. A home is an ideal place for a child to learn about almost everything that interests him. When his interests broaden, the community surrounding home simply becomes part of the learning environment. Unlike a large class, a family is very mobile, and can utilize the community very effectively in the educational process.

In talking with parents and teachers about alternatives in education, including homeschooling, over a period of years, I have found that foremost on the minds of many of them is how to prepare the child for school. What parents and teachers worry about is not what the child is learning, but, rather, will he be able to perform in school at a later date? What about next year? What if I move or get a job? What about junior high or high school? Essentially, their concerns are stated something like this: If a child's needs are met consistently, if he is provided with a great deal of personal freedom, how will he ever adjust to a public school classroom? The assumption is that in most classrooms, the child's needs cannot be met with any consistency; the task may be either too difficult or too simple, and the structure of the classroom will be very controlling. This assessment of classrooms gives rise to the question of why we consider putting our children in them in the first place.

Parents, then, must grapple with whether their primary goal is (1) to provide their child with useful and interesting educational experiences; or (2) to prepare him for school. If you are an adventurous sort, you can always opt for goal number one and rely on your child's ingenuity and good fortune to see him through whatever educational experiences he might face in the future, including formal schooling.

Assuming that you are a risk-taker and opt for designing a program around your child's individual needs, you may want to begin your work with a self-evaluation process. An independent or individual approach to education jettisons you out into uncharted territory. The following questions are organized into four groupings to help parents clarify their goals and make an assessment of their resources. The groupings are as follows: 1. What are my personal and social goals for my child? 2. What skills do I want my child to learn? 3. What kinds of childhood experiences do I believe are important? and 4. What are some of the community resources available to us?

1. Personal and social goals: What character traits and personal goals would I like to promote in my child? What kinds of experiences might help with these? Is it important to me that I spend a great deal of time with my child? Does my child have special problems which I must address, such as a physical handicap, temperament, or social difficulties? What family traditions or religious practices would I like to see continued by my child? What kind of relationships would I like my child to have — with other children, with other adults, with family members?

Learning to work and play with others is an important part of every child's life. This is often given as a primary reason why children should attend school. Children do not necessarily learn to work together in school, however. They work simultaneously and are actually discouraged from collaborating on their work. Collaboration is usually called cheating in school. In your own program, you may want to give considerable thought as to how to provide children with experiences in working together with siblings, friends, and other adults in a creative and cooperative manner.

The experience of playing with others in school is also an experience of questionable value. There is often too little supervision for too many children. Instead of learning how to play through exploration and interaction with others, children are often "assigned" a role or a stereotype early on that stays with them for years. The social structure generated by the children mirrors the rigid classroom and tracking systems laid down by the adults in the school, and can be just as stifling. Smaller play groups tend to make this kind of segregation unnecessary and unlikely.

2. Skills: What would I like my child to be able to do? What would my son or daughter like to be able to do? What are his or her special abilities or talents? Who is available for teaching some of these skills in addition to myself? Can my child help with a family business or with a family hobby or project, i.e. sailing, gardening, or building a room addition?

The basics - reading, writing, and arithmetic - are important skills for children to learn, but realistically, they are only a portion of the skills a child might acquire. The vast amount of time that most students spend on academic skills is probably attributable to "teaching" them to children much before they are ready to learn them, and to the instruction being given in impossibly large groups. Children do need instruction to learn these skills, a disciplined approach will be useful for most, but the task need not consume the better part of childhood.

3. Childhood experiences: What do I remember best from my own childhood? Who had a significant influence on me? Which of my current interests and hobbies stem from my childhood interests and experiences?

What is my child interested in? How can I help him to pursue his interests? How can I help him broaden them? Our own memories are probably a good curriculum guide. Chances are if you have a clear memory of an event, it was an experience that taught you something. Incidents which have faded into obscurity may not be worth remembering.

What kinds of experiences are unique to childhood? Children are so much more willing to experiment with novelty than adults. It is unusual for an adult to try a new and different kind of physical endeavor or an art or dramatic activity. It appears that certain kinds of pursuits, not given root in childhood, will likely wither away altogether.

4. Community resources: What kind of organizations might provide valuable learning and social experiences for my child? Girl Scouts, Boy Scouts, soccer, Little League, Blue Birds, 4-H... this list is virtually endless. Instead of being just another appointment the family races off to after an already busy day, these kinds of organizational activities can become an integral part of the homeschooling process.

What kinds of classes and lessons would my child enjoy? Piano, art, violin, karate... this list is also endless.

Is there anyone with whom a slightly older child might become a part time apprentice? Participating in a small business even on a very limited basis can be a fruitful experience.

Are there friends, relatives, or professionals who might provide tutoring for a fee or a swap of some other service? Retired or former teachers might be of help both for tutoring and for satisfying legal requirements.

What kinds of record keeping systems and curriculum aids can I purchase? For most people, this is not an exciting wheel to re-invent. Shop a while and find something workable.

No school, public or private, will give the kind of consideration to your child as an individual that you can as a parent. The transition from family member to becoming part of a larger group need not be an abrupt change. Exercising judgement and control over a child's social experiences is a parental responsibility which protects and nurtures the child. Parents are educators who have a meaningful investment in the child's future. Parents are unlikely to waste their children's time with irrelevant curricula, make-work tasks and stop-gap disciplinary measures which create more problems than they solve. Parents do not need to administer timed tests and pop quizzes to find out what lessons have been learned. Most importantly, parents have the best chance of helping children become involved in the planning and direction of their own education.

The education of a child is a little like a ship on a voyage. The course must be constantly altered to accommodate new circumstances, correct errors, and incorporate new information. The ship might even change its destination, but when the whole crew has an investment in the well-being of it's members and in the outcome of the journey, success is imminent. This does not mean that parents must perform every task themselves, but they can instead coordinate the efforts of many to insure a happy, safe, and exciting voyage.

Letting Them Learn

—— Judson Jerome ————————————————————————

Now that all of our children except one are old enough to be beyond the grasp of compulsory education, it's safe to come out of the closet. We have, for the most part, kept our children out of school. Many families may have been reluctant to try this alternative, perhaps intimidated by the law, or by the bother and complexity of setting up an alternative curriculum which their local school system would approve. We more-or-less evaded the law, and let our children educate themselves as they pleased.

In the late sixties I had some notoriety as a radical educator at Antioch College, where I was a Professor of Literature for 20 years. But while I had written, among other things, that schooling has nothing to do with education, my wife and I had done little except grumble and comply with the system in regard to the schooling of our own five children.

Why were our children in school? I suppose the answer was that's where they wanted to be. Compulsory non-schooling would be as much a perversion as compulsory schooling. When children live in a neighborhood in which all their friends go to school, and they want, above all, to be perceived and to have their family perceived as "normal," who would force them to stay out of school?

Would that be some kind of sacrifice of their right to self-determination in the name of parental ideas of freedom? I don't believe in forcing children to do anything, least of all appear as oddballs among their peers.

But in 1971 our lives changed dramatically. One of our daughters, Jenny, multiply handicapped, was having increasing difficulties in the special education programs available to us as she reached "school age." After our family went through some grave self-examination we concluded that it would be best for Jenny and the rest of us if she were to enter a residential program, one of the Camphill Special Schools in Glenmoore, Pennsylvania. The "villagers," as the special students are called, live with staff families in houses which are simply extended family homes. With great security in their country setting, the children move freely between their houses and school and other activities. Jenny, just before she turned seven, was the youngest child ever admitted to the program.

Far from the negative experience we dreaded, placing Jenny at Camphill proved to be a salvation for our family. The setting and atmosphere and staff were so ideal for her needs that we found ourselves strangely envious. "Jenny," we said, "has found her place. Now it is up to us to find ours." We wanted our children to be free, if they chose, to simply stay home. So we bought a farm and started a commune, partly for that reason.

As soon as we moved to the farm we applied for a license as a private school with two students: our twelve year old daughter and soon-to-be six year old son. The application forms amused us, with their elaborate questions about laboratory and gym facilities, and separate sleeping and toilet arrangements for boys and girls, and square feet per pupil of classroom space, but we filled them all out with straight faces and paid our $25.00 application fee, which was to be returned if our application was rejected. In the subsequent twelve years it has never been accepted or rejected, and I guess it is time now to ask for that $25.00 back — the best investment we ever made!

In the early years the state went through motions toward acting on the application. We had to submit a floor-plan of our farmhouse, with study areas indicated. We had to send in the credentials of our faculty -- ourselves and our fellow communards who had college degrees, some of them with teaching certificates and experience. Officials came out and tested the water in our well. An engineer came to measure the light in our classroom and check our furnace. We learned that he was on his way to the farm, so we hastily set up a desk on a sun porch, where a matronly woman was teaching Topher mathematics when the man drove up. His light meter went bananas over the sun on the porch -- a room unusable in winter, by the way, but he didn't notice that.

Then years would pass without further visitations from the authorities, and no one ever raised any questions about our faculty, most of whom had long since moved on to other places, or about any education which might have transpired at the farm. We had sketchily defined a curriculum in the application, carefully including the requisite credits in state history, hygiene, and what-have-you. No one ever inquired about whether we followed it. Each year the local superintendent would send his ritual inquiry, and ritually we would reply that they attended Downhill Farm School, license applied for, and that would be the last we'd hear from the authorities for that year.

Thus we never did anything actually illegal; we always indicated that we were willing to comply with what the state asked. But we obviously raised a problem for them that they didn't want to deal with. The law didn't prohibit a private school with no tuition and just one student, but it was obviously not intended to permit such an arrangement, either. They had no grounds for denying the application, and we, like Bre'r Rabbit, lay low and did not insist on approval.

By the time Topher was ten, and had spent five years at Downhill Farm without schooling and substantially without the company of other children, he was lonely. We recognized that his need for the company of his peers was becoming serious. From the beginning we weren't worried about academic learning. But how could an isolated child have any relationship with his peers? The best choice seemed to be to pull up the family roots temporarily and move to a place where there were children at least somewhat like him.

That was only partly true of the little school run by our sister commune, whose students were mostly children from town who had problems in the public schools. At least they were children, and they were accepting of differences. We have always treated our children as adults, always given them adult responsibilities along with adult freedoms. Our children have often found their counterparts in the "straight" world immature. Topher was always excited about going to school, and he took the academic part seriously, but he was dismayed to find that the other children groaned and complained about every assignment, cut corners, or simply didn't do their homework. He liked and was liked by the other kids, he enjoyed playing as much as any of them. But we could tell he was discouraged and considered the schoolday mostly a waste of time, though he was very appreciative of having friends -- especially after school.

At one time I went through a programmed text in algebra with Topher, who was 13 at the time. It was intended for college students, but it was so incredibly boring and repetitive that we finally abandoned it. It is hard to believe to what lengths professional educators go simply to fill babysitting time. The text was programmed more to fill a semester than to teach algebra. Four years later Topher and one of the girls bought themselves a computer and began actually to learn a little algebra. I'm sure that if they encounter situations in which algebra is actually relevant, they will learn more soon enough. But to teach such a subject in the abstract is like teaching music without using instruments or song or listening to recordings; it is just a bunch of relationships, easily remembered for a short period and quickly forgotten. After a few months we returned to our farm, where other children joined our school.

Topher spent much time at the commune where his sister lives, helping out on runs of a huge truck which carries food to and from Boston for a cooperative, joining in the haying and other chores of the dairy farm, and taking part in a Bread and Puppet pageant before crowds of thousands. At 17 he moved there, taking the computer and the bookkeeping work for our wind chimes business with him.

Of course, we think our children are outstanding, but that's not the real explanation for why they have done so well without schooling. If children live in a stimulating environment, among involved and stimulating adults, they are almost bound to learn more at home than they ever could at school.

Much of what we have done would be impossible for other families, as it depended on the combination of a quiet isolated rural setting and group living. Moreover, of course, the laws and degree to which authorities enforce them vary a great deal from state to state. But it is good to remember, too, that in many cases you have as much freedom as you choose to find the space for, and that too conscientious a compliance with the law, or too much idealistic effort to change it to suit your circumstances, can eat up the little space you have in your life with your children.

While I would not recommend outright confrontation with the

law, the years that parents have with their children are too short and precious to spend in litigation with a slumberous monster -- it is possible to sidestep a great deal and delay one's way to freedom. Erosion is my favorite force for social change.

Homeschooling Older Kids

—— **Mark and Helen Hegener** ———————————————————

Teaching your children to read, to write and to calculate with numbers is relatively simple, most parents feel fairly competent about handling the challenge. But what about the older child, who has already learned more about math than you ever knew, and now wants to know about biology, government, and the historical significance of the Middle East? Or worse yet, doesn't want to be bothered with any more lessons, and feels as though they've had plenty of education already?

Adolescence can be a difficult time of life, both for the youngster trying out new and unfamiliar emotions, and for the family learning to cope with and understand them. Patience is a daily necessity, and tact becomes a finely honed skill. Adolescence is the age of trial and error. It's trying on being an adult while not quite ready to give up being a child, and the results can be both trying and hilarious. (It's difficult not to laugh when a child who's taller than you stomps through the house crying, "You won't let me grow up!")

You should recognize that this young person is an individual, and due the respect you would give any other individual. It's important that their unique interests be acknowledged, and that they are actively involved in their own educational decision-making. Ask them what they want to learn-and why. Then use their interests to develop a suitable learning program. Negotiation can play an important role here, it might be fair to let the parent choose half of the courses and to let the child choose the other half.

It's important to remember that this is a "hands-on" age. By the time your children are teenagers, just reading about something isn't enough. They want to see, to touch, to experience.

There are special challenges in teaching the older child, but they are complemented by very special rewards. The parent-child relationship is gradually changing, and with luck and plenty of communication a sense of friendship and mutual understanding is growing. Finding curriculum materials might require a little more imagination than with the elementary ages, but there's also more flexibility. With a higher reading level the whole world opens up for use, and the increased ability to absorb information makes the "educational value" of museums and historical sites double what it is for younger children!

Sometimes, however, it might be advisable to throw formal instruction out the window and just get to know this interesting young person. Find a hobby to share, or a new skill to learn together. Travel can be especially rewarding with an older child, as they absorb all the sights and sounds of new places. Go to the beach together, play video games, or just take long walks together and enjoy this wonderful age of discovery!

Our Home Study

—— Patricia Smith Carsten ————————————————

My daughters and I were living in Oaxaca, Mexico. It was one of those nights that church bells and fireworks started proclaiming a saint's day at midnight. Scruffy little Busti had lulled us to sleep at 10:30 with his usual barking warning to the world outside the stone walls surrounding our apartment house and garden. The soldier from the barracks at Santo Domingo Church woke us for a few moments at 4:30 a.m. when he started his bugle practice. And on the dot at 7:30 a.m. Hernandez let the aluminum ladder fall with a metal clang against our second floor balcony. As usual he would be climbing onto the roof to check the water level in the cistern. It was a typical night in Oaxaca.

There was little water in Oaxaca in April. Some official had absconded with the money put aside for the new water system the community badly needed to get through the hot dry months before the rainy season started. We were lucky--Hernandez filled the cistern from La Duena's well every morning with a hose wrapped with dilapidated tape and full of holes. Being Americans, we had chosen an apartment house with conveniences. Most of Oaxaca went without water for weeks at a time. Even finding drinking water was a task.

It was a long call from back home where we had started our Home Study in Vermont and where Wendy and Jessica, 13-year-old twins, had lived their whole lives. It was the year I had been dreaming about. Wendy, Jessica and I did a Home Study. We sold our house in Vermont and used the money to support our travel. Besides six months in Mexico (November through April, 1990), we were to spend two months in Chicago, one month in New York, and one month traveling through northeastern North America visiting Toronto, Providence, Washington, and historically interesting places.

Certified as an elementary educator and a reading specialist, I had taught in public schools for seven years when we started the year of Home Study. The girls had completed seventh grade in a public school. My children needed more individuation, more challenges, more experiential learning than they were receiving in school. Even though they were motivated and great students, they were becoming less confident as each year went on. They are artists and found art class boring. They love basketball but weren't allowed to play more than one or two minutes per game. They were memorizing lists and tables in science to pass quizzes and had no idea what they were memorizing. Though their seventh grade history and English teacher had them reading advanced literature and introduced them to the study of racism, she was their teacher only 90 minutes each day. It wasn't enough. They were feeling less and less empowered. They were not learning how to be leaders, only followers.

The first big risk we took was leaving Vermont where they had lived their whole lives. At first they were not ready to leave and were skeptical about Home Study. They had a picture in their psychological picture albums of what eighth grade would be like but no picture of what it might be like in Mexico doing Home Study with their mother. They did feel positive and curious about travel. We had worked together in an after-school program where I was the teacher/director and they were helpers. We had worked together at a food co-op, scooping peanut butter, labeling bags of herbs and dried fruit, mopping the floor and doing the dishes. But we hadn't left the country together, except to visit nearby Montreal and Quebec City for weekends. They thought they would miss their friends.

It was a process in itself "psyching" them and creating new pictures that would be needs-satisfying for their eighth grade year. We consciously set about creating new needs-satisfying pictures. For one, they liked the idea of visiting friends in Mexico City, Toronto, Wisconsin, New York, and Chicago. When we visited Jennifer in Toronto, her father took us to his workplace. He was the special effects person in the television crew of "My Secret Identity." He introduced us to the stars of the show and took us on the set. When Wendy and Jessica met and talked with Jerry O'Connell, the teenage star, they came to the conclusion that this trip might be fun after all. Ironically, by the end of the year, this event lost its glamor. It was dwarfed by the experience of Mexico. But it served an important purpose. The girls felt what they were doing was unique and they felt important. It was their first opportunity to experience that taking a big risk, leaping into the unknown, could be more satisfying than plodding along in the old tried and true.

There is no substitute for the real thing. I handed Wendy the road atlas and asked her to get us to Washington, D.C. from Vermont via Spring Valley, New York, and she did. She made only one mistake -- when we were circling D.C. at rush hour. On the way home after Mexico Jessica directed me from Chicago to Vermont via New York.

There is nothing as motivating as survival. We were looking forward to learning Spanish-- we had to learn it. We wanted to find a nice apartment to live in and buy food like the natives. We wanted to get to know some people, talk to Mexicans. We enrolled in intensive language courses in Universidad Benito Juarez which met for five hours every day for a month. None of the teachers spoke a word of English, and after about two weeks of this we started dreaming in Spanish. People in the dreams were hurling word after Spanish word at us and we could understand nothing. Schoolwork had always come easily to Wendy -- she had expected to be fluent in Spanish in a month -- but it was a much greater task than she expected, and that was a good lesson. The girls learned that Spanish is not just English translated. We had discussions about the nature of language, about specific words, about the meaning of certain phrases, and how it was the meaning which was translated was not the specific words and sentence syntax. This was new to them, since they had only one language. They started to become aware of the relativity of English and the existence of other cultures. They learned that some meanings are better expressed in Spanish, and that some things couldn't be translated.

Months after returning, we sometimes still think in Spanish, especially in those areas where we had to struggle to meet our needs, physical or psychological. Licuados are still the favorite drink. Elote con mayonesa y queso and gorditas are favorite foods. "Danzas con Lobos" is the name of the movie Kevin Costner got so many Oscars for.

The girls at first let me do the talking and listened hard. When they were in our apartment they felt safe enough to tease each other in Spanish. There was lots of incorrect Spanish spoken in our home, but regardless we were integrating a new language into our lives. After four months our dentist Eva remarked to Jessica, "Pareces perico." ("You're like a little parrot.") Wendy was less willing to take the risk of making mistakes but she listened hard and understood a lot.

One day out shopping I stopped outside a market where Zapotec Indian women were sitting on the steps selling bunches of herbs and tortillas. I asked if anyone had epazote. One of them rapidly replied, smiling and slapping her forehead.

"Huh?" I said.

Jessica said, "Oh, she said she had a bunch which she left on her table at home and she'll bring it tomorrow." Wendy nodded her head to confirm this translation.

"Oh, you understood her?" I was amazed and disconcerted. I had two more years of speaking Spanish under my belt, but youngsters, I kept being told, pick up languages faster than older folks.

We experienced being part of an ethnic minority. We looked Northamerican. As Northamericans it was assumed we were rich and therefore justifiable prey for robbery. This was sometimes painful for us, but the girls never took it personally. They had a healthy attitude and used to do spontaneous skits, acting out actual scenes and making up new ones. Laughing helped put it all in perspective.

"Mira, voy a robarle," one tiny old Zapotec woman said to another across the aisle in Mercado Benito Juarez one day when I tried to buy zucchini from her. "Watch, I'm going to rob her."

There were many instances of market people forgetting to give us back the correct change. We had to insist that we were owed 10,000 or 20,000 pesos more. The girls' counting skills got very sharp.

It was strange to be the brunt of racial jokes. It made us think very hard what it must be like to be black or brown back home where color is such an issue.

The girls became skilled shoppers. They were fluent in numbers and currency and knew what things cost. If they thought the price asked for a bunch of bananas or a head of lettuce was inflated, they would move on to the next stall or the next until they got the right price. Our new lifestyle required bargaining for food and services. At moments we didn't feel like shopping and bargaining, but out of survival had to. It was because of this our greatest language skills are around shopping: foods, prices, numbers and money.

By the time we left Mexico Wendy and Jessica had learned how to assert themselves. One night Jessica went to the corner store to pick up a liter of milk. When she said she wanted milk, two half-liter cartons of milk powder were shoved in her hand and she was charged double what a liquid liter of milk cost. It took her four trips going from the store back home for coaching, but she finally managed to come home with one liter of milk and the correct change. She was met at the store each time by three Mexican women yelling "No falta, no falta" (We don't owe you anything."). They did owe her money and she finally got it. When Jessica got home the last time with the right change and the right milk, she felt proud and powerful. That was a turning point for her. After that she was fearless about leaving the house and eager to be alone on the streets of Oaxaca. She loved to do the shopping alone. Her confidence in herself took five giant steps. Wherever we went after that she was not afraid to ask for what she wanted. She also found that she made more friends if she put herself forward. Street life in Oaxaca prepared her well for entering high school in Providence in the fall.

Other than real-life street skills, the girls were doing a lot of reading, writing, and research. They devoted as much as 10 hours a day to school projects. They got deeply involved because they had so much choice and did not have their school day chopped into small periods. They did not have to make constant transitions. They could stick with what they were doing for hours, days, even months.

They did much more reading and writing than they ever did in school. They did this while getting lots of sleep and lots of nutritious fresh food, which was not the case when they were going to school. In school throughout all the primary grades, the length of time they used to have to line up for lunch, walk to the cafeteria, stand in line for the food or for milk, eat, and take their trays and rubbish back was 20 minutes. Needless to say, lunch was not much of a meal. Breakfast was not as relaxed as it should have been, either, with the time crunch to get dressed, washed up, feed and walk pets, eat, and walk to school by 8:00 a.m. Home Study allowed them as rapidly growing children to physically get what they needed. Old lingering colds and chronic coughs eventually went away, they girls put on a little weight and their cheeks were pink from feeling refreshed each morning.

Rested and nourished, they spent hours each day journaling, writing letters, history reports, short stories. Jessica worked on a book on lemmings, *The Adventures of Benjamin Tittle*. Wendy wrote a book on the mythology, art and life in ancient Greece. They often read 1,000 pages a week. They did research in the nearby American library. With all this practice their reading and writing skills advanced considerably. Jessica's handwriting changed from a careless sprawling scrawl to a calligraphic cursive, tiny elegantly formed letters, written in straight lines on blank journal pages.

Wendy and Jessica each completed two travel journals. The journals are works of art, recording how their sense of design grew over the year. They began to take great pride in their journals. The pages are mixtures of long-hand diary entries, illustrations of favorite pastries, fruit and street food, hotel rooms, Mexican lizards, dogs and plants, water color paintings of historical figures, red and orange pressed bougainvillea blossoms and pink roses, poetry (their own and others), comments on books they read, drafts of history papers, descriptions of Mexican life: the open air markets, the empanada lady, the Zapotecas with their baskets of hot tortillas, the beggars, the street vendors, the light, the heat, everything.

My daughters were not isolated from real life. We went to many art openings and got to know real artists. We took a week-long collage course given by a collagist from the southwestern U.S. Collage gave the girls an artistic technique to use to make statements about "burning issues." They used collage in letter writing, cardmaking, and in their journals.

We became friends with a woman from Chicago who lived in Oaxaca. An artist and a poet, she taught the girls how to use oil pastels on 'papel amate' (pressed bark available only in Oaxaca and Guerrero). We met an African-American woman who gave a collage and print exhibit in Oaxaca and who encouraged the girls when they were making collages with Civil Rights themes. The girls were taken seriously by these artists and, in turn, began to take their own art and social statements more seriously. They produced frenetically.

For science the girls read *Sand County Almanac* and Rachel Carson's *The Edge of the Sea*, and articles in the natural history magazines in the library. Our field trips consisted of snorkeling in the

Pacific at Puerto Escondido, swimming alongside the brightly colored fish being gently swept back and forth on the edge of the sea in their sheltered rock crannies. We explored different kinds of shores and the creatures and seaweeds that burrowed, clung, and were washed around close to shore.

For math the girls used a pre-algebra textbook. They also read *Math Equals*, biographies of nine famous women mathematicians starting with Hypatia of ancient Greece, and did units of each woman's math. They mastered the currency of Mexico and became familiar with metric measurement. Milk car ae in liters, fruit and vegetables in kilos. When we baked in the oven they converted the temperature and quantities of ingredients for me.

At the end of the year back in Vermont when Wendy and Jessica gave a presentation to about 20 people in the United Church of Strafford, both girls said that one of the best parts of Home Study was the freedom. They had felt ownership of their learning. My role as their teacher worked best when I acted as a resource person. I provided shelter and a quality learning environment, bought the books, helped them research in the library, taught skills when they needed that, guided them. The trick was to avail them of my knowledge and experience while being unintrusive.

One of the crucial parts was providing the right books and right places at the right time. Early in the year Jessica and Wendy both read *Firebrand* by Marion Zimmer Bradley, a historical novel about ancient Troy. They loved this book and yearned to know more about ancient Greece. We had brought with us the series on ancient civilizations put out by the Metropolitan Museum of Art, one of which is *Ancient Greece*. They dived into this next. They both ran off to the American library to see if by any chance there might be other books on the shelves about ancient Greece which they each felt they had discovered. Their sense of ownership was touching. Each was delighted to discover Homer's *Aeneid* and *Odyssey*, Bullfinch's mythology, books by Robert Graves and Mary Renault. Some they liked and read, some they didn't. Wendy devoted months to the study of mythology, art, and culture. Jessica went on to ancient Rome and Egypt. After reading *The Mists of Avalon*, also by Bradley, she became enthralled with the period when Christianity and Druidism were clashing in Britain. Both girls took eagerly to the study of matriarchal pagan religions. Jessica wrote a long report on the clash between the Romans' Christianity and Morgana of Avalon's Druidism.

Some of their research led us to discussions about linguistics. I often found myself doing research on subjects and issues I was eager to learn more about and had not had time for when I was working. We shared what we discovered excitedly, and our excitement was contagious.

We were in a great place for the study of ancient civilizations. Oaxaca is the center for Zapotec Indian culture, both ancient and contemporary. The indigenous people can be heros like Benito Juarez or the artist Rufino Tamayo, and, more commonly, are the gardeners, the maids, the people on the street corners with barefoot children dressed in traditional clothing, begging, selling, stealing sugar and salt from cafe tables.

The ancient Zapotec ruins in Oaxaca stand as a contrast to the present plight of these people. The ruins testify to their former greatness and gave life to the girls' study of ancient cultures. Jessica decided to become an archaeologist while crawling in the dark cool stone corridors and mazes of Monte Alban. They also came face to face with how destructive European Christian cultures were to the indigenous ones. They saw how the Spanish and the Indians had 'melted' into the Mexican culture. They witnessed this phenomenon in the way Mexicans practice Catholicism. The Indian influence was clear. Saints' days and religious holidays were huge parties which went on for days, sometimes were like carnivals. There were parades, candy stands, costumes, fireworks, dancing, drinking, and singing. Wendy and Jessica were familiar with more solemn ways to worship.

I had been shocked and saddened at how early and how much my girls (as females) had started feeling disenfranchised in school. Both of Marion Zimmer Bradley's novels are told from the point of view of women, Kassandra of Troy and Morgana of Avalon. They identified with these heroines, even as a couple of years before they gobbled up every Nancy Drew that came out but had no interest in the Hardy Boys series. I had come to the conclusion that in order to teach history to them, and to help them feel empowerment as citizens, the effective approach would be through books which they could *really* relate to as girls. As a teacher I tried to be ultrasensitive to their special needs. Being a woman helped.

Jessica loved *Mists* and combed the library for other Authurian legends. She read many and was turned off, remarking that in the others women were always seen in a bad light. Morgana was barely mentioned, only as King Arthur's sister, an evil witch. In *Mists* Morgana is a Druidic priestess who struggled to keep her religion alive in a world converting to Christianity. Jessica observed that she was ambitious, powerful and a politician. Wendy loved the role of the priestess in *Firebrand*. She was fascinated by the serpent goddesses and did a beautiful rendition of one on bark paper with acrylic paints. They needed female figures to emulate, for empowerment, to learn how to be women.

After Mexico we lived in Pilsen, the large Mexican neighborhood in Chicago. The girls saw firsthand the kind of poverty Hispanic Americans, and nearby African Americans, live in. They experienced our country's cultural, though segregated, diversity in a way that would have been impossible had we stayed in Vermont.

Another dimension of our trip was the museums and exhibits we constantly went to. Our sightseeing in Washington, D.C. in September consisted of visiting the White House and many of the memorials. The girls found the Vietnam Memorial moving. They were struck by the number of homeless practically living on the lawn of the White House. We toured the National Museum of American History where they wanted to see Dorothy's red shoes from the *Wizard of Oz* and the National Art Gallery. In October we went to the Metropolitan Museum of Art five times as the girls couldn't get enough of the European paintings. Wendy was dazzled by the Impressionists. In Chicago we visited the Art Institute. After Mexico the found the Field Museum of Natural History in Chicago instructive though we were disappointed over the minimal coverage of ancient Mexican cultures. After seeing "Dances with Wolves," we sat in the Pawnee Earth Lodge for a workshop, handled artifacts, and marvelled that so many items could be made from the buffalo. In Mexico we were surrounded by art all the time—from red and orange surrealist paintings and bas reliefs in touristy galleries, to the mountains of folk art everywhere, the plazas of Triqui women weaving, braiding, embroidering, the boys and old men selling polka-dotted vermillion carved wooden creatures next to fountains spurting polluted water.

The girls saw the ancient artifacts of Aztec, Mixtec, and Zapotec civilizations in the Museo Rufino Tamayo, the museum at the church Santo Domingo, and at the sites of the ruins. We stood in 16th century Spanish cathedrals with their ornate sculptures, jewels and gold, next to ragged barefoot natives on their knees crawling up to receive communion from priests droning mechanically from microphones. At the very end of our travels we drove through Lancaster County, Pennsylvania, to see the way of life of the Amish. We went to quilt exhibits and an exhibition and video at "People's Place." We did the car tour at Gettysburg National Park.

The Home Study year was a diverse year. It was a lot of fun. It was my dream come true. The last line of Jessica's end-of-the-year presentation was "Thanks especially to my Mom, who showed us just how much can be crammed into one year!" Wendy and Jessica grew in ways I do not yet fully comprehend. I am struck by their self-possession. While reciting their lines from Spoon River Anthology for their theatre class their voices are deep, strident, project. They have presence. They pace the apartment, enjoy spitting out the words, "I loathe you, Spoon River!" They are confident and dramatic, and prefer reciting their lines to watching cable television.

Entering high school in the fall, both girls have just turned 14. The school gave them an assessment test. Both were put into advanced English, theater, art, history, and Spanish courses. In math they entered Algebra 1. Even though they are two of the youngest in the school, an alternative school which does not have grades, they feel comfortable socially and are making friends with all ages of students. They are talking about finishing high school in three years and going to Israel to spend a year in a kibbutz before going to college to study archeology and art. Their lives have opened up considerably and they are still eager learners. They feel effective.

Support Groups

Support groups are the social side of homeschooling, and just what their name implies: a group of people who support and encourage each other, and who share their information about and experience with teaching their own children at home.

Homeschooling support groups can begin with two or more friends discussing their experiences and concerns, or they may be planned and coordinated from the very first meeting, with the groundwork laid out carefully beforehand and fifty or sixty people attending.

The purpose of support groups can range from those which simply serve as a community focal point for parents interested in teaching their own children to those which support grass-roots lobbying efforts to promote homeschooling. A well-organized support group can offer many valuable programs, and most arrange regular meetings in a convenient location, schedule field trips and special events, and publish a newsletter. In addition, many support groups watch the local legal atmosphere, keep their members advised of legislative developments, arrange pot-luck dinners and picnics, sponsor classes, seminars, workshops, curriculm fairs, conventions, and conferences, and promote public awareness of home based education. A homeschooling library is available within many groups, offering books, publications, and even curriculums to interested parents and their children. Many support groups distribute information packets, directories, special events calendars, and guides to local places of interest to homeschoolers, such as businesses which provide educational tours, or where to find learning materials and supplies.

Finding a support group is generally not difficult. You might begin by writing to a state organization and asking about groups in your specific locality. If none exist, or if you philosophically disagree with the existing group, starting a new support group is usually as easy as deciding on a time and place for a meeting and posting notices on community bulletin boards, or advertising in the local paper. When writing to support groups, please remember that they are usually staffed by volunteers, and a self-addressed, stamped envelope will be appreciated and will oftimes speed response to an inquiry.

Joining a support group is not a prerequisite to homeschooling, but the experience can enhance and broaden your family's learning opportunities.

The National Homeschool Association

The National Homeschool Association serves homeschooling families and the general public as an advocacy and information network. Through an annual conference, a quarterly newsletter, extensive nationwide contacts, and several service programs for homeschooling families, the National Homeschool Association is working to promote homeschooling on a national level.

The NHA strives to maintain a broad perspective, and encourages a wide-ranging involvement from the homeschool community. The NHA is a non-profit association, and holds as its statement of purpose: "to promote individual choice and freedom in education, to serve families who choose to homeschool, and to inform the general public about home education."

By using its national perspective, the organization monitors developments within the homeschooling movement and identifies issues that affect homeschooling families. Through the quarterly newsletter these issues are discussed and resources are provided to help homeschooling families make their own decisions.

Through its annual conference, press releases, news bulletins and informational brochures, the NHA informs the general public, government policy makers, and educational and business interests across the nation about homeschooling.

Membership in the National Homeschool Association is open to all interested persons. The benefits of membership include a one year subscription to the quarterly NHA newsletter, voting privileges for all elections, and access to the National Homeschool Association's service programs. Among the current programs offered are Nationwide Support Group Networking, a Homeschooler's Travel Directory, and a Resource packet.

For an informational package send $4.00 to The National Homeschool Association, Post Office Box 290, Hartland, Michigan 48353-0290; or call 313-632-5208.

Finding Resources

How do you go about sorting through all the curriculums, correspondence schools, teaching aids, educational materials, and other programs? How do you find out what's available, what each one is about, and most importantly, how do you figure out which program or materials might be best suited to your child's needs?

First determine the general approach you want to take. Decide whether you want to purchase a ready-made curriculum, or to assemble one of your own from various sources. Should you choose a correspondence school? Or would total freedom be most appropriate for your family?

Write for brochures and catalogs. A few postcards, sent to companies you're interested in, will bring an assortment of flyers, catalogs, brochures, booklets, sample curriculums, testimonials, order forms, and unabashed pleas for your business.

Many support groups sponsor regular "curriculum fairs," showcasing samples of supplies and materials. Most support groups also maintain a resource library, or a collection of curriculum samples and brochures. Or perhaps a support group can help you locate a homeschooling family who is already using a curriculum you're considering, and who would be willing to discuss their experience with it.

For Further Information

ORGANIZATIONS:

The National Homeschool Association
Post Office Box 290
Hartland, Michigan 48353-0290
313-632-5208

The Alliance for Parental Involvement in Education
Post Office Box 59
East Chatham, New York 12060-0059
518-392-6900

The Alternative Education Resource Organization
417 Roslyn Road
Roslyn Heights, New York 11577
516-621-2195

National Coalition of Alternative Community Schools
58 Schoolhouse Road
Summertown, Tennessee 38483
615-964-3670

PUBLICATIONS:

Home Education Magazine
Post Office Box 1083
Tonasket, Washington 98855
509-486-1351

Growing Without Schooling
2269 Massachusetts Avenue
Cambridge, Massachusetts 02140
617-864-3100

Circle of Correspondence
National Homeschool Association
Post Office Box 290
Hartland, Michigan 48353-0290
313-632-5208

Options in Learning
The Alliance for Parental Involvement in
Education
Post Office Box 59
East Chatham, New York 12060-0059
518-392-6900

The AERO-Gramme
The Alternative Education Resource
Organization
417 Roslyn Road
Roslyn Heights, New York 11577
516-621-2195

National Coalition News
National Coalition of Alternative
Community Schools
58 Schoolhouse Road
Summertown, Tennessee 38483
615-964-3670

BOOKS:

Barker, Britt *Letters Home* (Home Education
Press, 1988)
Beechick, Ruth *You Can Teach Your Child
Successfully* (Arrow Press, 1988)
Colfax, David and Micki *Homeschooling for
Excellence* (Warner Books, 1988)
Gelner, Judy *College Admissions: A Guide for
Homeschoolers* (Poppyseed Press, 1988)
Goldman, Jenifer *My Life as a Travelling
Homeschooler* (Solomon Press, 1991)
Gorder, Cheryl *Home Education Resource

Guide (Bluebird Publishing, 1989)
Gorder, Cheryl *Home Schools* (Bluebird
Publishing, 1990)
Hegener, Mark and Helen *The Home School
Reader* (Home Education Press, 1988)
Hendrickson, Borg *Homeschool: Taking the
First Step* (Mountain Meadow Press, 1988)
Hendrickson, Borg *How to Write a Low
Cost/No Cost Curriculum for Your
Homeschool Child* (Mountain Meadow
Press, 1989)
Holt, John *Teach Your Own* (Delacorte Press,
1981)
Holt, John *Learning All The Time* (Delacorte,
1989)
Kaseman, Larry and Susan *Taking Charge
Through Homeschooling: Personal and
Political Empowerment* (Koshkonong Press,
1990)
Leistico, Agnes *I Learn Better by Teaching
Myself* (Home Education Press, 1991)
Llewellyn, Grace *The Teenage Liberation
Handbook: How to Quit School and Get a
Real Life and Education* (Lowry House,
1991)
Moore, Raymond and Dorothy *Home School
Burnout* (Wolgemuth & Hyatt, 1988)
Moore, Raymond and Dorothy *Home Style
Teaching* (Word Books, 1984)
Moore, Raymond and Dorothy *Home Grown
Kids* (Word Books, 1983)
Moore, Raymond and Dorothy *Home Spun
Schools* (Word Books, 1983)
Mothering Magazine *Schooling at Home* (John
Muir Publishing, 1990)
Reed, Donn *The Home School Source Book*
(Brook Farm Books, 1991)

CHAPTER FIVE

Alternative Schools

Why Alternative Schools?

"It's difficult now, twenty years later, to remember the crisis proportions of the unrest that was sweeping the country during the late '60's and early '70's out of which the alternative school movement, as well as other grass-roots movements, was born. It was like the pre-Civil War years in intensity and, like them, the cause was oppression—oppression of blacks by whites, and, one hundred years later, of women by men, of children by adults, of students by administrators, of doves by hawks, of the poor by the rich—in fact, of the powerless by the powerful."
    –Lucia Vorys in
A Twenty Year Perspective
    on Alternative Schools
from *Challenging the Giant*
(Down-to-Earth books, 1992)

In the 1989-90 edition of *The National Directory of Alternative Schools*, published by the National Coalition of Alternative Community Schools, a brief article near the end of the directory poses the questions: Why should a parent send their child to an alternative school? What result can they expect?

Their answer? Generally speaking, an alternatively educated child will be self-confident. Alternative schools emphasize the positive, stressing accomplishments rather than shortcomings, reinforcing rather than punishing. The uniqueness and individuality of each student is encouraged and developed.

Because of the stress on individualization, students at alternative schools are exposed early to independent study, decision-making, and facing the consequences of their decisions.

Alternative schools stress democracy and the fair hearing of all sides. They are also non-discriminatory and have students and staff from a variety of backgrounds. Because they work with their teachers to jointly make decisions, they come to a better understanding of the adult point of view, as well as the feelings of their peers.

Students in alternative schools learn responsibility early by being part of the decision making process in all aspects of their schools. They are encouraged to help in any way they can. This includes everything from general maintenance to fund-raising; teaching classes to dealing with the disciplinary problems. It is no wonder that later in life they have no trouble getting and holding on to the jobs that they want.

Alternative schools encourage students to try new directions. They are not expected to fit the mold. Because they are able to stay in touch with their feelings they are better able to follow a truly new thought in a creative direction. They do not have to do things in a set pattern just to please the teacher.

Alternative schools not only stress the importance of good nutrition and exercise, but they allow students to learn in situations that are not stressful. Learning is not competitive. The dangers of things such as smoking, drugs, and alcohol are openly talked about. The atmosphere is relaxed, and positive physical contact and affection can be expressed.

Because of the democratic meeting structure, students in alternative schools learn to express their ideas and feelings on a continual basis. They are motivated to understand all that is being expressed in meetings because they know that real decisions are made there, and to the extent that they understand, and can express themselves, they become a greater part of that process.

Not only does the student in an alternative school become competent in the usual academic areas, but in areas that have broad range. Alternative school learners are open to new learning.

Perhaps most important, alternative school students become able to find the solutions to their problems. They are able to find the people, places, or materials they need to tackle a new situation. Their education grows with them, for they know that if they want to learn they do not have to wait to be taught.

"Modern compulsory public education systems were set up by cultural, political, and industrial leaders of the 1800's as a means of changing rural patterns of life into lifestyles fit for occupations in factories and commerce, and as a means for 'democratizing' diverse immigrant populations, especially in the United States, by making sure they all spoke the same language and had the same social habits. The enforcement of compulsory public education met with a tremendous amount of public resistance at first, requiring the calling out of troops upon more than one occasion. Almost from the start there were dissidents who criticized the program and started their own, 'alternative' schools."

–Introduction, *1992-93 National Directory of Alternative Schools*, published by the National Coalition of Alternative Comunity Schools

John Holt On Alternative Schools

The author and educator John Holt once wrote that he wanted to accomplish three objectives: he wanted to do away with the idea of compulsory learning, he wanted to change the idea that learning should be separate from the rest of life, and he wanted to break down the barriers that separated children from the work and concerns of adults.

Holt wrote that "It's okay to have some special places for kids, since they have special needs that in some respects are different from the needs of adults. At different ages they need different places to play, to run around, to make noise, to learn certain physical skills, and to mingle with each other. But they should not have to spend all their time in those special kid places. The adult world should be as far as possible open to them, and they should not have to go to the special kid places unless they want to."

Alternative schools are "special kid places." John Holt felt that the majority of alternative schools were only a little more subtle than the regular public schools in telling children what they should learn and in trying to make them learn it. He pointed the blame for this at the teachers, writing, "People say to me quite often, 'I want to work with kids.' What they really mean is that they want to work on kids, to do things to or for them, usually without their consent, which they think will do them good. I often say to these well-meaning people 'Why not find some work worth doing, and then try to find ways to make it possible for young people to join you in this work.' This is very different from starting an alternative school. Children should be able to see adults at work, and if they wish, to share in their work according to their energy and skill. If we want to call this place a 'school' then I suppose we can, but I would much prefer to call it something else. If we are inventing something new, and in our time this is new, I'd rather think of a new name for it than bend an old name out of shape to fit it."

The relationship between the teachers and the students in an alternative school seemed "deeply and dangerously ambiguous" to John Holt. He wrote that "In most schools the relation is stark and clear. School is the Army for kids. Adults make them go there, and when they get there adults tell them what to do, bribe and threaten them into doing it, and punish them when they don't. When the teachers in an alternative school try (as they should) to give up this bad relationship, it is very unclear what they put in its place.

If they are not there to tell the children what to do, what are they there for? To 'help' the children? Did the children ask for this help? Can they get away from it? Sometimes alternative schools talk about students and teachers being equal. If so, why are the adults paid? And to do what? One of the reasons teachers burn out so quickly at alternative schools, even faster than at regular schools, is that their position, task, and function are so unclear. Are they the students' servants, or their bosses, or if neither, then what?

"Is the task of adults in alternative schools to think up interesting things for the students to do and then try to seduce or cajole them into doing them? Is their task to be available if the students want their help, but otherwise stay out of their way? Neither of these seems to me like a good life-time work for serious adults."

Holt wrote that he would hate to be in the position of having to think up things for children to do and then find ways to get those children to do them. He often showed children things that he liked to do, but disliked the idea of doing things that he personally found boring in the hope that some child would find his actions interesting. He wrote, "I am always glad to play my cello with children around and to offer them a chance to play it if they want. But if they don't, that's fine with me; I am not trying to 'get them interested' in the cello. I am not going to take up painting in the hope that, seeing me, children will get interested in painting. Let people who already like to paint paint where children can see them."

Alternative schools come in many sizes, shapes, and forms, and many of them struggle daily with the questions of "who's in charge and what are their real responsibilities" which Holt perceived as crucial. The people in these schools, both the teachers and the students, are trying to find a way through the jungle of teaching methods and procedures, curricula, seating arrangements, grading, attendance records, testing, tracking, and a thousand other concerns that have come to be associated with schooling.

As a society, we seem to be groping our way unsteadily toward the bright vision of education which John Holt and many other alternative educators have seen so clearly. Alternative schools are helping to light our way.

A. S. Neill and Summerhill

Alexander Sutherland Neill was born in Forfarshire, Scotland in 1883. Son of the village schoolmaster, Neill started work at fourteen, studied for the ministry, found it not to his liking, and went on to specialize in English at Edinburgh University, where he graduated with honors and an M.A. in English Literature in 1912.

Neill worked as a teacher in Scotland, and it was during this time that he began to question traditional education theory and to form his own opinions about children and learning. He wrote about these ideas in his four "Dominie" (schoolmaster) books: *A Dominie's Log* (1916), *A Dominie Dismissed* (1917, *A Dominie in Doubt* (1922), and *A Dominie Abroad* (1923).

In 1921 Neill, with several others, set up an international school in Dresden, Germany. When revolution broke out the school was moved to Austria. There Neill encountered opposition and harassment for his unconventional curriculum and methods, and the school was finally moved to Leiston, Suffolk, about a hundred miles from London, in 1924.

Summerhill, a co-educational, self-governing boarding school, has been described as "the most unusual school in the world," and "the world's greatest experiment in bestowing unstinted love and approval on children."

Summerhill was the first truly free school. Children were not compelled to attend classes, and could stay away from them for as long as they cared to. And yet, to the utter bewilderment of the traditional educators, the children of Summerhill actually learned. In a report of the British Government Inspectors it was reported that one lad stayed away from classes for thirteen years - yet went on to become an expert toolmaker and precision instrument maker.

Neill was a severe critic of his times. He stated that "We are living in an insane society" and "most of our religious practices are sham." He felt that a choice must be made between educating a child to be socially and materialistically successful, or to fill a niche in life as a happy, well-adjusted person. To Neill, children were innately wise and realistic. He suggested that if left to their own without adult interference, children would develop as far as they were capable. He put his own goals rather succinctly: "I would rather see a school produce a happy street cleaner than a neurotic scholar."

Neill's "radical approach to child rearing" was simply to un-
mask the system of fear and control which paraded as authority.
He contended that the aim of education - and of life - was to work
joyfully and find happiness. Neill wrote that intellectual development must be matched by emotional development, and that the
child must learn to face the world as an individual.

While the Summerhill model of education has been widely criticized, it has also been widely emulated. In his book, *Summerhill*,
published in 1960, Neill wrote, "I do not think that the world will
use the Summerhill method of education for a very long time - if it
ever uses it. The world may find a better way. Only an empty
windbag would assume that his work is the last word on the subject. The world must find a better way. For politics will not save
humanity. It never has done so. Most political newspapers are
bristling with hate, hate all the time. Too many are socialistic because they hate the rich instead of loving the poor.

"How can we have happy homes with love in them when the
home is a tiny corner of a homeland that shows hate socially in a
hundred ways? You can see why I cannot look upon education as
a matter of exams and classes and learning. The school evades the
basic issue: all the Greek and math and history in the world will
not help make the home more loving, the child free from inhibi-
tions, the parent free of neurosis.

"The future of Summerhill itself may be of little import. But the
future of the Summerhill idea is of the greatest importance to humanity. New generations must be given the chance to grow in
freedom. The bestowal of freedom is the bestowal of love. And
only love can save the world."

A.S. Neill died of pneumonia in 1973. His daughter, Zoe Neill
Redhead, continues his work at Summerhill School. Neill's prolific
writings on education and child psychology include *A Dominie's
Log* (1916), *A Dominie Dismissed* (1917), *A Dominie in Doubt* (1922),
A Dominie Abroad (1923), *The Problem Child* (1926), *The Problem Par-
ent* (1936), *Is Scotland Educated?* (1936), *That Dreadful School* (1937),
The Problem Teacher (1939), *Hearts Not Heads in the Schools* (1945),
The Problem Family (1949), *The Free Child* (1953), *Summerhill: A Radi-
cal Approach to Child Rearing* (1960), *Freedom-Not Liscense!* (1966),
Talking of Summerhill (1967), *Summerhill: For and Against* (1967),
Neill! Neill! Orange Peel! (1972).

National Association of
Alternative Community Schools

Since 1976, the National Association of Alternative Community Schools (NCACS) has coordinated a networking effort for alternative, community, and free schools across the United States and around the world. A completely voluntary effort, this far-flung web of people, schools, programs, families and communities strives to maintain communication channels, coordinate an annual international conference, and to publish a directory of alternative schools and programs and quarterly newsletter.

From the introduction of their 1992-93 Directory comes this description of the National Association of Alternative Community Schools:

"The individuals, schools, and organizations presented in this directory are a living storehouse of innovative educational techniques and practices. They represent a cross-section of the cutting edge of the educational community."

From the 1987 Directory comes this definition: "Alternative community schools and programs differ from traditional schools and programs in significant ways. A main distinction lies in who started the schools and who controls them. Parents and teachers, and in some cases, students founded the schools during the sixties and seventies, forming the basis for the free school movement. They opened in cities and in suburbs, in ghettoes and in rural settings. They are run by people most directly involved in their programs, by the people who teach in them and are served by them.

"The schools are small, frequently serving fewer than fifty students total; they maintain low student-teacher ratios. They offer a wide variety of activities to learners as part of the everyday fare; open learning environments, apprenticeship programs, overnight trips away from school, the use of the community as the classroom and more. They are alternatives to conventional schooling."

Perhaps the best way to gain an understanding of the true nature of these schools is to "visit" a few of them through their brochures and booklets. For the address of each school see For Further Information at the end of this chapter.

Sussex School - Missoula, Montana

In 1971, a group of parents wishing to actively participate in the education of their children founded Sussex Cooperative Pre-

School. Two years later, realizing the need for a long-range commitment to alternative education in Missoula, they organized an elementary school.

In 1985, Sussex decided to eliminate its pre-school program and concentrate its resources on the K-8 elementary program which now enrolls over sixty students. Sussex School is incorporated as a non-profit educational organization and is licensed by the State of Montana. A Board of Directors, elected each May, consists of seven parents, one student, and one member from the community. Each student, parent and teacher at Sussex has a meaningful voice.

Sussex is a learning community whose fundamental values include love and respect for each person. The School believes that education should nurture the creativity and natural desire to learn that is inherent in each child. Sussex strives to develop the whole person, the student as both an independent, inquiring intellect and as a member of the community.

Sussex promotes the development of self-discipline, high self-esteem, and clear self-expression. Children become confident of their own authority and are expected to assume responsibility for their own behavior. Sussex helps children to develop a strong social consciousness which assists them in group problem solving. This balance of personal and social goals requires a low student-teacher ratio, which varies according to subject area and the age of the student.

Sussex focuses on a student's interest in his education. Children are encouraged to share in shaping the curriculum and each child is given a voice in this.

Sussex offers a flexible curriculum which allows students and teachers to structure a course of study that is best suited to the particular needs of the individual child. The structure at Sussex enables students of different ages to work and play together. Children are encouraged to be children, to dream and to use their imaginations. Compliance and conformity are not demanded, which permits each child to express his or her individuality.

Teachers are chosen for their commitment to the principles and values of Sussex, as well as for the depth and variety of their training and experience. Teachers are expected to be creative and flexible and to value process over product. Sussex expects teachers to teach mainly subjects of their own special interest and strength.

From the School's inception, parents have played an integral part in the direction, operation, and maintenance of Sussex. A decision to join Sussex School is a commitment to become involved in a large community dedicated to the positive growth and development of its children. Parent involvement adds to the charm and excitement of Sussex. Parents contribute in-depth knowledge about their interests and careers and thereby enrich student understanding of the world and their future. Parents are required to contribute a prescribed number of "parent participation hours" per quarter. These hours are extremely important to the School and its efficient operation.

Sussex does not discriminate on the basis of race, color, national or ethic origin in the administration of its educational or admission policies. The School admits children from ages five through fourteen. A balance is maintained between the number of boys and girls, as well as between age groups. Sussex has a sliding scale tuition policy to insure a balanced socioeconomic mix. Parent participation hours, tuition, donations, interest from a generous endowment, and fundraising support the School.

Horizon's Edge School - Canterbury, New Hampshire

What is the essence of Horizon's Edge School? What makes it unique? The answer is its people! The students who bring their fresh energy and enthusiasm and the staff who bring their expertise and commitment to the academic and social growth of their students. Horizon's Edge School is a community where everyone is contributing toward the common goal of creating a caring and trusting environment where children have access to the resources that they require to continue their growth as joyful human beings. The school derives its name from Walt Whitman's *Leaves of Grass* in which he describes this process of "becoming."

Horizon's Edge was founded in 1960. With 13 acres of land and access to an additional 1200 acres of fields and forest, the school is well situated for the active lives of its students and staff. Eight modern buildings, thoughtfully designed for living and learning with children, have been built through the years blending with the natural environment amidst the stone walls and sugar maples familiar to New England.

Children from Canterbury and surrounding towns, as well as boarding students from all parts of the U. S. and abroad, choose to come to Horizon's Edge because of its high academic standards, the individual attention possible in small classrooms, its supportive atmosphere, experiential approach and extensive arts, music and environmental science programs.

Day and boarding students enrich one another's lives. Boarders are frequent guests of day students and have the opportunity to experience family life in a New England community. Boarders bring a wealth of experiences to Horizon's Edge. Some have come from far corners of the world and share their culture and customs with us. Students flourish in this supportive environment.

Horizon's Edge School exists to assist its students in their development as whole individuals possessing qualities of self-assurance; the academic skills, discipline and motivation required by higher educational challenges; an appreciation for the arts; the ability to join and help groups in their cooperative work; an openness to recognize and value one's own gifts and those of others; a sense of stewardship of our natural environment; and the ability and desire to resolve conflicts nonviolently. The nurturing and care that is provided in the classroom, on the playing field, or in the family setting in the dormitory encourages the children to grow to their maximum potential thus setting the foundation for continued growth throughout life.

The primary goal of the academic program is to develop in children a love of learning such that it becomes a way of life, not merely a required activity. Hand in hand with this, we encourage children to strive to fulfill their potential and to develop the skills and knowledge that provide a solid foundation for higher learning. Our expectations for academic achievement are high, and preparation for admission to the secondary school of the student's choice is another important objective of the Horizon's Edge School program.

The value of each child as an individual manifests itself many times daily, from acknowledgement of a job well done in the morning to a bedside chat or "tuck-in" at night. As contributing members of the school community, children take responsibility for household chores and often volunteer to help with the cooking or with feeding the farm animals. Each individual's involvement, student and staff alike, contributes to a stronger sense of community and teaches valuable skills.

The Neighborhood Schoolhouse - Brattleboro, Vermont

The Neighborhood Schoolhouse offers a rich and varied experiential learning program where individual attention is given to each child's growth and style of learning. The comprehensive curriculum integrates academic and applied skills.

Children age 5-9 come together each morning in mixed-age homerooms to begin their day with a silent circle and a group activity. Emphasis is placed on working well in groups of mixed age level and on development of reading skills.

During the day they spend time working alone or grouped by skill level. Their learning takes place through creative play, self-directed projects and innovative academic teaching. Some of their favorite things to do include afternoon writing and publishing, electronics and experiments, field trips to museums, music, ensemble and contra dance, foreign languages and cultures, weaving and science studies, hiking and camping out.

The Middle School program for children ages 10-14 consists of academic requirements, electives and an apprenticeship. It's designed for children who are self-motivated. The core academic program includes language arts, creative expression, mathematics and science. The Apprenticeship allows students to work one morning a week in the community with an adult who is selected on the basis of his or her ability to work with children. Morning work experiences are discussed in the group in the afternoon. Work sites may include a food co-op, library, pottery studio, day care center, radio station, or weaver's studio.

Electives allow students to pursue special interests in depth. They may be offered by community resource people. Electives differ from year to year and may include foreign languages, music, art, photography, weaving, sports, computer, gardening, social studies, science projects and student's suggestions.

At the heart of The Neighborhood Schoolhouse philosophy is the understanding that we are all students as well as teachers. We trust one another and take risks together from which we emerge changed. We want our children to gain knowledge, skills and attitudes that help them lead useful, satisfying lives. We want them to be confident and comfortable with their own growth.

On the playground, in the garden, on a camping trip or in the classroom, we want our children to care about the world around them, about themselves and others.

The School Around Us - Kennebunkport, Maine

The School Around Us is an ungraded, community co-operative day school which has been in operation since 1970. The primary site is a schoolhouse built by parents and friends on eighteen acres of beautifully wooded land in Arundel, Maine. It is a small school, capable of enrolling up to thirty children. The small size affords many advantages, one being that the student/teacher ratio can be kept low (e.g., 7/1). The teaching staff consists of qualified teachers and parents. In addition, volunteers, parents and interested community people offer special classes and activities in science, gardening, environmental studies, social studies and a great variety of arts and crafts.

Since September of 1985, The School Around Us has offered preschool through third grades. Our goal is to provide a stimulating, creative environment in which children can learn and grow. The school environment consists of a brook, woods, playground, library and areas for science, art, blocks, dress-up, and water play. The schedule contains time for group talking and sharing, play time, project time for building and creating, storytime, art class and time for learning about the outdoors.

The name of The School Around Us is a clue to its philosophy - we are all constantly learning from the world in which we live. The parents and school personnel work together to create a partnership between home and school that will support the child throughout the school experience.

The School Around Us applies a developmental approach to learning where the children are able to work at their particular level of development and through their own learning style. Children are recognized as dynamic learners who are actively engaged in learning through their involvement with hands-on materials. The classroom environment is a planned, child-centered one which encourages this exploration and discovery in a self-directed, self-motivated manner. Divergent thinking is encouraged and children learn there is often more than one "right" answer.

At The School Around Us, we use an integrated curriculum which revolves around a unit theme. Each unit contains themes which are based on particular interests of the children and the teachers. The unit themes are planned according to seasons, developmental ages of the children involved, and community resources available. The themes, at times, reflect the values and interests of the community involved thus concentrating on environmental, social and cultural issues. Concepts, skills and projects are developed in relationship to the core theme. Together, teachers and children engage in a process of inquiry and discovery.

Throughout the year there are field trips to various civic, historic and environmental sites and museums. The school focuses on an appreciation of and the importance of the environment. Much of our school time is spent exploring the outdoors. The children use their senses, the people, and library resources available to explore and develop an appreciation of wildlife, an understanding of our ecology and a concern for the world around us.

The School Around Us is a not-for-profit corporation. Like any institution that is not funded by private tax revenues or by private life-time endowment, The School Around Us relies on fund raising, donations, and tuition. Families are busy with fund raising projects throughout the year and donations are raised through an annual fund raising letter. Tuition is determined by the annual budget. Parents may either pay tuition or contribute to the operation of the school by assuming a paid job (teaching, administration, maintenance) and applying the proceeds towards tuition. Time and energy is also put into committee responsibilities, forum discussions, work days and business meetings.

The Farm School - Summertown, Tennessee

The Farm is a cooperative community on 1750 acres in beautiful middle Tennessee. Founded on principles of non-violence and reverence for nature, it is one of the most respected and stable intentional communities. Visitors from around the world contribute a global view of life within the community and school.

The goals of The Farm alternative school are quality academic achievement, competence in new age technologies, development of research techniques, personal and creative expression, fostering of artistic talents, development of physical skills, project oriented education, and achieving a global perspective. The Farm's Home School Study Program brings these goals into the home, providing an opportunity for independent work and close interaction between students and their families.

Students in the Home Study Program are reminded to keep an ongoing log of activities, to average four hours a day in home study, to collect work samples in each subject to submit at evaluation time, and to evaluate regularly. Students need to have a teacher and a curriculum for each subject, books and resources are available from the Home Study Library, and new books can be ordered through The Farm Alternative School. Each year in the spring standardized tests are administered for all day school and home study students.

Students enrolled in the Home Study Program may take day school classes for $2.00 per hour and may visit anytime with prior phone arrangement. Conference and evaluation includes progress report, curriculum advice, and collection of records.

Classes are grouped as pre-K, primary, intermediate, middle school, junior high school, and high school, with combined classes allowing for more individualized and interactive learning. The Farm School curriculum tries "to give our students a planetary consciousness in addition to the basics, so they can understand the problems of the world and possible solutions." They incorporate field trips, international and local guest speakers, and an apprenticeship program for older students. Over the years The Farm School has produced a high degree of creativity in students as well as academic excellence and a sense of worth in its graduates.

For further information about the National Coalition of Alternative Community Schools write to NCACS, 58 Schoolhouse Road, Summertown, TN 38483; 615-964-3670.

Upattinas Educational Resource Center

—— Sandra Hurst ——————————————————————————

The Upattinas Educational Resource Center is both a place and a program of events designed to promote and foster learning for people who choose to have control over their own education or that of their children. It is an environment for exploration and contemplation; sharing and searching. It is a resource for finding people, books, equipment, ideas, and support for designing one's ongoing education.

Located in rural northwestern Chester County, west of Philadelphia, the facility for the Resource Center is a large old stone building with six and one-half acres of meadow and woodland including a small stream. The building includes a large meeting room and several smaller rooms. It also has a full kitchen. The rooms include a seven-thousand volume library with textbooks and learning materials for people of all ages and stages of learning as well as the blocks and toys which are the materials of learning for growing children. The large meeting room lends itself to drama, dance, improvisation and larger group experiences such as conferences and retreats.

The people involved in the Upattinas Educational Resource

Center include homeschooling families; people who want to graduate from high school while also pursuing interests such as art, music, ice skating, car mechanics, home-making... people who have particular interests in any of the varied programs available. They are teachers in search of students and students in search of teachers. They are learners in search of a community of learners and people who want to design their own learning situations. They are participants in the process of the Resource Center as well as in their own evolving education.

The Upattinas Educational Resource Center began as an alternative school in 1971, formed by families and teachers who were interested in experimenting with a combination of free school and open classroom ideas. It grew and developed as a school for the next nineteen years, waxing and waning with the times and the need for alternative kinds of schools.

During those years, a growing number of people who liked the philosophy of such schools, but who either lived too far away or did not have the funds to support private schooling for their children, began to school their children at home. It was an unpopular thing to do and many of these people found themselves in need of some sort of umbrella organization that would help them to find their way through the maze of laws and customs that impeded their progress toward their goals. At the same time, many families who had other philosophical reasons to keep their children at home also began to home school.

Because of our philosophy of empowerment of families to work with their children according to their own beliefs and ideals, Upattinas School became a resource for many of these people. We provided counseling as to working with their school districts, helped with preparation of letters of intent, and loaned textbooks to those who felt that they needed them. We were told clearly by the state officials that we could not permit homeschooling - only the District Superintendent could do that. But we could provide a resource and educational consultation for them.

The school has undergone a metamorphosis and has become still more of a resource for people who wish to get their education outside of traditional schooling. While still working with people who homeschool under the confines of their state laws and more structured traditions, Upattinas has become a resource for those who prefer to "unschool"; that is to say, to learn in ways natural to themselves and their environments without restrictions as to hours or credits.

This takes the form of counseling with people to help them see what they do in their everyday lives that is already educational., encouraging their active involvement in their neighborhoods or environs. We support children of all ages being involved in the work of the family or in jobs outside of their homes - real jobs - not classes about getting jobs. We support and sponsor travel programs which take young people farther away from home and into the natural world. We encourage their use of all the many different kinds of learning places available to them - community colleges, museums, art centers, YM/YWCAs, individual tutors, friends, community members.

When it is important to either the family or the individual student, we also allow involvement in classes which are a part of the on-going life of the Center. These classes are developed according to the needs of the people involved in any given year. They may be academic or elective types of classes, but all are developed with the involvement of the students who will be taking them. They are taught by people who know and understand the philosophy of participant involvement in decision-making and who are prepared to work with students according to their individual needs.

Students who wish, at the high school level, may work toward a diploma by collecting the credits needed to fulfill the requirements of the Commonwealth of Pennsylvania. They do this in their own time, according to their own needs and interests. They may fashion their own independent study courses with the help of staff at the Center, or they may take classes in any of the above mentioned educational institutions, or at Upattinas. For each credit they wish to receive they must write an essay evaluation of the work done and present some of that work to a staff member. When they have completed all the requisite credits they are graduated with a diploma which is recognized as a diploma from a licensed private academic school. The Center has a full roster of certificated teachers for facilitating this program.

The Upattinas Educational Resource Center also has two computers available for use by our families and is currently working to get a grant for more computers. These can be made available for individual use by enrolled students, but they are also available for people who want to try out the programs we have in academic areas to see if they are appropriate for a given student. We have a resident expert who can advise about and teach computer skills.

Because our Center has lovely space for meeting and playing, we also carry on a series of workshops and parent support groups and special programs for children and adults. These take the form of groups sitting over tea and chatting while children play; actual specific things like math and science; art and craft workshops; experiential days for exploring musical instruments; and virtually anything suggested by our community. We also anticipate developing several-day retreats for those interested in immersing themselves in special interests. For example, one of our families is developing a performance in drums, dance, and the experience of African American people. We expect to have a two-day workshop with them which will involve all of the participants in whatever aspects of the experience they might enjoy - from actually participating in the dancing and drumming, to sharing readings and discussions about what they experience.

People who enjoy working with others or sharing their special gifts and interests offer their services to the Resource Center. A chamber music group which needs to test out its new concert series will do its dress rehearsal here for our families; people who write poetry will bring their poetry reading group here so that we can listen in; a staff member who loves esoteric movies has organized a movie night at the Center. We are limited only by the imaginations of our community.

Our Center is funded by a variety of sources: tuition, individual class fees, rental of spaces, donations for specific programs and donations to the over-all program, and occasional foundation grants. We are a 501C3 non-profit corporation which is co-operative in nature. Our board of directors is elected from the constituent group and other interested community members. Our community includes anyone who is interested in becoming involved and who accepts our basic premises: co-operative, non-coercive learning; participant control through democratic process; non-discrimination as to race, religion, sex, or other individual difference.

One Alternative Setting: Clonlara School

___ Pat Montgomery _____

His cherubic countenance beamed up at me as I stood above his crib. I picked my waking baby up and sat cradling him, his one year old sister by my side. "Imagine," I thought to myself, "in five short years they'll both be trundling off to school." The thought left me numb. Self accusations raced through my mind. "What have they done to you that you would abandon them to a life in school?" Oh, sure, they kept me awake nights and dribbled their food but nothing so severe that it merited punishment. I shared these thoughts and feelings with Jim, their father, as soon as he arrived home from work. We mulled.

If not to Burns Park Public School across the street, where would they go at ages five or six? We researched the alternatives. Except for Catholic and Lutheran schools, the only other school in town was a Montessori school. More research.

Finally, a decision. I had taught for eight years in Catholic schools and six years in public schools by that time; I would, very likely, return to teaching sometime in the future. Why not start a school for Chandra and Chai, my children? One that reflected our own style and values and hopes for them. And so began Clonlara. The name is taken from the small village in Ireland where my father, John Clancy, attended school as a child. It translates from Irish as "the meadow of the mare."

And so began new doubts. I had never been in business; I had never operated a school. How would I know what to do, how to do it? It didn't take long to develop confidence. I had only to recall the administrators and teachers with whom I had worked. I had only to put the results of their labors and mine into perspective. I had only to examine now from a distance the construct of public (and most private) schools: the "system." The conclusion followed logically: If my efforts failed, if the school I started proved to be a disaster in any way, it would still be better than the ones I had taught in and researched for my children.

I finished my master's degree at the University of Michigan with a definite focus: child development and "new school" creation. I visited A. S. Neill in Leiston, England in 1967, probably because I wanted to see first hand a do-it-yourself, long-lived place for inspiration, and for verification that my goal of establishing a school was reachable.

"Don't start a Summerhill," he remarked. "There's already one of those. Each one of us has a school inside. Start that one. Don't be a disciple of anyone."

The temptation was strong, though, to do just that. Buy into the Montessori name; become a Waldorf school. Societies existed already. The proverbial wheel need not be re-invented. Brochures lauded this educational approach and that, this teacher-training institute and that. I read on.

In my journeys to the feet of the masters and in my almost ceaseless reading, visiting, and envisioning, I was able to sort through the experiences of others and select those which most closely reflected my dream. The world was my classroom, veritably. Teachers were everywhere, eager to share with an eager student.

Jim and I imagined a place where children of all creeds and races and ages might learn and grow in an unpressured, relaxed atmosphere, free of coercion. A place where the very democratic principles upon which our country was built would become a reality in the everyday lives of students and adults -- one person, one vote. No discrimination based on age. A place where parents would share intimately in the life of the school and in the education of their children, where they would be active participants, not passive observers and cookie bakers for PTA meetings.

The school would be small, enrolling fewer than 100 students, more like a family than an institution. There would be ample opportunity to learn academic skills as well as problem-solving methods and conflict resolution. Children would be free to make mistakes, to learn by their mistakes, and to grow in the process. Adults would be free to learn and to grow, too. All would be respected as thinking, feeling human beings and treated humanely.

The issues affecting our lives daily -- the environment, war and peace, world issues -- would be part of the curriculum. Travel would be, too. Every aspect of a student's growth -- physical, spiritual, mental, and psychological -- would receive attention.

And so it began in the fall of 1967. And so it is today -- a place for five year olds through eighteen year olds. Does it work? Was the dream realized? I am a tad biased, so I'll let others answer.

A Japanese teacher who visited Clonlara said, "In every other school I have visited in the United States and in Japan, the children have two faces, one for the teacher and one for the other children. At Clonlara, the children have only one face."

Bill, a graduate of our high school, said, "For a person to believe that a coercive atmosphere is better (for learning)... is to believe that might makes right. (Such an atmosphere) has a way of destroying creativity... In order to develop creative, life-long learning, it is necessary (for one) to be in a non-coercive, interest-initiated, learning centered atmosphere (like Clonlara)."

Sue, a Clonlara teacher, said, "This is the only school I have ever experienced where a teacher is 100% autonomous. We are expected to be sensible, mature people; we are respected as sensible, mature people; and we, in turn, can treat the students like sensible, mature people. That's how it works!"

Betty, parent of a Clonlara student, said, "If I had had a school experience like this when I was a child, my whole approach to solving problems and to life in general would have been totally different."

In recent years, Japanese parents and educators have become interested in alternatives to their present system of education. They are looking for innovative, humane ways of teaching their children. In 1981 the Hokkaido Shibun Press in Sapporo, Japan sent Yasushi Ohnuma, a reporter, to tour the alternative schools in America and collect information. His first stop was John Holt's office in Boston; John sent Yasushi to Clonlara. Upon his return to Japan, he had his findings published in both newspaper and book form. Clonlara was featured as a model school.

Since then, many Japanese have become interested in Clonlara's approach to education as an alternative to their highly competitive system of schooling. Twice they have invited me to Japan to give lecture tours promoting Clonlara's unique schooling. A number of Japanese reporters, educators, and a television crew have visited Clonlara to examine and report on us first hand. Two Japanese mothers have moved from Japan to Ann Arbor with their children so that the children could attend Clonlara. Eriko Miyazaki, a high school teacher from Tokyo, took a leave of absence from her post to spend that year as an intern at Clonlara. The bonds are continuing to grow.

Ben Hogan, director of an Australian television program, "Beyond 2000," wanted to visit Clonlara to videotape the campus, interview, and to tape an actual homeschool in progress. He had read about Clonlara in *Omni* magazine (October, 1985). The shows he directs are mostly about science and technology, but he wanted this one to focus on education. Alan's lighting director had accompanied him; he had been a student at A. S. Neill's Summerhill in England when he was twelve to sixteen years of age.

Clonlara was a pivotal player in the development of the only national group of alternative schools and homeschools, the National Coalition of Alternative Community Schools. The 1978 organizational meeting was held here in Ann Arbor; I served as President of the NCACS from 1978 to 1985.

My own two children have grown to adulthood. The plain fact is that Jim and I did not start Clonlara for our children only. At least I didn't. More and more, I realize that I started it for me. It was "the school in me," as Neill said, that needed to come out. It is very like all of those other alternative schools which were, and are, started by parents and teachers and students (or some combination of those) as an answer to the crying need to change the ways in which our society rears its children.

Sudbury Valley School: Where Ideals and Reality Cross Paths

—— Daniel Greenberg ————————————————————

The time was 1967. We were a small group of parents living near Framingham, Massachusetts, and we had been hunting all over the country for a school that met our requirements. We had travelled far and wide, visited and read about all sorts of places-- and come up empty-handed.

The one (and only) thing we all had in common was a deep commitment to a new style of childrearing, and the unshakable conviction that the existing educational system would do our children irreparable harm. We knew we had to do whatever was necessary to provide the kind of environment we wished the school to have. So it was that Sudbury Valley School was founded in 1968.

The starting point for all our thinking was the simple, revolutionary idea that a child is a person, worthy of full respect as a human being. To us, this meant that the child's agenda for its own life takes priority over anyone else's agenda—parents, family, friends, or the community.

As we were raising our children from infancy, this guiding principle led to a whole new approach. Time and again we were called upon to accommodate ourselves to the reality of our children's independent existence. They ate when they were hungry, not when we thought we should feed them. They slept when they were tired, not when we wished them out of the way. They learned to crawl, sit, walk and talk in their own good time, not when some expert thought that they ought to.

And so it was that we came to realize that, above all, the school we would either find or found for our children would have to extend to them, as a matter of principle, the same basic respect that we had been extending during the early years. At every point, their inner needs would have to be given the highest priority in their education.

As a practical matter, this meant that our children's activities at school would have to be determined by their own initiatives, not someone else's. There could be no set curriculum, no requirements, no externally imposed time periods, no outside dictation of what they should be doing with themselves. The school had to be a nurturing environment in which the children themselves schedule their times, choose what they wish to do.

The idea of personal respect leads almost directly to the concept of democracy as an institutional imperative. Democracy alone is built on the solid foundation of equal respect for all members of the community, and for their ideas and hopes. And so it became a cornerstone of our philosophy to involve everyone, without exception and including the parents, in the full process of running the school. For any way we looked at it, parents definitely had a place in children's education.

What is the school we founded like? At Sudbury Valley, children look adults straight in the eye, with no fear. They are friendly, curious about newcomers, nurturing each other. The atmosphere is open and lively. There is virtually no vandalism or theft, though there are no locks. The entire campus is freely accessible to everyone, as is the right to come and go. School opens at 8:30 in the morning, closes at 5:00, and people arrive, leave, return and do as they wish all day, subject only to the state's laws on compulsory school attendance.

Sudbury Valley is a school with completely open admission at any time of the year: we neither know nor care about the prior experiences of the students. The tuition is extremely low; at $3,500 a year for the first child in the family and less for others. The students we get are your normal, everyday, flesh-and-blood people. And yet, the quality of the children's minds has to be experienced to be believed! What a transformation occurs in "common" people when they are given their freedom! Their brains work overtime, opening into new experiences, delving now here, now there.

The inevitable question is: after eighteen years, how are we doing? What has happened to our graduates and to those who moved on before graduation? And, without requirements, without grades or report cards or school evaluations of any sort, how can they go on to college and other schools of higher education?

To begin with the last question: every graduate who has ever wanted to go to college has gotten in, usually to the college of first choice. Most schools welcome to their ranks a student who is self-motivated, self-directed, and self-possessed. Our graduates have been admitted to liberal arts colleges and specialized institutions all across the country. Many have gone on to gain graduate degrees.

The others go on to productive lives in the arts, trades, and in business. They learn to cherish each other as human beings, not as "college preps" or "voc eds." The friendships and bonds formed by students in their years here remain strong for the rest of their lives.

After reading and hearing about the school, many people still wonder and ask what a "typical day" is like at the school, both for the students and for the staff. We have trouble responding to such a question, because the people at the school are so different from each other, and there is such total freedom.

The variety is truly amazing! One person will settle into a perfectly predictable pattern for months on end, always doing the same things in the same sequence at the same times—and then suddenly change to another predictable pattern. Another person will do something else each day, or many things each day. Another person will go on a series of short term binges—a few intensive weeks (or months) of this, followed by a few intensive weeks (or months) of that.

Some people play all day. Some people talk all day. Some people paint or study or cook all day. Some people do a little of each of these things, according to some schedule they have for themselves.

Time assumes a different aspect at Sudbury Valley. Here there are no bells, no periods, no terms, no grades, no "freshmen," "sophomores," "juniors," "seniors," "preschoolers," or "postgraduates." Time belongs to each student in a very personal sense. Each student learns to understand and work with his own unique internal rhythm, pace and speed. No one is a fast learner, no one is a slow learner. All have in common the quest for a personal identity that is whole and individual, and that, once found, makes all reference to time seem trivial.

And that is the heart of the matter. By combining absolute respect for self with a deep sense of community, Sudbury Valley has put into practice the ideals we struggled for. It is the stuff dreams are made of, brought to life.

For Further Information

ORGANIZATIONS:

National Coalition of Alternative
Community Schools (NCACS)
58 Schoolhouse Road
Summertown, Tennessee 38483
615-964-3670

The Alliance for Parental Involvement in
Education (ALLPIE)
Post Office Box 59
East Chatham, New York 12060-0059
518-392-6900

The Alternative Education Resource
Organization (AERO)
417 Roslyn Road
Roslyn Heights, New York 11577
516-621-2195

The Global Alliance for Transforming
Education (GATE)
4202 Ashwoody Trail
Atlanta, Georgia 30319
404-458-5678

PUBLICATIONS:

SKOLE, The Journal of Alternative Education
72 Philip Street
Albany, New York 12202

The AERO-Gramme
The Alternative Education Resource
Organization
417 Roslyn Road
Roslyn Heights, New York 11577
516-621-2195

Options in Learning
The Alliance for Parental Involvement in
Education
Post Office Box 59
East Chatham, New York 12060-0059
518-392-6900

National Coalition News
National Coalition of Alternative
Community Schools
58 Schoolhouse Road
Summertown, Tennessee 38483
615-964-3670

Holistic Education Review
39 Pearl Street
Brandon, Vermont 05733-1007
802-247-8312

The GATE Newsletter
The Global Alliance for Transforming
Education
4202 Ashwoody Trail
Atlanta, Georgia 30319
404-458-5678

Changing Schools
c/o Colorado Options in Education
98 N. Wadsworth Blvd. #127, Box 191
Lakewood, CO 80226
303-331-9352

Rethinking Schools
1001 E. Keefe Avenue
Milwaukee, WI 53212
414-964-9646

ALTERNATIVE SCHOOLS
listed in this chapter:

Clonlara School
1289 Jewett Street
Ann Arbor, Michigan 48104
313-769-4511

Horizon's Edge School
Shaker Road
Canterbury, New Hampshire 03224

Sudbury Valley School
2 Winch Street
Framingham, Massachusetts 01701
617-877-3030

Summerhill School
Leiston, Suffolk
1P16 4Hy England
0728-830-540

Sussex School
1800 South 2nd West
Missoula, Montana 59801
406-721-1696

The Farm School
50 The Farm
Summertown, Tennessee 38483
615-964-2325

The Neighborhood Schoolhouse
Box 119
Brattleboro, Vermont 05301
802-257-5544

The School Around Us
RR 1, Box 1912, Log Cabin Road
Kennebunkport, Maine 04046
207-967-3143

Uppatinas Resource Center
429 Greenridge Rd
Glenmoore, Pensylvania 19343

BOOKS:

Deal, Terrance E. and Robert R. Nolan
  Alternative Schools: Ideologies, Realities,
  Guidelines (Nelson-Hall, 1978)
Dennison, George *The Lives of Children: The*
  Story of the First Street School (Random
  House, 1969)
Graubard, Allen *Free The Children: Radical*
  Reform and the Free School Movement
  (Pantheon Books, 1972)
Greenberg, Daniel *The Crisis in American*
  Education: An Analysis and A Proposal (The
  Sudbury Valley School Press, 1970)
Greenberg, Daniel *"Announcing a New*
  School..." A Personal Account of the
  Beginnings of The Sudbury Valley School
  (The Sudbury Valley School Press, 1971)
Greenberg, Daniel *Outline of A New*
  Philosophy (The Sudbury Valley School
  Press, 1987)
Greenberg, Daniel *The Sudbury Valley School*
Experience (The Sudbury Valley School
  Press, 1987)
Greenberg, Daniel *Child Rearing* (The
  Sudbury Valley School Press, 1987)
Greenberg, Daniel *Free At Last: The Sudbury*
  Valley School (The Sudbury Valley School
  Press, 1991)
Greenberg, Daniel *A New Look at Schools*
  (The Sudbury Valley School Press, 1991)
Hemmings, Ray *Children's Freedom: A.S.*
  Neill and the Evolution of the Summerhill
  Idea (Schoken Books, 1973)
Hentoff, Nat *Our Children Are Dying*
  (Viking, 1967)
Herndon, James *The Way it Spozed To Be*
  (Simon & Shuster, 1968)
Kohl, Herbert *36 Children* (The New
  American Library, 1967)
Kohl, Herbert *The Open Classroom* (New
  York Review of Books, 1969)
Kozol, Jonathan *Free Schools* (Houghton
  Mifflin, 1972)
Leue, Mary *Challenging the Giant: The Best of*
  SKOLE, The Alternative Education Journal
  (Down-to-Earth Books, 1992)
Miller, Ron *What Are Schools For: Holistic*
  Education in American Culture (Holistic
  Education Press, 1990)
Neill, A. S. *Summerhill* (Hart Publishing,
  1960)
Popenoe, Joshua *Inside Summerhill* (Hart
  Publishing Company, 1970)
Reimer, Eric *School is Dead: Alternatives in*
  Education (Doubleday and Company,
  1971)

CHAPTER SIX

Waldorf - Montessori

Waldorf and Montessori

Rudolf Steiner, an Austrian educator/philosopher/mystic/scientist, and Maria Montessori, an Italian doctor/educator, founded two very influential educational movements around the turn of the century. Today there are over 100 Waldorf schools and approximately 4,000 Montessori schools in this country alone, and both movements continue to influence education in many parts of the world.

Both Montessori and Steiner defined the education of a child as an unfolding, an awakening from within, and both identified several distinct stages of development. They each saw a need to provide a purposefully prepared environment for learning, with strong leadership provided by the teacher and a great deal of structure, regimen, and discipline within the classroom.

And yet both approaches depart from the public school model in their encouragement of individuality and creativity, critical thinking and personal development. Waldorf and Montessori schools are both noted for the enthusiastic participation of the students, and for the lack of a dictatorial atmosphere in the classroom. Teachers and students share a willingness to work together which is all too often lacking in the public school classroom.

By emphasizing wholeness and respect, rather than materialism and control, these movements provide two very hopeful and holistic alternatives to traditional schooling models.

"Both Maria Montessori and Rudolf Steiner recognized that the young child should not be taught cognitive work directly. Montessori said that the child should be taught through the body; hence the wealth of special equipment (not called *toys*) in a Montessori program, for teaching such concepts as geometric shapes, weights and so forth. Steiner went even further and said that concepts shouldn't be taught at all to children before the change of teeth. He placed the emphasis on creative play, imagination, imitation, movement games and fingerplays, crafts and artistic activities until the physical body is more developed and the energy needed for its intense early growth is freed for forming mental pictures and memory work."

Rahima Baldwin in *You Are Your Child's First Teacher*

Rudolf Steiner (1861-1925)

The name "Waldorf Education" derives from the Waldorf-Astoria cigarette factory in Stuttgart, Germany. It was the director of this factory who, in 1919, approached the Austrian social philosopher and visionary Rudolf Steiner with the request to develop a school for the children of his factory workers. Steiner, who had gained a following for his work in spiritual research, was being asked to apply his unique insights to many fields by the students of his social philosophy, including doctors, scientists, artists, farmers, theologians, pastors, businessmen, and teachers.

Steiner trained the faculty of the Waldorf-Astoria school, and developed a curriculum which reflected his belief that a child's development is marked by three seven-year growth periods. Briefly, Steiner believed that from birth to about seven years of age children learn primarily through imitation; that from seven through fourteen years of age the curriculum should focus on and awaken the child's emerging feelings; and that after fourteen the child's developing powers of independent thought should be addressed. Steiner believed that the individual soul of each person should be allowed to develop its capabilities in complete freedom, and that spiritual and cultural matters should be kept separate from the influence of economics or politics. This led him to believe that schools should be run by teachers and parents, and should foster the growth of freedom in children by addressing the growth of the whole person. Steiner wrote, "Our highest endeavor must be to develop free human beings, who are able of themselves to impart purpose and direction to their lives."

Steiner recognized in young children a basic need for an authority figure, who could nurture a relationship with the child based in love and respect. As the child grows older, the need shifts to close association with non-authoritarian adults. Steiner believed that children need to prepare for self-awareness and the capacities for individual judgement and self-expression, and that they need to grow into these abilities gradually. Waldorf schools are designed around this philosophy, and, ideally, a Waldorf teacher accompanies her class from grade to grade, thus maintaining a carefully built and nurtured relationship with the children.

Textbooks are not used in classic Waldorf education, rather the child makes his own books as he progresses through the classes. Early efforts are simply artwork and copying from the teacher's work, but these eventually give way to very individualized volumes reflecting the young author's development. Much of the substance of early Waldorf education is artistic, and includes art, crafts, singing, music and what Steiner called eurythmy — an art form he created in which movement corresponds to musical or spoken sound.

At around the age of nine, as the child develops an awareness of himself as separate from the rest of the world, a need to test authority and push limits calls for study of the outside world. Science, local history and geography, and social relationships are explored, giving the youngster a new focus for his rebellious attitude. Another transition point at about age twelve accompanies the child's physical and emotional development. At this time the child's growing ability for abstraction is presented the challenge of looking beyond his immediate surroundings to the world at large. At each stage of development, the goal of the Waldorf approach is to interest the child, and to satisfy his longings by recognizing their deeper spiritual sources and implications.

Steiner emphasized that education - being a spiritual and cultural concern - should remain free from economic and political influences. He wrote, "One should not ask, 'what does a person need to know and be able to do for the existing social order?' but rather, 'What gifts does a person possess and how may these be developed in him?'" He went on to explain that a new social order should "be alive with that which each fully developed individual brings with him into life," rather than weighted down with the baggage piled on by a society which expects each person to conform to the existing social organization.

Steiner's philosophy is rooted in the belief that we all live within a deeper reality we call spiritual, and that this spirituality is the source of all the world's great religions and teachings. Steiner taught that mankind all but forgot these spiritual realities as our scientifically oriented culture produced a materialistic world view. But Rudolf Steiner (among others) saw the interconnectedness of each phase of mankind's development, and believed that this scientific materialism was a part of the entire process, allowing mankind the chance to develop true inner freedom. Through his influence in education - as well as in medicine, art, business, farming, and other practices - Rudolf Steiner's inspiration has aided in that development.

On Waldorf Education

—— Susan Nelson ————————————————————————

Even if you never quite get the hang of pronouncing "anthropo-sophical," you may find yourself intrigued and perhaps even changed by the writings and practices of Rudolf Steiner and his followers.

Rudolf Steiner lived and worked in Germany from 1861 to 1925. He is reported to have studied and worked in the fields of philosophy, psychology, sociology, agriculture, art, medicine, drama, architecture, and education. He developed a theory of understanding man which he called anthroposophy. The rather inauspicious beginning of the Waldorf education movement was a result of Steiner's being asked, in 1919, by the owner of the Waldorf-Astoria cigarette factory in Stuttgart, Germany, to set up a school for the children of the factory workers--hence the name Waldorf.

Waldorf educator and author Francis Edmunds, in response to a request for a brief statement on Waldorf education, gave this truthful answer: "Since Waldorf education builds on an entirely new consideration of man and since this view of man reaches into all details of the teaching given, aiming at new results, there can be no simple and conclusive answer to such a question."

Since Rudolf Steiner lived only six years beyond the formation of the first Waldorf school, it has been primarily the followers of Steiner who have fashioned from his anthroposophical beliefs the practical methods and basic ideology of the Waldorf schools. Today there are approximately 350 Waldorf schools worldwide. Waldorf teachers feel that it has been especially difficult to gain a foothold for the movement in the United States. There are 71 schools here, located mostly on the east and west coasts. This compares with 71 schools in West Germany, a country roughly half the size of California and with a population only about one-fourth that of the United States. Literature from the Rudolf Steiner College in Fair Oaks, California, however, indicates that there were 175 schools worldwide in 1978 and 350 only seven years later in 1985; statistics which indicate at least a fair growth rate in recent years.

"Our modern knowledge rests on theories and deductions which fail to reveal the true being of man." --Rudolf Steiner, circa 1920. The difficulty in reading literature about Waldorf education for a person with a "modern" education is that there is a decided lack of commonly held definitions for much of the terminology used in these books. It is unrealistic to approach these readings with a purely information gathering motive and expect to make sense out of them. Steiner's statement that "The child is beginning to feel his skeleton. There is not yet harmony between the spirit and the bony system," is an example of the "language gap" which exists between the Waldorf literature and more conventional descriptions of child development.

If the reader is determined, however, to understand what Francis Edmunds termed the "Waldorf impulse," it helps to walk an imaginary mile or two in anthroposophical shoes. That is to say, the reader can cease looking for definable terms and verifiable facts and simply attempt to absorb the message.

Through reading enough Steiner philosophy and descriptive material about Waldorf schools, one comes to understand that the formation of the schools gave substance to the philosophical leanings of Rudolf Steiner. The school was probably not originally intended to play this role, but it is likely that without the Waldorf schools, Rudolf Steiner would be a significantly lesser-known personage than he is presently.

Waldorf education is based on anthroposophy and anthroposophy is based on a belief in reincarnation, specifically, reincarnation taking place in a particular way. According to Steiner, the material of the human body is replaced every seven years and this causes or coincides with a change in mentality. The changes in mental functioning are most pronounced in children. Anthroposophy holds that a child is "not ready for any intellectual pursuits whatsoever" until he or she receives his or her permanent teeth. Another change in thinking occurs at age 13 or 14.

Interestingly enough, these first three stages of mental growth are congruent in terms of years, and somewhat in terms of function, with Piaget's three stages of intellectual development. These stages also parallel Jerome Bruner's three modes of representation or instructional styles designed for children of increasing age. In simple terms, very young children understand actions better than words or symbols; somewhat older (school-age) children can make good use of both pictures and actions; and still older children (from puberty on) can begin to deal with pure abstractions, that is, ideas not represented by pictures or actions. The similarities in Steiner's perceptions of children's developing intellects to contemporary educational theorists would seem to indicate a measure of intuitive observation on Steiner's part which lends some credence to his educational proposals.

Some of the elements of a Waldorf program which distinguish it from more traditional schools are 1) the practice of keeping elementary children with the same teacher for eight years; 2) its emphasis on arts and feelings; 3) the teaching of subjects in "blocks (2 hours per day for 3 to 4 weeks); 4) the teaching of eurythmy; 5) the teaching of writing before reading.

Waldorf educators speak of curriculum relative to the child in this way: curriculum should be developed around a child like the rings around a stone thrown into a pond. Each ring is a little larger and encompasses a little more of the outlying area than the last. Curriculum begins with the immediate environment of the child and moves outward as the child grows and learns. This kind of curriculum avoids topics which have no real meaning for the young child.

The approach to science within the Waldorf method is thought-provoking, and easily understood and applied. The principle idea is to observe creatures and events in nature without disturbing them. So rather than collect insects or leaves of various types and label and display them, a child would be taken outdoors, perhaps with a notebook, to observe the patterns, behaviors, and relationships found in the immediate environment. This method of observation and study can, of course, be applied to geology, meteorology, the health sciences, or any other field of study. The student, in this way, becomes more of a naturalist than a scientist, but perhaps a naturalist will be the most valuable of scientists on a planet which has suffered interference to the point where some scientists fear for the survival of any of its life forms.

Waldorf education also give a great deal of attention to spoken language. One of the ways in which this is done is through the use of literature. There is a delightful practice in Waldorf schools of reading or telling a story many times over so that the children can participate in the story by reciting certain lines. Children can also be given certain "parts" to play within the story. Over a period of time, the story becomes a real possession to the child. Actions and dancing are also incorporated into the story and serve to further enhance its meaning. Eurythmy is a form of movement which is unique to Waldorf education. Nina Sagall, a Waldorf teacher who is trained in this specialized form of movement, describes it as "making visible the sounds of speech, giving form to sound." Eurythmy also incorporates tone and musical sounds.

The Waldorf schools have most likely been sustained by their underpinnings of respect and consideration of the child. Maria Montessori also spoke of the need for respecting the child, and Montessori methods have similarly gained a significant following in the world of education. But the Waldorf people address this basic notion in more religious or philosophical sounding terms, and may use phrases like "nourish the soul" or "speak directly through the feelings to the heart." Whatever the rhetoric, thoughtful and careful treatment of children is likely to engender a following of conscientious parents, wherever and whenever it occurs.

The religious leanings and unscientific language of the Waldorf methodology will almost certainly prevent its ever being given any consideration by public schools. Homeschooling parents, on the other hand, are in an ideal position to be as eclectic as they like in studying and incorporating a variety of philosophies and methodologies.

An easy to read introduction to Waldorf philosophy is Elizabeth Grunelius' *Early Childhood Education and the Waldorf School Plan*. For information regarding Waldorf education and the school-age child, Roy Wilkinson's *Commonsense Schooling* is a concise explanation of the Waldorf philosophy of education. This book also contains a chart which outlines the Waldorf curriculum. In addition, there are two magazines, *Childhood-The Waldorf Perspective*, published in the United States, and *Child and Man*, published in England, which deal with Waldorf methods.

Waldorf literature is anything but easy to locate. Two addresses which may be of help are: Anthroposophic Press, Bell's Pond, Star Route, Hudson, New York 12534 (telephone 518-851-2054); and Rudolf Steiner College, 9200 Fair Oaks Boulevard, Fair Oaks, California 95628 (telephone 916-961-8727). There is also a correspondence course for homeschoolers which offers a variety of independent study services based on the Waldorf approach to education. Write to Oak Meadow School, PO Box 712, Blacksburg, VA 24060.

Teaching the Waldorf Way:
Finding Resources to Support
the Waldorf Approach to Education

Finding resources for and about Waldorf Education can be as simple as a trip to your local library or bookstore. Rudolf Steiner was a prolific writer, and many of his books and articles are still widely available. Waldorf Education has also became one of the more popular alternatives to public schooling and the traditional private school, and if you live in a large metropolitan area there may be a Waldorf school located near you which could become a primary resource.

For those seeking publications on the Waldorf approach to education there is *Childhood*, a quarterly magazine providing a format for sharing ideas on holistic and spiritual alternatives in parenting, schooling, and homeschooling with a focus on the Waldorf philosophy of child development, Waldorf inspired initiatives, and intuitive parenting. Filled with articles on teaching and learning, parenting, handwork, festivals, and children's books, *Childhood* is a helpful source of ideas and inspiration. For example, this excerpt from an article by Ruth Bruns in the Summer/Fall, 1991 issue: "The formative pattern of life's journey is reflected in the yearly cycle. In the Spring we rise into the light, Summer sees us drinking in life's activities, and by Autumn we have the opportunity to begin the evaluation process. Fall is the maturing time of the year. We harvest our share of life's experiences and glean from them the kernels of Truth, Beauty, and Goodness."

The Peridot is a tabloid biannual, an independent newspaper published by the Rudolf Steiner Educational Association of Florida, Inc., a secular, non-profit organization whose major purpose is the support of the Waldorf School of Gainesville, Florida. *The Peridot* is produced to inspire, stimulate and share creative educational ideas which harmonize with the education and development of the whole child. Articles usually cover educational views, festivals and celebrations, crafts, fairy tales, calendar activities, nature and much more.

An article by Mark T. Brown and Barbara J. Reilly in the Spring/Summer, 1990 issue of *The Peridot* explains the value of a Waldorf Education: "We believe there is a rhythm to life and that it needs to be reinforced in all areas of life: from the daily activities of learning, playing and sharing, to the yearly seasons, to the cycles of human aging. In all of these things the Waldorf educational philosophy also believes. In no other educational environment does the education of the total child--head, hands, and heart--receive such attention. The Waldorf approach stresses a strict order and methodological approach that is tuned to the child and the rhythms of childhood. The progression of academic subjects and the complexity with which they are tackled is synchronized with early childhood development. The subjects taught are not much different from other schools except that art, music and two foreign languages are considered as important as math and reading. The differences are in the order in which they are presented and the techniques employed to enlighten and maintain the child's interest."

In the introduction to her Waldorf-inspired book on child development and child-centered awareness, titled *You Are Your Child's First Teacher*, Rahima Baldwin writes, "We need not another authority or set of rules by which to raise children, but a new way of seeing and understanding the human being. If we can enlarge our understanding of child and adult development to encompass the whole human being -- body, mind, emotions and spirit -- then we will be best equipped to make our decisions based on a combination of cognitive and intuitive knowledge."

This book takes a unique viewpoint that addresses the total picture of the child as a developing human being - inspired by the teachings of Rudolf Steiner and his Waldorf approach to education. Steiner taught that "Our highest endeavor must be to develop free human beings, who are able of themselves to impart direction and purpose to their lives." With a thorough explanation of incarnation - that Steiner-inspired awareness of the gradual process of unfolding and achieving adult consciousness - the author explains the developmental stages of childhood and how we as parents can respond to them in the most loving and welcoming ways.

Rahima Baldwin is the mother of three children and is a Waldorf early childhood teacher. She is the author of *Special Delivery*, co-author of *Pregnant Feelings*, and the founder of Informed Homebirth/Informed Birth and Parenting, a national nonprofit organization providing workshops for childbirth educators, midwives, and parents. In *You Are Your Child's First Teacher* she offers counsel and advice as from a warm and caring friend, never condescending or authoritative, but encouraging, supportive, suggesting new approaches and offering her own experiences for consideration.

There is an emphasis throughout the book on the child's process of unfolding. For example: "It is obvious that children do not reason as adults do. They are able to come up with amazing statements, both about how the world works and about how something they shouldn't have done managed to happen. Logical thought and problem-solving ability are slow to develop. Very young toddlers lack "object permanence" and will look for an object where they have repeatedly found it hidden rather than in the place where they have just seen you put it. Children before the age of six lack the ability for what Piaget calls "concrete operational thinking." Rational thinking does not develop until age ten or eleven as observed in Piaget's studies. So it has long been documented that the ability to reason and to think logically is a gradually unfolding power that children grow into. As adults we have forgotten what it was like to live in a nonlinear, nonsequential world. We expect to be able to reason with our children as soon as they are verbal. We reason with them about everything from their behavior and its consequences to why the sea is salty. And indeed, some five-year-olds show great ability to conduct such conversations with their parents - but they have learned it through imitating years of that type of interaction with their parents. Young children do not yet think rationally, and reason has little impact on changing their behavior."

Other books about the Waldorf approach to education include the *Waldorf Parenting Handbook* by Lois Cusick (St. George Publications, 1984), which includes a section on early childhood and a complete description of the Waldorf curriculum. Check your local library or bookstore.

Maria Montessori (1870-1952)

Born in Chiaravelle, Italy, in 1870, Maria Montessori graduated with a degree in medicine from the University of Rome, the first Italian woman to gain the degree of medical doctor. In 1899 she began a study of the problems of handicapped children. Working on lines first laid down by the French physician E. Seguin, she achieved startling results, and the children under her tutelage passed the state examinations in reading and writing for normal children. Dr. Montessori concluded that similar methods might be applied even more successfully to younger normal children, and she began to work with toddlers in private and public schools in Rome. Traditional schools in Europe were dominated by authoritative teachers, and she encountered opposition from proponents of the orthodox system of education. Her method encouraged freedom of movement, and was considered destructive of discipline, but she was warmly supported by the enthusiastic reformers of her day.

For her times, Maria Montessori had very foresighted and modern ideas about children, introducing such revolutionary concepts as child-sized furniture and the notion that a young child could be interested in exploring his environment. She believed that children of 3, 4, and 5 have one intuitive aim: "self-development." She maintained that progress should always proceed from the simple to the complex, from the concrete to the abstract.

From 1900 to 1907 Montessori lectured on pedagogical anthropology at the University of Rome. In 1909 her work led to the publishing of *Scientific Pedagogy as Applied to Education in the Children's Houses*. Describing her work with special education treatments and a prepared environment, this book attracted great interest in the United States, but the popular beliefs at the time included the notion of "fixed intelligence," that heredity alone determined a child's development. Many people felt that the extensive study and training in special methods were not warranted for preschool age children.

But as Maria Montessori continued her work and founded the first Montessori schools in Europe, she developed a following in many parts of the world. In 1915 she was enthusiastically welcomed to America, where she lectured and taught, and where a Montessori class was set up at the San Francisco World Exposition of 1915. She returned to Europe, and was appointed government inspector of schools in Italy in 1922.

Maria Montessori lectured in many countries, supervising training courses in Spain, India, England, and the Netherlands. She received many honors for her work, and died in 1952 at the age of eighty-one.

Three books by Maria Montessori on her methods were first published in English as *The Montessori Method* (1912), *Dr. Montessori's Own Handbook* (1914), and *The Advanced Montessori Method* (1917). Her major works have been republished, many in paperback, and her later books, related to those on her method, include *The Absorbent Mind* (1967) and *The Discovery of the Child* (1967).

Maria Montessori believed that education begins at birth, and that the first few years of life are especially important. She felt that since these are the most formative years, both physically and emotionally, even the smallest baby should be cuddled and talked to and exposed to a wide variety of experiences. She felt that too few people saw the baby as an intelligent human being, capable of great learning abilities. Her "discovery of the child" was a true awakening and advancement in early childhood education. She called the young child's mind "the absorbent mind" because of its great ability to learn and to grow from interactions with the world around it. Believing that the child absorbs learning from his environment, Montessori created the "prepared environment," but was quick to point out that "the environment should reveal the child, not mold him."

Montessori felt that there should be freedom in the prepared environment for the child to develop his own physical, mental, and spiritual growth. She stressed the need for beauty and quality in the materials a child was exposed to. And she felt that the primary duty of the teacher was to observe, to gently guide the child and to keep his enthusiasm for learning high, rather than to tediously instruct and demand conformation. She felt it was important to nurture a respect for the child and his privacy.

In a classic Montessori school four primary areas of development are addressed: care of self and the environment, sensory and motor education, reading and writing skills, and premath teaching. A key component of Montessori education is encouraging students to exercise self-motivation and self-education. The kinds of fantasy and imaginative free play generally associated with young children are not encouraged, and emphasis is placed on the proper use of tools and materials. Children at a traditional Montessori school are often industriously engaged in their "work" while the teacher maintains a low background profile. An article in *The New York Times*, Sunday, October 4, 1964 described a Montessori classroom as "...a place of almost mysterious silence and concentration. A visitor finds 20 or more tots bending over some private occupation in deep absorption like so many doctoral candidates researching their theses."

This seeming regimentation of the young child's education has been soundly criticized by many, who claim that those children who exhibit individuality or a rambunctious nature are summarily dropped out or transferred from the program. But while the austerity and regimentation of of the traditional Montessori classroom have caused concern, Maria Montessori's teachings and writings have generated a widespread respect and admiration for her work. Her ideas were revolutionary seventy-five years ago and many can see in her writings an important message for today. In her book *The Absorbent Mind* she writes, "The immense influence that education can exert through children has the environment for its instrument, for the child absorbs his environment, takes everything from it, and incarnates it in himself. With his unlimited possibilities, he can well be the transformer of humanity, just as he is its creator. The child brings us a great hope and a new vision. There is much that we teachers can do to bring humanity to a deeper understanding, to a higher well-being, and to a greater spirituality."

Montessori Curriculum

—— Susan Stephenson ——————————————————

Curriculum, in Montessori language, refers to the child's complete path through the first twelve years of life. It is the continuing study of how each child lives and learns much more than it is an outline of what he must learn.

How? Independence, concentration, and purposeful activity are some of the guideposts along this path. Giving a baby, the young child, the middle child, freedom to explore, respecting his concentration in whatever he has chosen to work on, providing activities that command the use of his brain and hands at the same time, all these things are part of the curriculum at all ages.

What? No matter what the child's potential or future vocation, Montessori believed in giving him an overview of how the Earth was created and how every living and non-living thing and every situation came to be from the very beginning to the present and with thought to the future. Life is presented as a great puzzle with every piece, including each child, playing a vital part for the functioning of the whole.

This is called "Cosmic Education." This part of the curriculum is divided into five "Great Lessons:" The Creation of the Earth, The Coming of Plants and Animals, The Coming of Man and His Tools: Language, and Math and Invention.

Before the age of seven, the child is invited, never required, to participate in motor and sensorial (not intellectual) activities within this curriculum which are fun, fulfilling, and appropriate to his or her age and development.

Between the ages of six and twelve, the child is required to do only that work which is required by the state's board of education. Beyond that they are free to explore, inspired by a very well-trained Montessori "directoress," in whichever directions his or her natural talents and interests may lead.

In the first few weeks of each year in the 6-12 class, the five "great lessons" are presented with experiments, timelines, charts, etc., to the whole group. These inspire the children to further research on their own or in small groups which they may form. It becomes obvious that everything man may choose to study has a relationship to everything else. An interest in one subject can lead to an interest in almost anything else.

In the Montessori Elementary Class, age 6-12, almost nothing is required but that the child work, because that is what will fulfill him or her. The choice of work, for the most part, is left to the child. There is an exception: whatever the state wherein the child resides requires, very basically, must be met. It is the teacher's job to find out what it is, have it available, and help each child develop his or her own method for scheduling and recording this work.

The first lessons in the Formation of the Earth come from nature... non-verbal experiences of the sun and wind, playing in sand and water and mud, seeing the sun rise and set, watching the stars at night, visiting the seashore, the child's own collection of rocks, sorted by color, size, type and texture. A rich first environment and time to explore and observe are the best inspiration.

This is not the age for many explanations and discussions. Instead we place in the environment sensorial materials for the child to work with as much as he or she desires, in that way absorbing the basic principles which will lead to later interest in the study of the creation of the earth.

A solar system mobile can be hung in a gentle breeze in a baby's room. Puzzle maps give practice in recognizing the shapes of continents, countries, and oceans. A globe or wall map can be referred to whenever a part of the world is brought up in the family and classroom. Sand and water play can be a vehicle for discovering islands, lakes, bays, mountains, and other land and water forms. The infant and young child's exploration of the world and their work and play with magnets, bubbles, electric circuits, and objects which sink and float will teach them about the basic principles which were active in the past and which are active in the present and always changing the earth.

Experiments, models, charts, research papers, field trips, reports which may include poetry, drama, dance and any other form of creativity, express the child's research and understanding of The Creation of the Earth. The 6-12 teacher gives a presentation in the beginning of each year which may last for days, in which he presents the story of the creation. With charts and experiments ending with the explosion of a volcano, he shows how all the elements follow the will of God (or whatever his teacher wishes to call the divine source of this miracle) in this wonderful creation.

Some elements are attracted to each other, some repel, some particles flow and fill every nook and cranny and some flow upward into the air, but each obey the laws of nature written for it, and plays its particular part, fulfilling its Cosmic Task.

The work that inspired this First Great Lesson continues through the year as children study Physics and Chemistry, Geology and Astronomy, whatever direction each chooses to go. The teacher does not require specific work, but guides the children as individuals or self-formed groups in doing research following their own interests, and in creating and finishing research projects and in finding a way to express them.

The Second Great Lesson, The Coming of Plants and Animals, begins with a great, inspiring lesson given in the beginning of the year with experiments, charts, stories, a long timeline of the evolution of plants and animals from the beginning to the present, all "Keys" to inspire the child's own research.

The work revolves around the evolution of plants and animals, their needs and how they are satisfied, the functions of the organisms and their various parts, and the classification of the amazing and wonderful variety of life on earth.

A nature table in the home or classroom, changed in some small way daily, is a good place for children to put special treasures--rocks, eggshells, a vase of wildflowers, a piece of bark--and for the adult to bring something special to the attention of the child, a sprouting seed, "phototropism" (a plant growing toward the sunlight), any lesson or experiment. This table can get very dirty, but the child can learn to care for it, to empty and wash it. After all, we are showing them the beauty of nature. The child above the age of six, who wants to know the inside workings of everything will be interested in dissecting flowers, plants, and a dead animal found in the garden. This is very appropriate for this age but would be disturbing for a younger child.

At all ages children can express their experiences in nature in art forms--drawings, paintings, stories, sculpture, poetry, drama, etc., and beautiful and scientific books can aid them as far as they wish to go in research and discovery and creative expression.

In the beginning of each year the Third Great Lesson, The Arrival of Man, is presented, introducing the study of man with charts, timelines and research guides. The child moves from the general to the specific: At age 6-8 the emphasis is on prehistoric life, the development of the physical environment and plants and animals. At age 8-10 the emphasis is on early civilizations, from tribal cultures to the development of cities. At age 10-12 the emphasis is on the child's national and state history. Of course all of these studies are going on at the same time and the child is free to follow his or her interests, no matter what the age.

In a Montessori school the history of man on Earth is taught through the study of the physical and spiritual needs and the mental tendencies of man. The physical needs are food, clothing, shelter, transportation and defense. The spiritual needs: self respect and self love, love of others (culture), creative love (art), and the love of God (religion). The mental tendencies are: exploration, orientation order, exacting work, perfection, invention and communication.

The history of man is studied both objectively and subjectively. For example as the child learns about how man obtained food in the past, he learns to grow and prepare that and other food. As he learns about clothing of the past, he may learn to knit or make costumes. As he learns of the famous and not famous explorers of the past, he himself explores in many directions. He studies the arts of the past while developing his own musical and other artistic talents and while studying the cultures and religions of the past he is, at the same time, exploring his own relationships and ways to express love to friends, family, and to God.

The Fourth Great Lesson introduces the exciting exploration of Language. It is given in the beginning of each year in the 6-12 class to touch the imagination and start children on their research. Through stories, charts and beautiful, carefully chosen books, we enable children to see the path traced by language, the growth and development of language - through travel, colonization, commerce, war, etc.; how man has given a name to everything he has found or made and how this process continues; how language changes; and that language is an expression of the creative force of man.

And, for the child's own use of language, we do not require him to read and write every day, but we must fire his imagination in all subjects so that he thirsts for information and is forced by this to explore through reading and to express, record and communicate his discoveries.

When a child is first beginning to read words, we do not ask that this be done aloud. That would add another complication and frustration. Instead we give him a few handwritten labels to match a few objects of which we are sure he knows the name. This is called "The Object Box." He goes on to read the labels to hundreds of objects in picture form--household items, plants, animals, and so forth. The child can check to see if he has done this correctly by adding a second card with the label on it. These are called "classified reading cards" or "three part cards." He then goes on to match sentences and paragraphs to pictures. It is not until much later that children are asked to read aloud, and then with drama and expression.

In The Fifth Great Lesson, in the beginning of each year the elementary children are introduced, with stories, books, and examples, to the exciting history of math. Objects were first kept track of, not by counting, but by comparisons, a notch made in a piece of wood as each sheep returned home, a stone put in place for every member of the group. When actual counting began it was associated with parts of the body, as in base ten from man's ten fingers. It is important that we help the children realize that mathematics has evolved and is still evolving from a practical need and the spoken and written language of math from the need to communicate that which was calculated. Geometry arose from the practical need for reestablishing planting boundaries after the annual flooding of the Nile in Egypt. In "geometry," "geo" stands for "earth" and "metry" for "measure." Children of this age love to reach back into history with their imaginations and reconstruct these needs and solutions and the creation of language. The Hindus introduced the use of zero--let the child try and do math without it! As a result of this lesson, the children will want to invent their own math and geometry. They will make up their own problems for themselves and their friends and come to a very clear understanding of the function and value of this area of knowledge.

There are hundreds of kinds of Montessori classes for children. The use of the word "Montessori" can mean that the school has bought Montessori materials and no one has any training, or it can mean that it has the best teachers in the world and the happiest children. It is very important that you go and observe and see if it is what you expected from your readings or from hearing about Montessori schools. A teacher can have the best training and a school can have the best materials, but if the children are not happy, kind and busy on self-chosen uninterrupted work, your child will not experience all the wonderful benefits of attending a real Montessori school.

The other aspects of the school, cost, administration, parent involvement, are as varied as any other type of school. Some are private, some religious, some magnet schools within public school systems. In all these areas look for what you want and need and choose carefully. Your child will be entering a second family.

For Further Information

MONTESSORI:

American Montessori Society
150 Fifth Avenue
New York, New York 10011

Association Montessori Internationale
1095 Market Street
San Francisco, California 94103

International Montessori Society
912 Thayer Avenue
Silver Spring, Maryland 20910

North American Montessori Teacher's
Association
2859 Scarborough Road
Cleveland Heights, Ohio 44118

American Montessori Publishing
P.O. Box 5062
Rossmoor, CA 90721

Publications:

Public School Montessorian
230 10th Avenue South
Minneapolis, Minnesota 55415

Michael Olaf's Essential Montessori
Post Office Box 1162
Arcata, California 95521
707-826-1557

Books:

Gettman, David *Basic Montessori*
(Christopher Helm, Ltd., 1987)
Hainstock, Elizabeth *The Essential Montessori*
(New American Library, 1978)
Kramer, Rita *Maria Montessori: A Biography*
(Addison Wesley, 1988)
Montessori, Maria *The Absorbent Mind*
(1967)
Montessori, Maria *The Discovery of the Child*
(1967)
Montessori, Maria *From Childhood to
Adolescence* (Schoken Books, 1948, 1973)
Orem, R.C. *A Montessori Handbook* (G.P.
Putnam's Sons, 1065)
Spietz, Heidi Anne *Montessori at Home*
(American Montessori Publishing, 1988)
Spietz, Heidi Anne *Montessori at Home I - 6-9
Years* (Am. Montessori Publishing, 1989)

Spietz, Heidi Anne *Montessori at Home II -
10-12 Years* (American Montessori
Publishing, 1990)
Standing, E.M. *Maria Montessori: Her Life
and Work* (New American Library, 1984)

WALDORF:

Organizations:

Anthroposophic Press
Bell's Pond, Star Route
Hudson, New York 12534
518-851-2054

Assocation of Waldorf Schools of North
America
17 Hemlock Hill
Great Barrington, Massachusetts 01230

Rudolf Steiner Institute
Post Office Box 1925
New York, New York 10025

Rudolf Steiner College
9200 Fair Oaks Boulevard
Fair Oaks, California 95628
916-961-8727

Waldorf Institute
260 Hungry Hollow Road
Spring Valley, New York 10977

Waldorf Teacher Training Program
Antioch/New England Graduate School
Roxbury Street
Keene, New Hampshire 03431

Publications:

Childhood
Route 2, Box 2675
Westford, Vermont 05494

Child and Man
6334 Gaston Avenue, Suite 212
Dallas, Texas 75214

The Peridot
921 S.W. Depot Avenue
Gainesville, Florida 32601
904-375-6291

Waldorf Kindergarten Newsletter
9500 Brunett Avenue
Silver Spring, Maryland 20901

Books:

Baldwin, Rahima, *You Are Your Child's First Teacher* (Celestial Arts, 1989)
Cusick, Lois, *Waldorf Parenting Handbook* (St. George Publications, 1984)
Edmunds, Francic L., *Rudolf Steiner Education* (Anthroposophic Press, 1987)
Grunelius, Elizabeth, *Early Childhood Education and the Waldorf School Plan* (Waldorf School Monographs, 1974)

Hahn, Herbert, *From the Well-Springs of the Soul* (Rud. Steiner Schools Fellowship, 1966)
Harwood, A.C., *The Recovery of Man in Childhood* (Anthroposophic Press, 1958)
Masters, Brian, *Rudolf Steiner Waldorf Education* (Steiner Schools Fellowship, 1986)
Steiner, Rudolf, *The Education of the Child* (Rudolf Steiner Press, 1965)
Steiner, Rudolf, *The Essentials of Education* (Rudolf Steiner Press, 1948)
Steiner, Rudolf, *A Study of Man* (Anthroposopic Press, 1947)

CHAPTER SEVEN

High School and Higher Education

Continuing the Learning

For the child who has been alternatively educated, higher education is not necessarily defined as going on to college. When a child has spent his life learning at home, in an alternative community school, or in a Waldorf or Montessori school, the tremendous variety of opportunities in the world becomes somehow more available, more accessible, and more appealing than it is to the student who has spent his or her life within the regimen of public school. The alternatively educated child knows that there are often many different ways of arriving at the same goal, and he or she will seek them out with enthusiasm. And that may or may not include the help of an educational institution such as college.

For those who do wish to pursue a college education, an alternative education can be a tremendous asset. Having been taught to challenge the system, to think creatively, and to believe in and rely on their own abilities, these students often excel in the academic atmosphere of college.

Finding an apprenticeship or a mentoring situation, embarking on travels, taking college courses by correspondence, building a business, volunteering and community service work, or simply continuing to explore life on one's own are all paths to a higher education.

"Don't sell your books and keep your diplomas. Sell your diplomas, if you can get anyone to buy them, and keep your books."
Walter B. Pitkin

Exploring Life Without College

—— Britt Barker ————————————————————————————

After twenty years of life, most of which have been lived outside of institutionalized settings, I find myself now mixing with
those raised more within the systems of our society. Having lived
away from the mainstream, one of the most popular questions I
am asked is in reference to my schooling: "If you could change one
thing about your upbringing, what would you change?" People
are very interested to find out if I would have gone to school, had
my parents "let" me. They always look eager when I reply, "Yes,
there is one thing, but only one, that I would change in my life up
to this point..." and they are often surprised when I tell them that
if anything, I wish I hadn't attended school the three years that I
did. It's not that I really have so many feelings about those few
years of school (they actually bring back no vivid memories at all),
but I find it is a way of helping people understand that I have no
regrets about not having attended school since I was nine years
old.

Being educated at home was simply the way I lived my life and
I never gave it a great deal of thought. Now that I'm spending
more and more of each year away from my family, I find this is an
aspect of my life that many are interested in. While traveling
through Switzerland in November, 1986, I met a Canadian film
producer who even wanted to do a documentary about my homeschooled life! He liked the combination of homeschooling, my
deep love for classical music and my non-electrified farm life. This
was the first time I began to think about the fact that my life had
been any different.

Not being in school through the years has enabled me the time
to pursue interests that the demands of high school or college
would have rendered difficult, if not impossible. Traveling and
naturalist work are two areas of interest that have caused me to
leave my cozy farmstead and explore the world beyond my warm
family nest.

My first naturalist opportunity beyond the farm came my way
through John Holt (author of many books on alternative learning).
I had asked him for ideas about work in the field of biology, beyond schools or government agencies. He put me in touch with
naturalist writer/artist Aleta Karstad and her field biologist hus-

band, Fred Schueler. I joined them in travels across Canada, camping in their van and gathering data for the new book they were doing on endangered habitats across the north country. My time with these two good people was a wonderful first step from my home. I learned much about watercolor art from Aleta and was able to put it to use with sketching in making my journals come to life. From Fred I learned of field data-collecting as I peeled snake specimens from the road, recorded measurement data, caught crayfish and frogs. Fred and Aleta had been trained to dissect their world as part of their biological research technique. My entire existence had always been one of integrating the world - seeing it as a whole. I found myself wanting to reject the field of biology if this was what it meant. So, in spite of the affection I had for the Karstad-Schuelers, I decided to leave them after my apprenticeship. I rejoined my family on one of their backpacking treks in the Chisos mountains of the Texas-Mexico border. Back with my family, I again became immersed in my music and my love for the natural world.

After a few months on the farm, I found myself again drawn to the wild. This time I was to join a team of Italian biologists as they tracked wolves in the Appenines mountains of central Italy. I loved working with the Italians. They seemed to experience the world as a whole as they gathered data and analyzed the animals they were studying. My time in Italy was exciting and enlightening, as were the following seven weeks of travel throughout Europe and Britain (recounted in detail in *Letters Home*, published by Home Education Press, 1990).

I returned home with a clearer idea of what I wanted to pursue and a little more informed about my world beyond the farmstead. Two months after my return from Europe I was off again, studying shorebirds in Bodega Bay, California. I found these winged creatures a delight to work with as I learned of different field techniques. Focusing on Dunlin, we mist-netted these little birds at night out on the salt marsh in which they roosted. We disentangled them, then weighed and took them back to the lab for measurements and banding before releasing them. This work was of a "hands on" type more than the observational experience with the wolves. I further developed my identification skills, enabling me to take in my surroundings with a new awareness. An awareness not as pure and perfect as just being, but one which would make me useful as a "field technician." How awakening it was to learn of the abundant life thriving beneath the mud, completing the cycle, as those lively winged creatures flitted above. Such an intricate ecological balance!

The biology graduate students I met on the shorebird project directed me to Point Reyes Bird Observatory, a good place, I was told, to gain experience in this work. My friend Sarah arranged for me to interview with the head biologist at the Bird Observatory who soon discovered that I had no college degree, no high school records, no graduate program I was pursuing. He then had to interview just me, the person sitting before him. We discussed my previous experiences with animals and I felt the importance of "common sense" to be much greater than that of "chemistry." From that interview I was hired to work at the Palomarin field station for ten weeks, beginning in September. So far I had found that, if anything, my not being in school made me available at time when other people were not.

While at Palomarin I found that I could integrate my life to include all of the things I loved. During six hours of five days each week I ran mist nets. This meant checking each of twenty nets every thirty minutes or so, disentangling any birds, bringing them back to the banding lab where they were weighed, measured, checked for fat content, wing wear, molt and age before being banded and released. Other times I biked the four miles of enormous coastal hills into the town of Bolinas to practice the piano or listen to chamber recitals. I jogged along the beautiful coastline; played Bach on my guitar with wonderful seaside acoustics; sketched the things around me, bringing them intimately closer through careful observation; and wrote of the things I loved for my local Ohio newspaper, sharing my experiences with others. I was also able to take advantage of the local library which gave me a chance to delve into the minds of great thinkers.

From my work at the Palomarin Bird Observatory I was offered a position working with elephant seals on the Farallon Islands, 30 miles off the coast of San Francisco. I agreed to work a six week position through December to mid-January. Between the two California jobs, I joined my family in the beautiful canyon country of the southwest for six weeks of invigorating hiking. It was during this time that I "stumbled" across yet another opportunity. While attempting to arranging a flight from the mountains of the Big Bend/Rio Grande area to El Paso, I fell to talking about birds with a pilot whom I learned had spent over 1000 hours tracking bald eagles from the air. Since one of my passions is the joy of flight, I jumped at this idea... and before I knew it, I was on a team of biologists radio-tracking these magnificent birds along the Verde River in Arizona. I would join these biologists and their leader with his own airplane and love of flight, as soon as I finished working on the island...

Spending six weeks on the 100 acre Farallon Islands, with no other people except for the three biologists I was working with, was a memorable experience. I worked with massive two-ton male elephant seals, creeping up behind the sleeping animals to mark and tag them. I immersed myself in creating a harmony, in attuning all of my senses to the rhythms of the island. It was here that I had a chance, had the clarity of mind, to stand back and take a close look at what I was doing with my life. Sitting atop the lighthouse hill, surrounded by the vast blueness of the Pacific Ocean with a thousand gulls riding the wind currents around me, I was able to explore life beyond ordinary reality. I became more aware of myself and my position in life's great web.

Had I ever before thought that perhaps my ready acceptance of biological positions was becoming an "institution" in itself? Perhaps I was narrowing myself by diving into the parameters of "field technician"? Sitting near a great rock we called Raven's Cliff on West End Island, I had a flashing thought which I had to write down: "...I look out upon a constant rolling, musical sea and brown rocks jutting to meet its white spraying surf. A gull stands upon a rock and, in a sudden instant, looks like a man. A human being standing there and immersing himself in the ancient rhythms of eternal song. And I think of how many times I have done just that as a young child, have greatly loved the laughter of nature. And yet, it seems that as I go deeper into these opportune jobs in field biology, perhaps I am losing something precious - something essential. That love which so fills me with happiness for life, sometimes slips away as I become too busy with the nearly habitual processes like data collecting..."

Am I becoming dissatisfied with my life? No, I am exploring the meaning, attending carefully to each thing I do. I am realizing that one can become institutionalized in very subtle ways. I have always seen life as something to be loved and when I do something, I examine closely "is this exactly what I want to be doing," continuing only when I can answer truthfully "yes." What else is life for, except to grow in love, to flow in perfect harmony both within and without?

From six weeks of glorious solitude on the island, I flew inland to the desert and reservoir area of the Verde River, Arizona. Here

I adjusted myself to the pattern of a bald eagle pair, following their daily actions from dawn until dusk as they built their nest, foraged and lived their free life. I camped with three other biologists, in the field for ten consecutive days, our site accessible only by boat. Other days I flew the airplane for hours while my boss tracked the eagles below us.

The more I thought, however, the more doubtful I was about this "line of work." Why, exactly, did I love field technician work? I examined my reasons: to observe closely the lives of our wild kin, and to be near the earth, doing "meaningful" work. I began to realize that I could follow these loves of mine without stopping every five minutes to jot down data, without disentangling captured birds from nets, without disturbing the birthing elephant seals by constant making and tagging... Was my Love becoming a trap encouraged by society's labels? I think about the opportunities open to me in this field: work at an Australian Bird Observatory, work with red deer in the Hebrides... and yet I must follow my own deepest feelings, keep my mind as open and fertile as it was cultivated to be when I was very young outside of the institution of school.

I have just returned from Costa Rica, a glorious venture into the tropical lushness, the cultural vitality of the south. Near-future plans take me to the farthest reaches of the globe as I feel a need to touch various cultures in other parts of our earth, my home. What is more important at this time than exploring life, tangibly experiencing this fragile planet upon which we live? I continue to flow with life as I have always done, living each day to its fullest. I am grateful for everything life has given me and delve with appreciation into its offerings as I move ahead.

High School at Home--Away From Home

—— Donn Reed ————————————————————————

The many challenges of homeschooling seem to multiply as our children reach adolescence. Responding to inner biological clocks, pre-set when civilization was much simpler, our teenagers may feel ready to leave the family nest long before we think they're adequately prepared for the larger world.

Most of us have several well-meaning relatives who won't hesitate to remind us that "You have to let them go sometime," but the question remains: When?

Cathy, our oldest, made the journey through adolescence and high school at home with relative ease. She had part-time jobs, social activities, and close friends. At 17, she received our Brook Farm School diploma with our full confidence that she was a mature and responsible young adult. Now 20, she has lived and worked near home and away, has travelled in Mexico, and is now back home for a while. She enjoys independence but still also enjoys our family life.

Karen, at 16, was much more restless; she felt smothered by country life and by high school at home. Rural friends and small-town jobs didn't interest her, she longed for the fast-paced glitter and excitement of New York City. Academically, she had completed all high school subjects with great success, but we felt she needed more mental and moral growth before tackling any big city on her own. She compromised by staying with relatives for a while, but soon rebelled and left them. As we had feared, the big city was ready to eat her alive. When we brought her home a year later, her dreams and determination had become near-disaster and resignation. That summer, she sorted herself out, then entered college, and is now earning top grades in several difficult subjects.

Susan, now 16, has become increasingly insistent about her need for more than we can give her - and we agree with her. Meeting her academic needs is easy, but our isolated family life can no longer meet her social and psychological needs. Most of her friends dislike learning, and have few interests beyond soap operas, rock stars, and weekend "parties." Susan has argued for permission to go to a public school, and we have refused. Like many schools, the local high school is impoverished intellectually and morally. We seemed to be facing a dilemma, with no solution in sight.

In desperation, we sent for catalogs of several boarding schools. One by one, they arrived - slick booklets with glossy photographs of laughing students, expensive buildings, and spotless dormitories; promises of excellence in college preparation - and tuition fees greater than our annual income.

Nearly lost in the fancy avalance was a small brochure which seemed to have the answer - not only for us, but perhaps for many other homeschoolers.

The Meeting School, in Rindge, New Hampshire, founded by Quakers in 1957, seemed to be exactly what we wanted - a small, friendly environment with strong moral values but without religious dogmas or indoctrination; a school with a philosophy of learning very similar to our own, with emphasis on development of the whole person - mental, physical, emotional, social, and spiritual.

Could such a school really exist? We decided to find out. With Cathy in Mexico and Karen in Florida, and leaving Jean and Derek to tend the cows and chickens, Susan and I tossed our suitcases into the car and set out for the beautiful hills of southern New Hampshire.

In the next week, I visited the school five times, and Susan was invited to spend several days and nights, living and working with the students. Both of us found the school to be everything we had hoped it would be, and more.

Physically, The Meeting School is not impressive. It's a small collection of old farm buildings - six rambling houses, a shop, two science laboratories, two greenhouses, a pottery shed, and a barn - surrounded by 150 acres of fields and woods. The house furnishings are simple and rustic. Housekeeping is clean and neat, but not fussy. Clothing styles are similar, ranging from neat-but-not-fussy to wrinkled-and-baggy. If you're looking for spotless dorms and rigid dress codes, don't look here.   The number of students varies, from about 20 to 30; the student-teacher ratio is about four to one. Faculty members, many of whom have preschool children, share their homes with the students. Members of each household - teachers and students - live and work together as a family, sharing equally in daily chores, cooking, cleaning, and decision-making. The students help care for the preschool children.

Formal titles and deference to arbitrary authority are as scarce as floor wax and neckties, but the principles of cooperation and peaceful resolution of conflicts are interwoven throughout all aspects of the school's community life.

Students are moved to high academic standards by stimulation rather than competition. The main classes of each trimester are centered around a particular theme - such as Biology, Physics, or Writing - which is then emphasized in many aspects of academic and community life.

The school's academic and work programs are flexible, encouraging self-motivation, allowing the pursuit of independent studies, and balancing family, social, and academic life.

Before my first visit was over, I found myself wishing we had discovered The Meeting School two or three years ago; in many ways, it's almost an extension of our own homeschool. The similarities are so many, in fact, that I wasn't surprised when one of the teachers told me that the school is now actively seeking enrollment by homeschoolers.

"Many teenagers are ready for independence from their own families," he said, "but still need some adult guidance. The family-centered living at The Meeting School offers a stable and nurturing environment, in which students can find their own identities and develop internal controls and integrity."

The teacher agreed that the cost of the school, although much lower than that of most boarding schools, may be prohibitive for many homeschoolers. On the other hand, no applicant is ever refused because of financial need. Although the school is very poor - in term of money - many students are granted financial aid, and the school is even willing sometimes to trade some tuition costs for goods or labor.

"That's also one of the reasons our basic subjects are centered in a trimester," the teacher told me, "rather than being spread over the entire year. The learning is more intensive, for one thing; for another, homeschoolers who want to study Physics or Biology in a fully equipped lab, or study writing under a qualified instructor, but who can't afford a full year, can receive a year's course in a third of the time - and at a third of the cost. At the same time, all the other benefits of our community life will be gained."

The Meeting School accepts students for grades 9, 10, 11, and 12. Susan's enthusiastic application for next fall has been accepted, and she can hardly wait. For her and for us, The Meeting School presents an ideal opportunity - high school at home, away from home.

I think we may even manage to pay for it without robbing a bank.

The Sheepskin

—— Thomas Kane ————————————————————

Rightly or wrongly, a high school diploma is considered proof of education. Many jobs are restricted to high school graduates, and colleges give them preference. But these requirements can be evaded—after all, a diploma is only a piece of paper, and many great people were high school dropouts. Still, a diploma is useful. School departments have a harder time justifying a demand that a high school graduate return to their classes. It gives a student prestige. For whatever reason, most people are impressed with an early degree. Many homeschoolers just want a high school diploma. And they deserve one. Here are several ways to get a high school diploma at home:

One common non-traditional diploma is the GED (General Equivalency Diploma). This is awarded on the basis of a test given by the state, so that people who are unable to attend high school can obtain a diploma later in life. It was originally designed for the Armed Forces, but was later made available to all people. Legally, the GED is the equivalent to a high school diploma. It is recognized in all fifty states. There is a perception that GED degrees are inferior to other high school diplomas, but several studies have shown that GED graduates have been at least as successful as traditional students. Passing the GED test will require some effort, but one of the many GED study guides could be helpful.

Some states award high school degrees to college students who have completed the equivalent of the Freshman year. A University degree supercedes a high school one, so Universities may be an alternative to high school. Most colleges and Universities allow people to take courses for credit outside the general curriculum, and neither a diploma nor a SAT score is required for these classes. Assorted classes may be taken over a period of time, eventually accumulating enough credits for a degree. Taking one or two college courses is not much more disruptive than, say, taking music lessons, but a disadvantage to college is that it IS a form of school, complete with teachers, peer pressure, and inflexible schedules. This bothers some families more than others. And the reaction of other college students is unpredictable. I have attended college since age 14, and most of my classmates ignore my age. However, I am tall, and look like them. A younger homeschooled girl in this area has entered college too, and the students dislike her. One professor warned her that "a lot of people here are coming to get away from children." College professors are usually unbiased about younger students. In fact, they seem delighted to have a student interested in the subject matter they are teaching instead of just in "grades." Getting admitted should not be a problem. When enrolling for individual courses, as opposed to entering as a freshman, one seldom encounters any trouble. In most cases they are anxious to augment their student bodies and welcome an applicant.

Correspondence schools are a third way to get a diploma. Some are highly respected, other school by mail operations are illegal. The only really useful diploma will be a legitimate one. Most schools and employers have lists of "diploma mills." A school's introductory literature can generally be used as a guide. If it seems to be actually teaching a subject, it's probably legal. Places that sell diplomas for money alone may be worthless. Some correspondence schools require classes to be taken by mail, while others allow the student to take a final exam; if the student can pass it, no further courses are required. This lets the student choose his own method of study.

The public and expensive private schools do not have a monopoly on high school degrees. The methods described here are accessible, and many children could graduate years before the traditional schools let them.

The General Educational Development Test

The General Educational Development Test, or GED Test, is often referred to as the High School Equivalency Test, as this examination measures your abilities against those of graduating high school students. The certificate earned is equivalent to a high school diploma for purposes of higher education, employment, promotion, and licensing.

The GED Test was developed during World War II, and was designed to allow veterans to go on to college without re-entering high school after service in the Armed Forces. In recent years more than one-half million GED Tests have been taken annually. The only requirements for eligibility are those of age and residency for the state, territory, district - or, in the case of citizens of Canada, province - in which the test is taken. There may be a slight charge, generally between two and ten dollars, and the test must be taken at one of the more than 3,000 official test centers in the U. S. and Canada.

The purpose of the GED Test is to measure how well you have mastered the skills and general knowledge that would be acquired in a four year high school education. Five subjects are covered: Writing Skills, Social Studies, Science, Interpreting Literature and the Arts, and Mathematics. In the Social Studies, Science, and Literature and the Arts tests, you often have to read a fairly lengthy passage before beginning the test, which is figured into the total time allotted for the test. Most questions are multiple choice, with five answer choices for each question. A short essay is also necessary for the Writing Skills Test, in addition to the Writing Skills multiple choice. It will take about 71/2 hours to complete all the subtests; some states prefer that you take these all at once, others will allow taking them over a two day span. Minimum passing scores vary from state to state. If one or more tests are not passed they can be retaken as many times as necessary, with a new set of test questions each time.

Many books on the GED Test are available, check with your local library or bookstore. For information on GED testing and preparation courses in your area, contact your local vocational education center, community college, superintendent of schools, high school counselor or librarian. Printed information on GED testing should be available at no charge, or you can write to General Educational Development, GED Testing Service of the American Council on Education, One Dupont Circle, Washington, DC 20036.

Apprenticeships

One of the oldest methods of learning a skilled trade - and still one of the best - is apprenticeship. Under the direction and guidance of an experienced "master," the apprentice is given a chance to learn about his subject of interest first-hand, with invaluable hands-on experience and exposure. According to the book *Guide to Apprenticeship Programs* (Arco, 1983), by William F. Shanahan, an apprenticeable occupation is a skilled trade which possesses all of the following characteristics: 1. It is customarily learned in a practical way through a structured, systematic program of supervised on-the-job training. 2. It is clearly defined and commonly recognized throughout an industry. 3. It involves manual, mechanical, or technical skills and knowledge which would require a minimum of 2,000 hours of on-the-job work experience (about 1 year). 4. It requires related instruction to supplement the on-the-job training.

In her book *Alternatives to College* (Franklin Watts, 1978) Linda Atkinson writes, "Many experts think that apprenticeship programs are the most efficient way there is to learn a trade. Though the heart of these programs is on-the-job training, it is quite different from the kind of training you might pick up on your own by working as an assistant to someone with experience. Apprentices are taken, step-by-step, through every aspect of the trade. They learn not just one skill but every skill the trade involves. When they complete the program, they are "all-round" workers, able to understand the trade as a whole and to work in any branch of it."

Many apprenticeship programs are supervised by the federal government through the Bureau of Apprenticeship and Training, Department of Labor. These programs are often lengthy, covering a two to four year program, but upon completion an apprentice is eligible for a Certificate of Completion of Apprenticeship, which guarantees their recognition throughout the U. S. as fully trained all-round workers. Their versatility and hands-on experience make those who have completed apprenticeship programs particularly valuable workers, and generally able to qualify for promotions rapidly. *Alternatives to College* notes, "A survey of companies in the construction industry found that 90 percent of the top company officials - presidents, vice-presidents, owners, and partners - began their careers as apprentices."

What kinds of occupations are offered through an apprenticeship program? The list is virtually endless, but among those for which registered apprenticeships are available: Airplane mechanic, bookbinder, bricklayer, butcher, carpenter, draftsman-designer, jeweler, optical technician, tailor, and wood-carver. Since an apprenticeship is a job, with the apprentice providing some useful and valuable labor and a growing amount of skill, the apprentice is paid for his time. Usual starting wages are about half what a fully trained worker in that field would earn, but increases come rapidly, generally about every six months, until full wage is being earned, at which time the apprentice is considered to have learned the trade.

Information about registered apprenticeship programs is available at your library, or through your local Job Service office. For more informal apprenticeship programs, contact your local library or community college, or just begin asking around.

Tutoring

Tutoring, another of the oldest forms of instruction, is simply one-on-one teaching. As explained in *This Way Out* (E. P. Dutton, 1972), by John Coyne and Tom Hebert, tutoring has a somewhat tarnished reputation: "In America there is a problem with the word tutor. The word suggests that someone is in trouble and that a worried parent has taken action. Ninety percent of the students using professional tutoring services are in academic trouble. For ten dollars an hour someone tries to get them out of it. And they do. Tutors we have talked with say that students who do not learn in classrooms generally start doing better work and get confidence in themselves working with tutors."

Tutoring differs from the apprenticeship method, but the differences are not well-defined. It's primarily a matter of who determines the lesson content. In an apprenticeship situation, the apprentice decides what skill or trade he would like to learn and then locates a person or a program that can help him learn it. From that point, he is pretty much told what he will need to pay attention to in order to gain the Certificate of Completion of Apprenticeship, if that is the goal. He may also progress through several teachers in his learning.

In a tutorial situation, the learner (and/or his parents) often determine the direction and content of the learning program, and then seek out someone who is skilled in that area of knowledge or field of experience. And the development of a close relationship between the tutor and his student is an integral part of the process. In *This Way Out*, Coyne and Hebert list four purposes for tutorials: "1. To give the student mastery over some material; 2. To allow the student to be creative; 3. To permit a close relationship to develop between a teacher and a student; 4. To build literacy in the student."

They also offer some particularly valuable suggestions about tutors: "You don't have to have a specific learning plan in mind when you first begin to work with a tutor. Let him assist you in your quest. Your ideas may still be 'floating,' which is fine. He will know his way around a bibliography, and can draw you out in early conversations to find why a particular area interests you."

Or this insight: "The tutor should have some enthusiasm for the subject. If the tutor isn't excited to some degree by it, dig around to find where the tutor's interests really lie. We found in our many conversations with tutors, that they all had some area that they were just itching to get into with someone. That's where the real learning for both of you may take place."

It will probably take some digging to uncover a good teaching/learning program, whether an apprenticeship or a tutorial situation. You might want to consider simply searching out your own leads with an ad in the local newspaper or in a trade magazine serving the area of specialization that interests you. A listing of many of these publications can be found in the professional writer's access guides, such as *Writer's Market*, available in the reference section of most public libraries. Intriguing special interest magazines such as *Air Line Pilot*, the magazine for professional flight crews; *Motor Service*, for professional auto mechanics; *The Dairyman*, for the commercial dairy industry; *Apparel Industry Magazine*, and hundreds of others will be listed and described. Locate a publication in the field you want to study, jot down the address and price, and send for a sample copy. You'll have a wonderful first-hand guide to the world you're interested in!

Perhaps the best way to "break into" a field is to find someone who's already skilled or experienced in your chosen area and ask their advice. Ask how they learned what they know. Ask them if they might be able to recommend someone who can help you get started. Most people are proud of their skills and knowledge, and more than willing to share their expertise with someone who's sincerely interested.

From Homeschool to College:
How to Succeed in Freshman Comp Without Really Lying

—— Craig Conley ————————————————————————

Most entering Freshmen are less prepared for English composition than they are for any other college class. The homeschoolers among them are no better off... but for very different reasons.

I have a somewhat unique perspective on this predicament: I have experience both as a homeschooler in college and as a college instructor. I was taught at home as a child, attended one year of high school before dropping out, and then went on to earn as B. S. in Journalism and an M. A. in English. During my Master's program, I had a graduate teaching assistanceship. It all seems very ironic in retrospect: with practically no classroom experience, I ended up spending six and a half years in college, and even found myself teaching Freshman Composition for three of those! How did I--with a built-in distrust of structured learning--manage to survive in an institution for so long? Experience is indeed the best teacher, and it alone helped me to deal with my almost constant frustration.

It is a similar frustration with institutions that prevents some homeschoolers from succeeding in composition class. They certainly aren't academically inferior, since these students regularly score higher on standardized tests than do their classroom counterparts. Whether homeschoolers use a correspondence course (I participated in the Calvert course during my first two years out of school), or custom design their own curriculum (as I did thereafter), they almost assuredly won't be prepared for the demands of English 101.

And it's all due to basic philosophical differences between individualized and institutionalized education. The reason seems simple enough, but the solution will take some effort on the student's part.

When I started college, writing was my life. I was constantly working on my own fictional stories, I enjoyed writing letters to pen pals, I was editor and publisher of my own magazine (read by family and friends in 17 states), and I submitted articles to the "Youth Focus" section of the local newspaper. Consequently, I had what was probably an above average amount of writing practice when I started college, and I was certainly comfortable facing a blank sheet of paper with pen in hand. In spite of my confidence, I nearly didn't make it through my first semester of composition class.

But you'll be a lot less frustrated if you recognize these four important factors (which I learned the hard way):

1. Your convictions. Always be yourself when you write, but don't assume that your teacher will understand your perspective. What you take for granted may be completely foreign to him. Homeschoolers usually have very strong convictions about education (and everything else, for that matter). By definition, they choose to learn in a non-traditional way. My parents assumed a huge responsibility when they decided to teach me at home, not to mention the fact that they were at odds with the local school authorities. We read all of John Holt's books, and subscribed to two magazines about home education. Most of our friends were homeschoolers. Therefore, I was accustomed to being around people who shared my deepest convictions. Each had his own reasons for being non-traditional, but all believed that homeschooling worked and that for one reason or another, school didn't. When I went to college, I didn't necessarily expect my teachers to agree with my philosophy, but I had no idea of just how strange (and I mean both foreign and peculiar) that philosophy was. The solution: before you state a generalization, lead up to it by briefly describing your unique background to your reader. Then, when you state an opinion, be sure to state exactly how and why you have reached

it. Assume that nothing is obvious. On the bright side, once your instructor gets a feeling for your point of view, he will very probably respect your uniqueness (if you could read everyone else's papers, you'd find that your competition is in no way stiff).

2. No soap boxes. I was accustomed to talking and reading about the virtues of homeschooling and the vices of public education. I was very tempted to try to convert my teacher, after all, I knew a lot about the subject. The solution: don't be an evangelist. Keep a low profile. If you feel you must write about homeschooling, dwell only upon your positive experiences (never on negative school experiences), and be sure to address the typical arguments of the opposition (socialization, "real world" experience, the qualifications of your parents, etc.). Show tolerance for different opinions, and express your willingness to hear about and learn from others' experiences. Having been a member of a minority for so long can make you defensive.

3. The essay. By its very nature, the essay is artificial. What you will be writing in class will undoubtedly have no useful purpose outside that class. You are essentially demonstrating to your teacher that you can follow certain models of discourse. He will speak often about your "audience," but when it comes down to it, you are writing to him alone. This will be stressful for you if you're accustomed to writing letters, or a journal, or fictional stories, or poetry. I was upset initially, but have come to respect the essay for the discipline that it teaches.

4. Creativity. What I say above seems to indicate that the essay allows for no creativity on the writer's part. Indeed, Freshman Composition is designed to prepare students for writing themes about literature. However, though an analytical paper may be very structured, there's still plenty of room for a student's personal insight. You probably won't ever write any fiction in that class, but remember that fiction isn't the only form of creative writing. This is true for homeschoolers perhaps more than most students. Topics which are run-of-the-mill for regular students will require you to muster every ounce of your creativity. For instance, my very first in-class assignment was to write four pages about "My Summer Vacation." My life had never been divided up that way. The following topic was "My Senior Prom." What a challenge--but I got to write fiction at last!

I don't have a single homeschool friend who didn't succeed in college. As a group, homeschoolers are self-confident and competent, but it can be discouraging when your very first class turns out to be the antithesis of everything you believe. John Holt once told me that the best preparation for a bad experience is a good experience. It's a tribute to homeschooling that so many of us can look back upon Freshman Composition in a positive way.

A College Survival Guide

Thomas Kane

___

It was after midnight, and my professor was telling me about the information packet he had to write for incoming freshmen on how to succeed in college. He said he thought faculty should get out of the business entirely and let students circulate underground manuals. These books would tell real stories out of academe, with all the juicy details on beating the system. They would, of course, be forbidden. Therefore, people would read them.

I still need a grade from that professor. Therefore, I wrote him his clandestine handbook.

To the Incoming Student:

You might as well ask, everyone else does. Yes, I'm a senior. Yes, that means I'm about to graduate. Yes, that means I'm thinking about careers. Yes, all my aunts, neighbors and friends' grandfathers like to ask me about these topics over and over again. If they think that endears them to me, then there really is a generation gap. But I think you're different, and I don't mind telling you about college. In fact, I want to show off my scars.

I went to college at the University of Maine in Farmington. Having seen Harvard and Dartmouth, I still doubt that the teaching faculty of any school in the country can surpass UMF's professors for energy or expertise. A scholar supposedly wants to tap that sort of genius. Only rules, customs and standard procedures stand in such a pupil's path. Therefore, no matter how good a student you are, you take a terrible risk every time you let the college make you do something the accepted way.

For example, in my second semester at UMF, I wanted to take a seminar course in writing. Unfortunately, it listed the mandatory English Comp class as a prerequisite, and I had not taken that course. At the advice of my parents, I went off to meet the Dean of English and ask for a waiver, carrying a portfolio of references, published articles and other trophies. Nobody at the college seemed to know what the word "dean" meant. Finally, a secretary figured out what I wanted and found the department head. He looked at my material, asked several questions, and then said that it was better for everyone to take the courses in their usual order.

I signed up for the seminar anyway and got an A in it.

That also fulfilled the English requirement, meaning I no longer needed to take English 101. Shortly thereafter, I began to learn what I had missed, as friends produced fifth and sixth revisions of papers on topics like "Resentment," "When I Conformed," and "The Blessedness of Inequality." My mother told me about her assignment to write a paper entitled "On Being Well-Bred." Teachers of mandatory courses can get away with that sort of project. As I realized this truth, I began my long struggle against the core curriculum.

The Core Curriculum

I will not even attempt to argue the justice or injustice of compelling students to study core subjects. I know all the practical and political reasons why universities establish required courses. Nevertheless, there is something outrageously presumptuous about a faculty member who feels entitled to impose his favorite subject on everyone who attends college. To probe the depth of this arrogance, try suggesting that the University should trust students enough to let them decide what classes they need to become "rounded out." Professors will not tell you that you are wrong, because they will not even understand your premise.

Therefore, evade the core in any way you can. A sympathetic professor makes everything easy. After English, I evaded Computer Literacy simply by asking for a waiver--writing my request on a word processor. Unfortunately, professors in certain departments know that without the threat of force, no self-respecting student would need to take their courses at all. To them, the fact that you already know what they have to teach is strictly irrelevant.

I grappled with the Physical Education requirements for four years, finding only barriers. With the exception of my mother, everyone I asked chuckled about the impossibility of getting an institution to accept substitutes for the health requirement. However, I walked four miles every day simply to go to my other classes, in addition to assorted outdoor work and athletics. If, after that, I succumbed and took Jog-Walk, Fly-Fishing, Body-Building or Aerobic Dancing, I would have no integrity left whatsoever.

As I searched for opportunities, I found myself drawn into a turf war between entire departments. The wording of the "fitness requirement" allowed students to fulfill the core by taking a gym course and a lecture in either "Health" or "Physical Education." Members of the Physical Education Department felt that only the latter course truly fulfilled the spirit of the fitness requirement. They raised the subject at a faculty meeting and proposed making PE 101 the only acceptable course for fulfilling the core.

The Health Department resisted, but seemed likely to succumb. Then, the powerful Education Department entered the field. Education majors need an unconscionable number of courses for their degree, and many would be unable to schedule them all without the flexibility of taking either Health *or* Physical Education. Education professors negotiated a secret bargain with the Political Science Department. If Physical Education defeated Health, then Education and Political Science would combine votes to strip the fitness requirement from the core entirely. This, of course, squashed the whole debate. However, I took the controversial Health lecture and felt that I stung my enemies in at least a tiny way.

That left the gym requirement itself. I finally walked into a Physical Education professor's office and suggested an Independent/Directed Study course in hiking. He accepted my suggestion at once. I kept a journal showing the progress of my personal wellness program which consisted of distance walking. The hikes, coincidentally, always came precisely half an hour before I had other classes.

Independent/Directed Study
Independent or Directed Study is, without a doubt, the most effective tool in existence for beating the system. What it means is that the student makes up a course he or she wants to take and tells the professor how to grade it. You can use Independent Study against the core. You can use it to get credit for projects you wanted to do anyway. You can make up a course with the same title as a regularly offered course and thereby avoid the usual professor. Be ready to consult several professors if the first one says no, but by all means, use Directed Study.

Independent Majors
UMF and many other universities allow not only Independent Study but Individualized Majors. Unless you want to pursue a

particular professional program, individualized degrees offer many of the same benefits as individualized courses. You get to decide exactly what the degree is called. You also get to decide what courses you want to take. I picked an individualized major with three titles, so that, depending on my mood, I can have a degree in Science, English Writing, or Foreign Policy.

By the way, people will want to know what you major in. They usually ask more than once, hoping, no doubt, for a fresh new response each time. Therefore, you should always claim to be studying "Nucleophillic Substitution." It's the only honest thing to say.

My experience, of course, deals only with the UMF Honors Program, but nearly every school has some equivalent. Our Honors Department advertises itself as a program offering especially difficult courses to students who consider themselves more intellectual than the average student body and who prefer rigorous study to the idle pursuit of careers or entertainment. Honors students go to a variety of lectures, awards ceremonies, formal luncheons and violin performances which the normal student body is not expected to attend. The Honors Department has a chronic problem with recruiting.

However, Honors Courses are worth investigating. I did not enroll in the Honors Program, but I took four Honors Courses by asking the professors who teach them for permission (which, incidentally, shows how easy that permission is to obtain). these courses consisted of impassioned discussions on all the topics which make lively conversation: war, love, religion and money. We also talked about baseball, Darth Vader and drugs. (Every time a professor describes a school of philosophy, someone will ask, "Did the guys who made that up do a lot of drugs?") Without going into details, these courses offer what college would offer in an ideal world.

Some instructors do remember that Honors Courses are supposed to be especially difficult. With that in mind, they assign three or four times the normal amount of reading. If you accidentally take such a course, you will see a beautiful example of civil disobedience in action. Honors Students, being the aristocratic clique that they are, have a tacit agreement to simply ignore any work which offends their delicate sensibilities. And just as Gandhi would have predicted, no professor can stand against the nonviolent resistance of his whole class.

There are Honors Courses with titles like, "Psycho-Social Implications of Early Abstract Expressionism," but if you sign up for one of those, you deserve whatever you get.

I mentioned that I took four Honors Courses out of sheer interest. Shortly afterward, I learned that if I took five, my transcript would list me as a sort of honorary Honors Student, although I was never subjected to the required courses or cultural enlightenment prepared for that lofty bunch. Therefore, I invented a fifth Honors Course, using Directed Study. Yet another reason not to sign up for programs the ordinary way.

What applies to Honors Courses applies to college in general. You can always assume that advanced courses offer more excitement, less drudgery and easier grades than their lower-level equivalents. Even in the physical sciences, prerequisites serve not so much to prepare students for the subject as to keep the riffraff out. You are not riffraff. If you want to study a subject, study at the highest level you can.

The Professors

Professors, of course, encounter stories like mine all their lives. As long as you avoid putting yourself in their power, you have no stronger source of allies. There are instructors who blur the distinction between courses they recommend and courses the college requires. Others--especially your faculty advisor--may simply not know the college rules. However, once you convince a professor that you genuinely want to pursue his or her subject, you have a friend. And as long as they do not have to admit it, the best professors always want to be co-conspirators.

Thinking of that last principle, I wrote versions of this manual for each of my professors. Naturally, every copy has its own expurgations. The fact that I am admitting this here means that you are reading the uncensored edition.

When Homeschoolers Say No To College

Patrick Farenga

Even though they have access to college, some teenage homeschoolers choose not to go and instead enter directly into a profession. Encouraged as children to pursue their interests in a disciplined fashion, so now they are encouraged as young men and women to explore and use the world to find their work in it. If college is part of that plan, fine; but, more often than not, the time and expense of a college degree is not necessary for these young people to find work worth doing.

Most children who are homeschooled start in grammar school and go back to school around high school. Andy Endsley did the reverse: he got through grammar school, but by the end of his sophomore year of high school he decided he wanted to be home-schooled. College admittance was a big concern for Andy's parents, and together they conducted research on home education.

Andy says that to feel comfortable about their choice in the beginning, he was enrolled in the Clonlara Home Based Education Program.

"My parents wanted me to have a diploma and transcript that looks traditional... But since that time we have found out that you don't need any of the conventional pre-requisites to get into college. You can do so without any degree, or even a G.E.D. You can work your way in through community colleges, even at a young age of 13 or 14, or you can go directly to a university - a very well, highly accredited school - and just approach them with your situation. Because you are unique and are not really comparable to the thousands of other students that have their high school transcripts merely listed as grades on a computer printout, you're an individual in their eyes, so that also gives you a step up above the traditionally schooled applicant."

Andy's interest in military history, and participation in historical re-enactments, consumed him during his school years. Fort Meigs, in Perrysbury, Ohio (his hometown), is a museum as well as a site for historical re-enactments.

"I was with [Fort Meigs] since I was 12. So I was still in school when I was with them, but I found as my interest in the time period of Fort Meigs grew, I continually looked forward to the weekends so I could get out of school. I could have lived twenty-four hours a day at this fort. That's really what kept me going through the last 2 years I spent in school -- just looking towards the weekend. If I could just make it through the next five days I was home free."

I was struck by his description of waiting for the weekend. It sounded so much like some adults I know who dislike their work and "live for the weekend." Fortunately for Andy, he and his family recognized the dead-end he was facing intellectually. The fort is open Wed. - Sun., and when Andy started to homeschool he was able to volunteer there for almost as much time as the paid staff was there. When he was 15 he was giving tours of the fort to high school seniors.

One of the important things about learning without school that Andy, and the other teenagers I will profile, demonstrate is how they can determine whether or not they want to develop a career and its requisite skills by actually doing it, rather than reading about it or being evaluated for it by a counselor.

"...I had a chance to work with a curator and his assistants, and other staff that work at the museum. I got to see first hand what a curatorial job actually was. Over time, even though I liked history, I thought that wouldn't be a job for me. I enjoyed traveling and going to other events around the country. You can't have a job like that and follow those travel interests because you work on the weekends. Monday and Tuesday are your rest days, and you can't schedule much travel around that."

Another common experience that Andy discovers as he learns in the real world is the importance of networking, of actually getting to know and stay in contact with people you like or people whose work you find interesting.

"You get to meet people from around the country through historical re-enactments. You support other historic sites. They send troops to your fort and you go to theirs. Within that experience I made contacts with people and kept in contact with them for when I felt I needed a change, to go on to something different. I was somewhat dissatisfied with the program at Fort Meigs at that time. I knew of some other groups that are considered the higher caliber as far as living history was concerned, they are recognized for their authenticity and the accuracy of their performances. So I hooked up with one of those groups and even before I got to go to one event with them, they were asked to be in the movie *Glory*.

"The captain called me and asked me if I was available to work one day as an extra in *Glory*. Since I wasn't in school I was able to go down on a weekday and spend time on the set working. As it turned out, and this happens on most films, they go over-budget and over-schedule and they needed people to stay for the following week. Most of these guys I do events with have 9 - 5 jobs they go to on regular weekdays, so they had to go home. But I was able to stay an additional three days because I didn't have that school commitment. That extra time allowed me to make friends on the crew. You know, behind the camera, support capacity. Just getting to know those people, and staying in touch with them, led to my opportunity to be in *Dances With Wolves*.

"For *Dances With Wolves* I also got paid better than being an 'extra.' I was classified as a "Re-enactor" since I brought my own equipment, as well as some knowledge of the drill and customs of the period."

The same method of contacts led to Andy being a re-enactor on a film starring Kris Kristofferson aired on Turner Broadcasting in December 1991 as a Christmas Special, *Miracle in the Wilderness*.

"On that film I got to ride as a cavalryman for two weeks. Up at four in the morning, feeding and watering the horses, brushing them down and saddling them, being on the set by six for breakfast and then not getting back to our cabin until 10 at night. A full schedule for those two weeks, but it was a nice experience...

"The more I learn about history the more I learn how little I know. It's a never-ending search. It might turn into a position on films sometime... Not as a historical consultant, but rather as a crew member. My bias is towards the camera, but my interests may lead me to something else in the business."

Andy is not blinded by his brush with movie stars - "Movie projects come up, but they also fall through the floor" - and he maintains a steady income by working in his father's business, which is a specialty food brokerage. His homeschooling enabled him to get a head start in his chosen endeavors because his work with his dad, as well as his volunteer work at Fort Meigs, earned him credit towards graduation from the Clonlara Home Based Education Program.

"I continue to follow my interests. Even though I officially graduated from Clonlara, and I'm out of the state's control now, nothing has really changed... I didn't use pre-set curriculum before, and now that I'm officially free and responsible for my own actions, nothing has really changed."

Andy does shipping-receiving work for his dad, as well as basic office work; he also travels across the U. S. helping his father sell his products. His father recently entered the business of selling inexpensive, reusable canvas bags to grocery stores. Andy learned to do silk-screening after his dad purchased the proper equipment, and that is how he now earns most of his money.

"I made lots of mistakes at first. I should have asked for help from our friends in the silk-screen business, but I decided I had to learn it all myself, on my own. Now I can print well without making errors. I learned by doing it, which I feel is the best way. You feel better about what you've done because you're not always asking, 'What do I do next?' or 'How do I do this?'"

He considers his work relationship with his father more of a partnership than an apprenticeship, and he bills his father for his time and expenses for each job. When asked if he considers going to college at all, Andy responds,

"I feel no matter what field I want to go into I can do it faster and with better results out of school than in any institution across the country... I enjoy the thought of that challenge...

"But another aspect of my studies has been Libertarian politics, both with a big 'L' and a small 'l.' I'm a party member as well. So if I go to any college it would be Hillsdale College, because I like their philosophy - pro-free market and pro-individual liberty - and they welcome homeschoolers...

"I would go to hear the thought of one professor, or to attend a specific class, but I don't think I would want a degree. Maybe I could some way, in a debating environment, further my abilities in expressing my ideas at Hillsdale. But I don't know why I would have to spend money to accomplish that whereas I've made some contacts in Washington D.C. and am thinking of doing an internship at the Cato Institute, a political think-tank along the lines of classical liberal thought of free markets and free minds. I can actually have a paid position that would just barely cover my expenses for rent and food in Washington. At the same time I would get to do work for them that would accomplish the same thing as going to college... I'd be working with people who are actively trying to sway the minds of the American public back towards liberty. I think that would be much more productive than going to a school environment."

Andy is using the world as his classroom and he has been able to develop a strong sense of identity and purpose that I doubt would be easy to find in the ranks of most 18-year-old freshmen. Certainly, he couldn't have done this as easily without his family's support. Yet it is so often one's family that pressures young adults to enter college when they would prefer to do otherwise.

In his wise and extremely useful book, *The Question is College* [Random House, 1989], Herbert Kohl writes about how families can be ripped asunder when a child decides not to attend college. Though Kohl writes a few sad stories of teens who wind up on the streets as a result of such fights, more often than not these young adults are able to find and pursue rewarding careers without college. Sadly, however, their relationships with their parents have been so strained over the college issue that they are no longer able to communicate with them. I recommend this book highly to anyone whose child faces college: it doesn't take the position that college is necessarily wrong for young people, but it also doesn't take the more typical position that after "bumming around" awhile every person needs to attend college to find their life's work. It contains excellent advice for getting involved in a field that interests you without going to college first. Andy Endsley describes the reason why this is a good thing to do:

"Even if you need a degree to do what you think will be your life's work, go and find out about that life's work really is before you even spend a dollar on school. When Kira, my sister, started to homeschool, she volunteered for two days a week at a veterinarians office. At that time she loved animals, and she still does, but she thought, 'Wouldn't it be neat to work with animals for my career.' She volunteered at the vets and found out that the actual work is rather routine and you meet the animals only when they're sick or need to be put to sleep. It wasn't as fun-filled, or rapport-building an experience with the animals as she thought it would be. Even though she saw it was a nice career, she saw it was something she didn't want to do. But if she had that false idea of what it was like all the way through high school, gotten her degree, then got into veterinarian school, then it's another seven years before you actually graduate and get into practice. By that time it's a little late to change your career plans. It can be a very expensive mistake.

"Even if you want to go into a field that's almost impossible to crack the degree expectations, you can learn more about it and get a head start on those who also want to get into that field by following your interests and working at that place beforehand."

Kohl's emphasis on communication and family support during a teen's struggle with the college question is amplified beautifully by Kendall Hailey, a young writer who, like Andy, couldn't wait to leave high school and avoid college in order to begin her education. She documents her early graduation from high school at 16 and "the advice, adventures, and acrimonies that befell me thereafter" as she learns to be a writer and actress in her bumptious book, *The Day I Became An Autodidact*. Hailey writes:

"I do concede that college is very useful for becoming a doctor, a lawyer, an architect, an engineer, or Madame Curie. But for people without such definite ambitions, college seems more a passageway from childhood to adulthood than a place to learn. And as rites of passage go, it would be hard to find a more expensive one. In general, the parents of my friends are going to be shelling out close to twenty thousand dollars a year. With plane trips home and all the items necessary to make a home away from home feel like a real one, I suspect in a few years an education at a private university will cost somewhere very near a hundred thousand dollars per child. Whereas being an autodidact is open to everyone.

"…Yesterday I read that the fear of escalating college costs has made some states adopt a system whereby new parents give the state a certain sum of money at their child's birth, and the state, in exchange, guarantees the child a college education in eighteen years.

What happens if they've raised an autodidact? Why must college be the only choice after high school? I think I am the only one of my graduating class not choosing it, but also the only one whose parents have not limited the choices to college or getting a job.

"So many parents seem perfectly willing to shell out all that money for an education, but so unwilling just to provide food and shelter and allow their children the opportunity to educate themselves or to get a head start on their chosen careers without the pressure to show immediate monetary gain. Or just time to take a look at this life we have been tested on so furiously for so long.

"Did you know that the eighteen-year-old leaving for the first semester of college has the highest incidence of suicide among teenagers? We are so terrified that the decision we make now will decide the rest of our lives. And we feel as if we have to decide everything by tomorrow. That should be what tomorrow is for. The point of tomorrow is it's a chance to change our minds."

Hailey has written the book quoted above, which is published by a major firm, and written and performed plays since she embarked on her autodidactic adventures. She has accomplished all of this at about the same time her age-mates would be sophomores in college.

Her point about the expense of college is important. "The latest survey by the independent College Board shows that a college education [average 4-year college costs] at a public university will cost more than $51,000 in ten years - and more than $108,000 at a private school." Homeschooling will probably be seen in coming years as a rational alternative to the monetary costs of schooling, as well as an alternative to the intellectual and spiritual costs it has for its students.

Further, since getting a college degree is no longer a safe bet for finding a high paying job, it is harder to figure out why it's worth going to college just because one has graduated high school. Our

poor economy and a surplus of college-educated adults are contributing heavily to this situation. It is a sad irony that much of the
work being done by people with college degrees now was done
quite well by people without them in the past. Stories of recent
college graduates who consider themselves lucky to find jobs
waiting on tables at $2.90-an-hour or as entry-level typists are
very common now. "Wherever the employment pipeline is monitored this year - among the fresh grads who have moved back
home, in the university placement offices, or in the personnel departments of small businesses and large corporations - the pulse is
the same. Faint."

Examples of young people who are finding other ways to find
work worth doing without going to college are more important
now than ever. Britt Barker wrote a series of newspaper columns
about her experiences as a young teenager who forgoes college.
Unlike Andy and Kendall, Britt never attended high-school, and
has been homeschooled for most of her life. Her book, *Letters
Home* (Home Education Press, 1990), tells us about her pursuit of
the work she loves, biology and music, and the meandering but
important routes her pursuit takes her. After seeing an exhibit for
Earthwatch at a Summer Opportunities Fair, Britt is thrilled with
their projects:

"All of them were real, in the field [ongoing] professional research projects... The Earthwatch representative I spoke to at the
fair encouraged me to complete a preliminary fellowship application, though it was doubtful anything would come of it since I was
neither a full-time student nor teacher as in their stated requirements.

"So many of the projects interested me it was hard to make three
choices...

"Their prompt written reply included a four page application as
well as a requirement to write two essays... about how I planned
to make use of my sketches, journal notes and Earthwatch experience, and the question, 'You have been given the opportunity to
study with the person of your choice either alive or dead for one
year. Who would you choose, what would you study, and why?'
In my essays I detailed my plan to collect material for my *Letters
Home* column. It seemed a perfect opportunity to not only do
meaningful work and meet interesting people, but also to see new
parts of the world and all the while writing...

"So with high hopes, but low expectations, I sent it all off with
photocopies of several *Letters Home* from Canada [where Britt had

earlier apprenticed with two naturalists doing field work] and a page of watercolors..."

Britt gets a full scholarship to study and track wolves in the Appenine mountains of central Italy through Earthwatch, and her descriptions of her travels and work provide a wonderful counterpoint to the grind and tension of competing for grades we normally read about people of her age. Britt arranges different apprenticeship opportunities for herself throughout her letters. Sometimes her role is clearly that of apprentice, other times she is an apprentice in an informal way, learning from incidents in her travels and meetings with people. Her father, Richard, writes in the afterward to *Letters Home* about Britt's self-education since her letters were published: two weeks as an Earthwatch volunteer at the Bodega Bay (California) Marine lab; a three month biology internship at Point Reyes Bird Observatory; her performance at the latter led to a six-week position tagging elephant seals on the Farallon Islands. Britt, without any traditional school credentials, has accomplished in one year what many students of biology can't even attempt until they complete four years of undergraduate course work. You may have thought studying biology was impossible outside of college, but, as I once heard a mother say at a homeschooling conference, "Nobody told me it was impossible when I did it."

Not all homeschoolers have the urge to write about their experiences as Britt does, but their experiences are nonetheless illuminating for contemporary life without a college degree. Darin Geisy, homeschooled through high school, tells how things didn't turn out the way he thought they would at college.

"I always planned to go to college. It was just a matter of finding a college that would take me. By the way, the people who say you can't cram for the SAT are full of it. I crammed for four weeks and got 600 verbal and 600 math...

"First I looked at Old Dominion University (VA) for some freshman courses, but they needed too much paperwork and felt that anyone who didn't go to high school couldn't possibly be prepared for college... I got accepted to Antioch... they seemed to rely heavily upon essay questions and interviews.

"...I was a theater major first... I started ballet in 1976 when I was 9. My mother, sisters and I all started lessons at the same time. It started as a family activity. I had just quit playing ice hockey at the time - it was just too hard to find ice in Virginia - and I said 'Sure, I'll try this.' Then I stopped cold turkey when I was 14.

No one was going to make me a dancer! I became attracted to the technical aspects of theater instead of the performing aspects...

"...But Antioch didn't have much of a theater program, so I switched to being a Video major, and then an Environmental Sciences major. I spent time in Canada doing field research for that one...

I got credit for my EMT class and firefighting class while I lived at Antioch. I was a member of the Antioch Fire Department, too. Antioch's co-op job program is a great idea... I went to my adviser asking to work in an emergency room; but the best he could come up with was to place me as an orderly in a rehab center in Boston."

While in Boston Darin decided to take up ballet classes again. He liked them so much that he decided to dance full-time again. He left Antioch and came to Boston, where he auditioned for and received a partial scholarship at the Boston Ballet. Since then he has been employed as a dancer by the Nevada Dance Theater, Hartford Ballet in Connecticut, and is currently working at Ballet Met in Columbus, OH. The ballet companies have all exhibited total indifference to Darin's homeschooling background since everything depends on what you can do, not what you can recite from memory. "They didn't even ask if I graduated high school," says Darin. Indeed, not going to college for professional dancers is more the rule than the exception. "Out of twenty people at Ballet Met I think there's only one guy who has a bachelors of fine arts degree," Darin says. He notes though, based on his awareness of advertised job opportunities, that there is a trend for college and high-school dance programs to want their teachers to have college degrees, "but a lot of them still say 'degree or extensive performance experience within the art form required.'"

When asked if college will enter his life again Darin says, "I certainly don't consider college a dead issue. I've known a lot of people who went back to college long after they were eighteen. In addition, Ballet Met and Hartford Ballet offer some free college courses to their dancers... If I go back, it'll be for a specific education, not to make the college scene... There haven't been any doors closed to me because of my lack of a college degree, at least none that I've tried so far... I've been toying with the idea now for a couple of years of becoming a physical therapist once I'm done dancing. Having spent a significant amount of time over the last four years in physical therapy in various places for various injuries, I've found there's a lack of people in the physical therapy profession that really understand dance. It is getting better in most places, but a lot of the time it's difficult to relate the dance vocabulary to the physical therapy vocabulary. Most therapists are trained to deal mainly with football or baseball players than dancers... Along those lines I've thought about working in a sports med clinic as an aide or something for a summer, but I can't pursue that now because I keep spending my summers auditioning."

John Holt, the late author, educator, and founder of *Growing Without Schooling*, describes the sort of university that Andy, Kendall, Britt, and Darin are attending this way:

"In the past twenty-eight years at least I've been the president of a university, and quite a good one. It has a student body of one - namely, me. The faculty of the university is made up of all the people from whom I think I can learn something that I think is important to me in terms of my own life's goals...

"When I find such a person, I quickly put him on my faculty. He doesn't know it. There are no salaries in my university. Some of the faculty in my university are alive, some are dead; some are known to me, some close friends, some are people I have yet to meet. I'm constantly hiring and firing on my faculty; there is no tenure in my university. Some of the people who at one time in my life were very important teachers to me no longer are. Perhaps I now see the world differently, no longer agree with what they told me. Perhaps I've simply absorbed what they had to tell me and moved on. Others of my teachers in the past are my teachers still.

"One might say that one of our important life tasks was to find our true teachers, to make our own university, and we can say of education that it is a process that ought to help us get better at doing this. Certainly to find one's own teachers, someone from whom we think we can learn something really important, is one of the really great pleasures of life."

While the stories of these "autodidacts" are still in the making, it is hard not to talk about them as living examples of what young adults can do without college. If they share any common thread it is their wide number of interests, their enjoyment of the pursuit of these interests, a flexibility to change course or seize opportunites as the need arises, and their abilities to turn those interests into marketable skills. Indeed, their specific job skills and overall work experience far exceed those of most college-age teenagers; their rich work resumes already indicate how industrious, self-motivated, and able to learn they are. Interestingly, none followed graded curriculums in their higher education, and Darin and Britt never followed them at all in their homeschooling. Yet all have developed considerable discipline and stick-to-it-ness to learn and get work done without the the carrot and stick method of traditional curricula. Their resumes and portfolios should impress any college admissions officer if they decide to attend college later in life.

However, they may never need to go to college. They are socializing with and learning about a wide variety of people by living their lives in the multicultural milieu of the real world; not through units of study or parties within the confines of a carefully selected campus crowd. While their age-mates are cramming to pass mid-terms, handling fraternity and sorority initiations, and reading the greatest works of English literature in twelve weeks, these young adults are experiencing life, controlling their own education, and discovering their dislikes and joys without college pressures. "Happiness," writes Kendall Hailey, "is like everything else. The more experience you have, the better you get at it."

And Then What? Some Thoughts About Higher Education For Alternatively Educated Students

Bobbie Groth

As the Director of Admissions and a faculty member at a small liberal arts (generally regarded as "alternative") college, I get many inquiries from parents of students or from the students themselves wondering how they can get into college, now that they have decided it is something that they want to do. Some of the students are homeschoolers. Some are students from alternative high schools and primary schools. Some are young single moms who left high school, and now feel that higher education is the only way out of the poverty cycle. Some are young - and not so young - men and women who entered the job force or the armed services directly after high school and now feel that higher education is the avenue to the next phase of their lives.

Some of these individuals have been in alternative high schools and cannot match their expectations or backgrounds to the admissions requirements or academic offerings of most colleges. Some have been traveling for a year or so after high school. Some entered college from any of the above scenarios, became highly discouraged, and dropped out. Whatever the reason, there is a whole sector of the population which has been educated in and out of school in a manner which does not fit them into the mainstream of the "higher education" chronology or content in the United States.

Many factors contribute to the lack of fit between this sector of the population and the opportunities offered by common denominator colleges and universities in this country. Many students do not have high school diplomas. Some may have quit high school; some alternative schools are not accredited. Many alternative high schools ask for different "shows of success," or graduation requirements, than public schools. Most homeschoolers not only do not have a high school diploma, but do not have transcripts, grades, teacher evaluations, etc. Some seekers of higher education may have credits and grades and papers from twenty years ago. And many of the students are so far away from the targeted population for standardized testing that even if they have taken the tests - their test scores make no practical sense.

Additionally, there is the "attitude factor" for the alternatively educated student. Many of these students have grown up in families where education is taken seriously and where expectations of success are quite different from the competitive public sector, which pits student against student in the search for regurgitated facts. Those who have survived by guts and determination are no longer willing to be spoonfed or ignored by a large educational system. These are the same students who have learned individuality, a touch of rebelliousness, and a commitment to group closeness which is not found in the media-broadcasted culture of the 1980's.

Alternatively educated students are usually different -- in all their aspects. They may be shy in large groups, or they may be a little too cocky for teachers unused to being questioned. They may have "spots" in their education -- excelling far beyond the "normal" student in some areas, while totally ignoring other types of subjects generally considered essential. The students may dress differently, act differently, and have very different expectations from their public sector peers and teachers. The parents who so lovingly provided them with the alternative education they believed in may find a child unprepared to survive in this world - or at least unable to comfortably "mainstream" into a "normal" college education.

When alternatively educated students decide to go to college, the first step is to find colleges where those students will succeed. There is no such thing as a person who fails -- there are only people who are thrust into situations which are not right for them. If students want a college education, they should be carefully guided to find the right medium -- i.e., college -- through which that education will become possible. Perhaps the student thrives on a structured environment; perhaps he does better where structure is left up to his internal workings, and he is given the freedom to determine his own program. Perhaps he prefers the workbook method of independent study with little social contact; perhaps he thrives on interaction with other students and professors. The student may be quite decided on what his future career will be, or he may be interested in developing more general skills so that he can change careers many times. The student may be highly technically inclined, or he may be interested in the Classics. Whatever his or her bent, an honest realization of it is in order. Then the school must be found which serves the student best.

The most logical place to start looking for the right college is the local public library. Several companies, such as Peterson's and Barron's, put out catalogues of colleges and universities. These include bare minimum free listings, plus larger, more in depth profiles for which the colleges pay advertising rates. In addition, these companies put out subsidiary manuals on specified topics -- alternative colleges, religious colleges, foreign colleges, nursing colleges, etc.

Many libraries also have a computer service which allows students to type in characteristics they seek from a college, and the computer will spit out a list of schools which "match" their needs. Public high school counseling offices also have these services. In addition, many students seek the services of private college counselors who work directly with the student to find a college and to proceed through the admissions procedure to enrollment.

Finding a college and sending for materials is one thing -- applying for admission is quite another. Colleges generally have applications which require certain documentation: diplomas, test scores, teacher evaluations. Most have cut-off points for standardized test scores, below which they will accept no one. Students without such standard documentation should search for a college with a more flexible admissions program. These colleges are to be found, and they dwell primarily on the motivation of the student and on other than standard admissions documentation. They may require written material, interviews, and letters of recommenda tion.

To put the best foot forward, the student should consider the following: type all written material. Have it proof read and presented in a "formal" style, such as would be done for publication in a journal. The power of a good looking application and manuscript must not be underestimated. The piece of work should accurately reflect the student's point of view, and be in the student's language. However, just as if the student were going to apply for a job, the appearance must be projected that the outcome of the process means something to the student. This will be better expressed by a neatly typed and proof-read essay than a "hand written on notebook paper" misspelled essay.

Students should become acquainted with the program offered by the school. They should thoroughly understand why they want to be at that school. They should be aware of the admissions deadlines; if they find out about the school close to deadlines, they should be prepared to put off entrance for a semester or more.

If letters of recommendation are required, get references from persons who can a) speak positively and in depth about the student, b) be able to attest to the student's ability to work and get things done, c) employers, family friends, religious personnel, etc. are preferable. For a student who is raised within the family and educated there, this may limit the number of adults who can testify as to his ability. If it is necessary for a family member to write a recommendation, make it as objective as possible. It should speak about who the student is, not who the family wants the student to be. Dwell on strengths, but recognize weaknesses and speak positively about how the student deals with them. As a parent or family member, show positive support for the student's new endeavor.

To flesh out the application of a student who is alternative, provide more, not less of what is provided -- more letters of recommendation, extra essays or creative writing, slides of artwork. If the student has special accomplishments in other arenas, include them with the application. The college is interested in seeing how the student can measure up in a situation where the student is expected to function independently, study, and contribute to the group as a whole.

How does one advise a student on college? I come from a particular slant, and I will make no bones about my support for the slant of the institution for which I work. I am also a graduate of this college and have personal experience with this type of education. I entered as an "early entrant" -- a student who had not yet graduated from high school. I was never one who particularly "fit in" to the public education mode, and had received most of my education from activities outside of school. At 16 I finally had the freedom to quit, and did so. With the advantage of a very good high school transcript,

I went almost directly into college. I thought I had clear career goals (I had always wanted to be a veterinarian), but being 16, these changed quite a bit. Because I enrolled in a liberal arts institution, changing goals was fine. I proceeded with my liberal arts education no matter what I envisioned my future to hold. I never wasted a bit of my education. All I did was learn more.

The college that I work for, Shimer College, is a Great Books school. We present a curriculum which uses the original works of the Great Books of the Western World as a starting point, then fleshes these out with other, more recent works. Whatever the drawbacks of the Great Books (they have been criticized as being overwhelmingly male, which is one reason we add other works to our curriculum), they are the original writings of some of the greatest trendsetting thinkers of all time. We take the stance that by understanding the thinking of the great philosophers, and by learning to analyze these works, one learns how to think and express one's ideas more clearly.

Our classes are group discussions of the materials we read. By discussing materials, agreeing and disagreeing on points of view, we feel the student learns to think on his feet, to express himself clearly, to solve problems, to formulate ideas. In so doing, one is able to then learn to do anything, or solve any problem, that one is given. This prepares one to accept technical knowledge and put it to productive use.

In addition to our academic curriculum, we have a system of self-governance in effect, where each member of the Shimer "community," be they student, faculty, or staff, have one vote in the governing body of the college, the Assembly. Persons who choose to attend Assembly meetings and vote have a direct say in the major policies of the college. The only major decisions not made by the Assembly are those of the Academic Standing Committee, which is wholly made up of faculty. Thus, students can have a direct say in policies which govern the school -- as well as an eye-opening experience with hands-on democracy.

We pride ourselves in teaching students "how to think, not what to think." As expected, Shimer appeals to a large population of alternative students; we offer an environment where their expectations are met in terms of the "different drummer," and where their intellect is challenged. Being so small (around 100 students), we seldom "lose" students in the paper shuffle.

We also offer a very different admissions procedure, which is personal in nature. We state that we take students from "where they are in their motivation to learn, not where they have been." This way, students who are alternative in background can enter the mainstream of college education (if Shimer can be termed "mainstream" in any sense of the word!).

So, college education is out there, after an alternative primary education, or after an interruption of the "normal" time framework of college preparatory high school work. The most difficult task is to allow the student's intellect, so carefully nurtured by the alternative education the child received, or so blatantly disappointed by that same system, to come to fruition through a carefully chosen college which recognizes the benefits of an independent education, and allows the student to expand strengths in a way which helps meet the demands of the world the student lives in.

The factors to look for are how well the college meets the student's needs, how flexible its admissions policies are, and how it prepares him for a future where obsoletism is rampant, and solid traditions ignored. A college with values echoing those which prompted the student and family to seek alternative education to begin with. This might include a general education teaching the student to develop his innate capacities and survival skills while not repressing his individuality.

Students need an education that accepts change as normal, but embraces it in ways that are solid and commonsense, not short-sighted or flimsy. Students need to be accepted, and well prepared to enjoy an uncertain future. They need a college which will work with them as individuals, and teach them to take responsibility for that uncertain future. All of these things will provide a capstone for the type of alternative education which has been fostered in the student. Hopefully, they also provide students with the personal skills to survive -- and enjoy -- their future.

College Level Examination Program (CLEP)

Since 1965, this widely available credit-by-examination program, sponsored by the College Entrance Examination Board, has tested the knowledge that a student has acquired through such nontraditional methods as television or radio study programs, correspondence study, reading, working or just living. The CLEP itself does not award credits, but thousands of colleges and universities in all 50 states have their own policies for awarding credits on the basis of CLEP scores, and many will grant the equivalent of one or two years of full study for a satisfactory performance on the CLEP examinations.

The tests are based, according to the Board, on "the assumption that many Americans know more than their academic credentials would suggest. This is because most people do not stop learning simply because they have stopped going to school. Many people are avid readers; many receive training on the job; many watch educational programs on television or take noncredit courses in adult education programs offered by their high schools, community colleges, churches, or clubs. In fact, most people learn on their own in more ways than can be counted."

Tests are given at over 900 test centers, usually located on or near college or university campuses, in the third week of each month. Two types of tests are available, General and Subject. The five General Examinations cover English Composition, Math, Natural Science, Social Sciences and History, and Humanities. There are also specific subject examinations in over fifty fields such as Accounting, Biology, Computers, English Literature, Geology, Medical Technology, and many others. The CLEP examinations are all formatted as multiple-choice questions; tests are generally scheduled for three hours in the morning and two hours in the afternoon. Some colleges might request an additional essay examination.

Originally designed for adult use, persons of any age may take the CLEP examinations. The examinations are somewhat difficult, but grades are not given. Preparation and estimating your own readiness for the examinations can be done with any of several guidebooks, such as the CLEP General and Subject Examinations; Descriptions and Sample Questions. For more information on the College Level Examination Program, check your local library or bookstore for a guide to the CLEP program, or write to the Program Director, College Level Examinations, College Board, Princeton, NJ 08541.

University Without Walls

An alternative plan for undergraduate education, the University Without Walls (UWW) is a program for people of any age group who want to learn outside the walls of a college or university setting. A time schedule and a curriculum which fit the student's needs and lifestyle is fashioned with the assistance of an advisor, and the student is left responsible for shaping his or her own education.

The University Without Walls program does not use a rigid semester or a prescribed curriculum. In place of grades in this program is a unique concept of joint evaluation by the teacher and the student, who keep ongoing journals recording the effectiveness of the venture. This evaluation becomes a learning experience in itself.

Students should approach a University Without Walls education with the understanding that they will have to learn to identify their own educational needs and will have to learn to satisfy them, with the guidance of teachers and advisors. They will need to recognize that furthering their own education is something they want to do; not something which they will simply be told to do.

For information on the University Without Walls programs offered by participating institutions write to University Without Walls, Union for Experimenting Colleges and Universities, Yellow Springs, Ohio 45387.

For Further Information

Programs and Organizations:

National Coalition of Alternative
Community Schools
58 Schoolhouse Road
Summertown, Tennessee 38483
615-964-3670

The National Homeschool Association
Post Office Box 290
Hartland, Michigan 48353-0290
313-632-5208

The Alliance for Parental Involvement in
Education
Post Office Box 59
East Chatham, New York 12060-0059
518-392-6900

The Alternative Education Resource
Organization
417 Roslyn Road
Roslyn Heights, New York 11577
516-621-2195

The Global Alliance for Transforming
Education
4202 Ashwoody Trail
Atlanta, Georgia 30319
404-458-5678

Intern Program
New Alchemy Institute
237 Hatchville Road
East Falmouth, MA 02536

Center for Interim Programs
P. O. Box 2347
Cambridge, MA 02238
617-547-0980

Time Out
619 E. Blithedale Ave, Ste. C
Mill Valley, CA 94941
415-383-1834

Apprentice Alliance
151 Potrero Avenue
San Fransisco, CA 94103
415-863-8661

University Without Walls
Union for Experimenting Colleges and
Universities
Yellow Springs, Ohio 45387

Program Director
College Level Examinations
College Board
Princeton, NJ 08541

General Educational Development
GED Testing Service of the
American Council on Education
One Dupont Circle
Washington, DC 20036

Council for the Advancement of
Experiential Learning (CAEL)
10598 Marble Faun Court
Columbia, MD 21044

Degree Consulting Services
P.O. Box 3533
Santa Rosa, CA 95402
707-539-6466

Publications:

SKOLE, The Journal Of Alternative Education
72 Philip Street
Albany, New York 12202

Holistic Education Review
39 Pearl Street
Brandon, Vermont 05733-1007
802-247-8312

Home Education Magazine
Post Office Box 1083
Tonasket, Washington 98855
509-486-1351

The American Journal of Distance Education
College of Education
Pennsylvania State University
University Park, PA 16802

Journal of Higher Education
Ohio State University Press
2070 Neil Avenue
Columbus, OH 43210

Books:

Atkinson, Linda, *Alternatives To College*
   (Franklin Watts, 1978)
Barker, Britt *Letters Home* (Home Education
   Press, 1989)
Bear, John, *Bear's Guide to Non-Traditional*

College Degrees (Ten Speed Press, updated annually)

Carlson, Laurie M., *Home Study Opportunities: The Complete Guide to Going to School by Mail* (Betterway Publications, 1988)

Coyne, John, and Tom Hebert, *This Way Out* (E. P. Dutton, 1972)

Gelner, Judy, *College Admissions: A Guide for Homeschoolers* (Poppyseed Press, 1988)

Gregory, Thomas B. and Gerald R. Smith, *High Schools as Communities: The Small School Reconsidered* (Phi Delta Kappa Educational Foundation, 1987)

Hayes, Charles D. *Self-University* (Autodidact Press, 1989)

Kohl, Herbert, *The Question is College* (Random House, 1989)

Llewellyn, Grace, *The Teenage Liberation Handbook: How to Quit School and Get a Real Life and Education* (Lowry House, 1991)

Parker, Gail, and Hawes, Gene, *College On Your Own* (Bantam, 1978)

Rheim, Sarah *The Teenage Entrepreneur's Guide* (Surrey Books, 1987)

Simasko, Susan *Earn College Credit for What You Know* (Acropolis Books, 1985)

Splaver, Sarah, *Nontraditional Routes To College Careers* (Simon & Shuster, 1975)

Thorson, Marcie Kisner *Campus-Free College Degrees* (Thorson Guides, 1989)

Appendixes

Contributor's Biographical Notes

Barker, Britt - Britt Barker Bennett is the daughter of homeschooling pioneer Penny Barker. She is a classical pianist, private pilot, naturalist, and lover of life. Author of *Letters Home*, a fascinating glimpse into the journals of a homeschooled girl who embarks on travels alone around the world at the age of sixteen, she is currently completing her second book, *Six Weeks on an Island*.

Carsten, Patricia Smith - Patricia Smith Carsten is a freelance writer, teacher and certified Reading Specialist. She has travelled extensively, living in Israel, France, Mexico, and several U.S. states. She and her twin daughters, Wendy and Jessica, currently live in Providence, Rhode Island.

Conley, Craig - Craig Conley offers this profile of himself: Latest accomplishment: authored an irreverent how-to manual entitled *"Graduate School Made Simple;"* Hero: Walt Disney; Night-table reading: Foucault's Pendulum by Umberto Eco; Favorite sport: spectator *Nintendo*; Hobbies: Collecting Disney memorabilia, creating anagrams and word games, travel, and reading. Craig also has experience both as a home schooler in college and as a college instructor. He was taught at home as a child, attended one year of high school before dropping out, and then went on to earn as B. S. in Journalism and an M. A. in English. During his Master's program, he had a graduate teaching assistanceship. Craig lives in Virginia.

Farenga, Patrick - Patrick Farenga is President of Holt Associates, the organization which has continued the work of John Holt since his death in 1985. Patrick is also Managing Editor of the homeschooling publication, *Growing Without Schooling*. He lives in Cambridge, Massachusetts with his wife, Day, and their daughters Lauren and Allison.

Gatto, John Taylor - A teacher for 26 years in New York City Public Schools, John Taylor Gatto was three consecutive times New York City Teacher of the Year, and was 1991 New York State Teacher of the Year. His success has been hailed in hundreds of media articles and interviews, and he has been commended for his work by four U.S. Presidents.

Greenberg, Daniel - Daniel Greenberg, a physicist, was a professor of physics and history at Barnard and Columbia, and one of the founders of Sudbury Valley School. He and his wife, Hanna, have three children, all of whom are, of course, Sudbury Valley graduates.

Groth, Bobbie - Bobbie Groth is a former Director of Admissions and a faculty member of Shimer College, Waukeegan, Illinois.

Hegener, Mark and Helen - Mark and Helen Hegener are the parents of five children who have always been homeschooled: Michael, Christopher, Jody Ellen, Jim, and John. The Hegener family's Home Education Press publishes books and a bimonthly magazine for homeschooling families. They make their home near Wauconda, Washington, where the entire family enjoys gardening, horseback riding and traveling.

Houk, Katharine - Katharine Houk is a Director of the Alliance for Parental Involvement in Education (ALLPIE), a grassroots, nonprofit, tax-exempt organization which emphasizes the importance of the family in education. She and her husband, Seth Rockmuller, live with their children near East Chatham, New York.

Hurst, Sandra - Sandra Hurst is an Educational Consultant with twenty-seven years of public and private school experience. She is also a member of the Board of Directors of the National Coalition of Alternative Community Schools, an international support group for organizations which are designed to share education in non-coercive and non-discriminatory programs.

Jerome, Judson - Jud Jerome, who passed away in 1991, was *Writer's Digest's* poetry columnist for more than 30 years. He was one of the earliest correspondents to John Holt's homeschooling newsletter, *Growing Without Schooling*, and was one of the first people Holt knew who was actually letting his children 'grow without schooling.'

Johns, Catherine - Freelance writer and homeschooling mother Catherine Johns lives with her family near Los Angeles, California.

Kane, Thomas - After public school and private school, Thomas Kane finished high school at home. He started college at 15 and graduated with a BA degree in three majors: Science, Writing, and Foreign Policy. After a childhood spent hating everyone connected with schools, he now finds that most of his friends want to be teachers. Tom says he's seen school from a lot of viewpoints. Tom currently flirts with graduate school. Meanwhile, he writes freelance for a variety of publishers. He has published numerous full-length books for use with role-playing games such as *Dungeons and Dragons*. In the non-role-playing field, Tom is a contributing editor for *Command*, a strategic-studies periodical. His work also appears in *Home Education* magazine. Tom lives in the woods of Maine with the bears and the killer birds.

Kaseman, Larry and Susan - Larry and Susan Kaseman's experience in alternative education includes learning with their four children through homeschooling since 1979 and their active involvement since 1984 in Wisconsin Parents Association, a grassroots homeschooling organization of which Larry is executive director. Perspective on "the other side" comes from Larry's earlier work as an administrator at a school of education and as a bureaucrat in the U. S. Department of Education.

Miller, Ron - Ron Miller was the founder (and for several years the editor) of *Holistic Education Review*, a quarterly journal which explores a person-centered, global, ecological paradigm in education. He has also written for several journals and books on alternative education and humanistic psychology. He was trained, and taught, as a Montessori teacher before pursuing graduate work in the cultural foundations of American education. He lives in Oakland, California with his wife Jennifer and young son Justin.

Mintz, Jerry - Jerry Mintz coordinates the Alternative Education Resource Center, and publishes the *AERO-Gramme* newsletter, which serves as a communications link between thousands of individuals and many different kinds of alternative education. Jerry travels extensively in the U.S. and overseas in his work with alternative schools and homeschoolers.

Montgomery, Pat - Pat Montgomery is a widely respected author and educator, a founding member and past president of the National Coalition of Alternative Community Schools, a Council Member of the National Homeschool Association, and the founder and Director of Clonlara School in Ann Arbor, Michigan.

Nelson, Susan - Susan Nelson is a free lance writer and curriculum developer who lives with her family in Ramona, California.

Olson, Becky - Becky Olson is a freelance writer, a long time homeschooling advocate, and a founding member of the National Homeschool Association. She and her husband Paul, the homeschooling parents of five, make their home near Tucson, Arizona.

Reed, Donn - Donn Reed is a homeschooling father and the author of several books on homeschooling, including the comprehensive volume, *The Home School Source Book*. He is a frequent contributor to publications in the U.S. and Canada.

Rockmuller, Seth - Seth Rockmuller is a Director of the Alliance for Parental Involvement in Education (ALLPIE), a grassroots, nonprofit, tax-exempt organization which emphasizes the importance of the family in education. He and his wife, Katharine Houk, live with their children near East Chatham, New York.

Stephenson, Susan Mayelin - Susan Mayelin Stephenson grew up in Indiana, in an English Country garden populated by German musicians. Inspired by her first child's happy response to attending a Montessori school, she went to London, England to take the Primary (age 3-6) Montessori Teacher Training Course at the Maria Montessori Training Organization, which was begun by Dr. Maria Montessori in 1919. Since then she has taken the advanced training (6-12) and has taught in Michigan, California, the Virgin Islands, and Lima, Peru. The Stephenson's three children have been and are being educated at home, in Montessori primary and elementary classes, in public and private schools and Universities, and out in the world, following their own interests. Susan believes that the most valuable use of the Montessori Method of observing children and discovering and meeting their needs is in the home, or with schools and home working together for the child and the future of society. Since 1983 the Stephenson's have produced an extensive catalog of Montessori materials, the Michael Olaf "Essential Montessori" catalogue.

Stevens, Earl - Earl Stevens is a freelance writer and a columnist for *Home Education Magazine*. He lives in Portland, Maine with his wife, Linda, and their son, Jaime.

Williams, Jane - Involved since 1974 with education (conventional, alternative, and homeschooling), Jane Williams shares her expertise through conference speaking engagements, workshops, media interviews and her Bluestocking Press/ Educational Spectrums catalog of books and educational products.

Selected Resources

PUBLICATIONS

American Education, Superintendent of Documents, Washington, DC 20402

AERO-Gramme, The Alternative Education Resource Organization, 417 Roslyn Road, Roslyn Heights, New York 11577; 516-621-2195

Changing Schools, c/o Colorado Options in Education, 98 Wadsworth Blvd. #127, Box 191, Lakewood, CO 80226; 303-331-9352

Childhood Education, 11141 Georgia Avenue, Suite 200, Wheaton, MD 20902

Childhood-The Waldorf Perspective, Route 2, Box 2675, Westford, VT 05494

Curriculum Review, Curriculum Advisory Service, 517 S. Jefferson Street, Chicago, IL 60607

Early Years, Box 1266, Darien, CT 06820

Education Digest, P. O. Box 8623, Ann Arbor, MI 48107

Education Week, Editorial Projects in Education, Suite 775, 1255 23rd Street N.W., Washington, DC 20037

GATE Newsletter, The Global Alliance for Transforming Education, 4202 Ashwoody Trail, Atlanta, Georgia 30319; 404-458-5678

Gifted Child Quarterly, 5110 N. Edgewood Drive, St. Paul, MN 55112

Gifted/Creative/Talented Children, P. O. Box 66654, Mobile, AL 36606

Growing Without Schooling, 2269 Massachusetts Avenue, Cambridge, MA 02140; 617-864-3100

Holistic Education Review, 39 Pearl Street, Brandon, VT 057330-1007; 802-247-8312

Home Education Magazine, P. O. Box 1083, Tonasket, WA 98855; 509-486-1351

Innovative Higher Education , 72 5th Ave, New York, NY 10011

Instructor Magazine, P. O. Box 6099, Duluth, MN 55806

National Coalition News, National Coalition of Alternative Community Schools, 58 Schoolhouse Road, Summertown, Tennessee 38483; 615-964-3670

Options in Learning, The Alliance for Parental Involvement in Education, Post Office Box 59, East Chatham, New York 12060-0059; 518-392-6900

Phi Delta Kappan, P. O. Box 789, Bloomington, IN 47402

Rethinking Schools, 1001 E. Keefe Avenue, Milwaukee, WI 53212 ; 414-964-9646

Skole, The Journal of Alternative Education, 72 Philip Street, Albany, NY 12202

Teacher's College Record, Teachers College, Columbia University, 525 W 120th Street, New York, NY 10027

BOOKS

Arons, Stephen *Compelling Belief: The Culture of American Schooling* (McGraw-Hill, 1983)

Ashton-Warner, Sylvia *Teacher* (Simon & Shuster, 1963)

Atkinson, Linda *Alternatives To College* (Franklin Watts, 1978)

Baldwin, Rahima, *Your Are Your Child's First Teacher* (Celestial Arts, 1989)

Barker, Britt *Letters Home* (Home Education Press, 1988)

Bear, John, *Bear's Guide to Non-Traditional College Degrees* (Ten Speed Press, updated annually)

Beechick, Ruth *You Can Teach Your Child Successfully* (Arrow Press, 1988)
− *The Three R's* (Arrow Press, 1985)

Bruner, Jerome *The Process of Education* (Harvard, 1960)

Carlson, Laurie M., *Home Study Opportunities: The Complete Guide to Going to School by Mail* (Betterway Publications, 1988)

Colfax, David and Micki *Homeschooling for Excellence* (Warner Books, 1988)

Copperman, Paul *The Literacy Hoax* (Morrow Quill, 1978)

Coyne, John, and Hebert, Tom *This Way Out* (E. P. Dutton, 1972)

Cusick, Lois, *Waldorf Parenting Handbook* (St. George Publications, 1984)

Deal, Terrance E. and Robert R. Nolan *Alternative Schools: Ideologies, Realities, Guidelines* (Nelson-Hall, 1978)

Dennison, George *The Lives of Children: The Story of the First Street School* (Random House, 1969)

Dewey, John *Education Today* (Putnam, 1940)

Dreikurs, Rudolf *Children: The Challenge* (Hawthorn Books, 1964)

Edmunds, Francic L., *Rudolf Steiner Education* (Anthroposophic Press, 1987)

Elkind, David *Miseducation* (Knopf, 1987)

Gatto, John Taylor *Dumbing Us Down: The*

Hidden Curriculum of Compulsory Schooling (New Society Publishers, 1991)

Gelner, Judy *College Admissions: A Guide for Homeschoolers* (Poppyseed Press, 1988)

Gettman, David *Basic Montessori* (Christopher Helm, Ltd., 1987)

Goldman, Jenifer *My Life as a Travelling Homeschooler* (Solomon Press, 1991)

Goodman, Paul *Growing Up Absurd* (Random House, 1960)
– *Compulsory Mis-Education* (Horizon, 1964)

Gorder, Cheryl *Home Education Resource Guide* (Bluebird Publishing, 1989)
– *Home Schools* (Bluebird Publishing, 1990)

Graubard, Allen *Free The Children: Radical Reform and the Free School Movement* (Pantheon Books, 1972)

Greenberg, Daniel *The Crisis in American Education: An Analysis and A Proposal* (The Sudbury Valley School Press, 1970)
– *"Announcing a New School..." A Personal Account of the Beginnings of The Sudbury Valley School* (The Sudbury Valley School Press, 1971)
– *Outline of A New Philosophy* (The Sudbury Valley School Press, 1987)
– *The Sudbury Valley School Experience* (The Sudbury Valley School Press, 1987)
– *The Sudbury Valley School Experience* (The Sudbury Valley School Press, 1987)
– *Child Rearing* (The Sudbury Valley School Press, 1987)
– *Free At Last: The Sudbury Valley School* (The Sudbury Valley School Press, 1991)
– *A New Look at Schools* (The Sudbury Valley School Press, 1991)

Gelner, Judy, *College Admissions: A Guide for Homeschoolers* (Poppyseed Press, 1988)

Gregory, Thomas B. and Gerald R. Smith, *High Schools as Communities: The Small School Reconsidered* (Phi Delta Kappa Educational Foundation, 1987)

Grunelius, Elizabeth, *Early Childhood Education and the Waldorf School Plan* (Waldorf School Monographs, 1974)

Hahn, Herbert, *From the Well-Springs of the Soul* (Rudolf Steiner Schools Fellowship, 1966)

Hainstock, Elizabeth *The Essential Montessori* (New American Library, 1978)

Harwood, A.C., *The Recovery of Man in Childhood* (Anthroposophic Press, 1958)

Hayes, Charles D. *Self-University* (Autodidact Press, 1989)

Hegener, Mark and Helen *The Homeschool Handbook* (Home Education Press, 1990)
– *The Home School Reader* (Home Education Press, 1988)

Hemmings, Ray *Children's Freedom: A.S. Neill and the Evolution of the Summerhill Idea* (Schoken Books, 1973)

Hendrickson, Borg *Homeschool: Taking the First Step* (Mountain Meadow Press, 1988)
– *How to Write a Low Cost/No Cost Curriculum for Your Homeschool Child* (Mountain Meadow Press, 1989)

Hentoff, Nat *Our Children Are Dying* (Viking, 1967)

Herndon, James *The Way it Spozed To Be* (Simon & Shuster, 1968)

Hillesheim, James W. and George D. Merrill *Theory and Practice in the History of American Education* (Goodyear Publishing Company, 1971)

Holt, John *How Children Fail* (Pitman Publishing, 1964)
– *How Children Learn* (Pitman Publishing, 1967)
– *Freedom and Beyond* (E. P. Dutton, 1972)
– *Escape From Childhood* (E. P. Dutton, 1974)
– *Instead of Education* (E.P. Dutton, 1976)
– *Teach Your Own* (Delacorte Press, 1981)
– *Learning All The Time* (Delacorte, 1989)

Illich, Ivan *Deschooling Society* (Harper & Row, 1970)

Kaseman, Larry and Susan *Taking Charge Through Homeschooling: Personal and Political Empowerment* (Koshkonong Press, 1990)

Kohl, Herbert *36 Children* (The New American Library, 1967)
– *The Open Classroom* (New York Review of Books, 1969)
– *The Question is College* (Times Books/Random House, 1989)

Kozol, Jonathan *Death at an Early Age* (Houghton Mifflin, 1967)
– *Free Schools* (Houghton Mifflin, 1972)
– *The Night is Dark and I Am Far From Home* (Simon and Schuster, 1975, 1990)

Kramer, Rita *Maria Montessori: A Biography* (Addison Wesley, 1988)

Leidloff, Jean *The Continuum Concept* (Alfred A. Knopf, 1975)

Leistico, Agnes *I Learn Better by Teaching Myself* (Home Education Press, 1991)

Leonard, George *Education and Ecstasy* (Delacorte Press, 1968)

LeShan, Eda J. *The Conspiracy Against Childhood* (Atheneum, 1967)

Leue, Mary *Challenging the Giant: The Best of*

SKOLE, The Journal of Alternative Education (Down-to-Earth Books, 1992)

Llewellyn, Grace *The Teenage Liberation Handbook: How to Quit School and Get a Real Life and Education* (Lowry House, 1991)

Maeroff, Gene I. *Don't Blame the Kids* (McGraw-Hill, 1982)

Masters, Brian, *Rudolf Steiner Waldorf Education* (Steiner Schools Fellowship, 1986)

Miller, Ron *What Are Schools For: Holistic Education in American Culture* (Holistic Education Press, 1990)

Montessori, Maria *The Absorbent Mind* (1967)

Montessori, Maria *The Discovery of the Child* (1967)

Montessori, Maria *From Childhood to Adolescence* (Schoken Books, 1948, 1973)

Moore, Raymond and Dorothy *Home School Burnout* (Wolgemuth & Hyatt, 1988)
– *Home Style Teaching* (Word Books, 1984)
– *Home Grown Kids* (Word Books, 1983)
– *Home Spun Schools* (Word Books, 1983)

Mothering Magazine *Schooling at Home* (John Muir Publishing, 1990)

Neill, A. S. *Summerhill* (Hart Publishing, 1960)

Orem, R.C. *A Montessori Handbook* (G.P. Putnam's Sons, 1065)

Parker, Gail, and Hawes, Gene *College On Your Own* (Bantam, 1978)

Pearce, Joseph Chilton *Magical Child* (E. P. Dutton, 1977)

Piaget, Jean *To Understand Is To Invent* (Grossman Publishers, 1973)

Popenoe, Joshua *Inside Summerhill* (Hart Publishing Company, 1970)

Postman, Neil, and C. Weingartner *Teaching As A Subversive Activity* (Delecorte Press, 1969)
– *The School Book* (Delecorte Press, 1973)

Ravitch, Diane *The Troubled Crusade: American Education 1945-1980* (Basic Books, 1983)

Reed, Donn *The Home School Source Book* (Brook Farm Books, 1991)

Reimer, Eric *School is Dead: Alternatives in Education* (Doubleday and Company, 1971)

Rheim, Sarah *The Teenage Entrepreneur's Guide* (Surrey Books, 1987)

Rousseau, Jean-Jacques (Trans. by Allen Bloom) *Emile* or *On Education* (Basic Books, 1979)

Simasko, Susan *Earn College Credit for What You Know* (Acropolis Books, 1985)

Smith, Vernon H. *Alternative Schools* (Pro. Educators Publ., 1974)

Spietz, Heidi Anne *Montessori at Home* (American Montessori Publishing, 1988)
– *Montessori at Home I - 6-9 Years* (American Montessori Publishing, 1989)
– *Montessori at Home II - 10-12 Years* (American Montessori Publishing, 1990)

Splaver, Sarah *Nontraditional Routes To College Careers* (Simon & Shuster, 1975)

Spring, Joel *The Sorting Machine: National Education Policy Since 1945* (McKay, 1976)
– *The American School: 1645-1985* (Longman, Inc., 1986)

Standing, E.M. *Maria Montessori: Her Life and Work* (New American Library, 1984)

Steiner, Rudolf, *The Education of the Child* (Rudolf Steiner Press, 1965)
– *The Essentials of Education* (Rudolf Steiner Press, 1948)
– *A Study of Man* (Anthroposopic Press, 1947)

Thorson, Marcie Kisner *Campus-Free College Degrees* (Thorson Guides, 1989)

Index

For Additional Copies:

Alternatives In Education, edited by Mark and Helen Hegener, revised fourth edition, published by Home Education Press, 1992, 288 pages, completely indexed, $16.75 plus $2.00 shipping. Send orders to Home Education Press, Post Office Box 1083, Tonasket, WA 98855-1083; (509) 486-1351.

"Perhaps more than at any other time since the beginning of public education in this country, parents and children are aware that they have the power and the responsibility to take charge of their education and their daily lives. Here, in this book, is both information and inspiration for those who are ready to act on that awareness."

Earl Stevens, from the Introduction

Also Available from Home Education Press

THE HOMESCHOOL READER

A unique collection of articles, answering questions on socialization, legal issues, higher education, accountability, compulsory education, selecting curriculum materials, and much more. From the pages of *Home Education Magazine*, 1983 through 1988. 164 pages, resource listing, indexed, $12.75 ppd.

I LEARN BETTER BY TEACHING MYSELF

This book, by homeschooling mother Agnes Liestico, is an introduction to interest initiated learning, also known as student-directed or student-led learning. A very reassuring and encouraging book for anyone interested in less structure in their home school. 152 pages, resources, indexed, $11.75 ppd.

LETTERS HOME

A fascinating glimpse into the life of Britt Barker, a homeschooler who embarks on travels around the world at the age of sixteen. Her experiences shed light on the question of how homeschooled youngsters might make the transition from the home to the outside world. 60 pages, $6.50 ppd.

HOME EDUCATION MAGAZINE

A bimonthly magazine for homeschooling families, featuring interesting and informative articles, feature sections on topics of interest, several regular columnists, letters from readers, interviews, feature-length book excerpts, an extensive resource section and much more. Bimonthly, 64 pages, $4.50 current issue; $24.00/yr.

For your free informative catalog of homeschooling
publications, send your name and address to:

HOME EDUCATION PRESS

Post Office Box 1083, Tonasket, WA 98855
(509) 486-1351